BJÖRN BORG
WINNER LOSES ALL

Lars Skarke

BJÖRN BORG
WINNER LOSES ALL

BLAKE

Published by Blake Publishing Ltd,
98–100 Great North Road, London N2 0NL, England

First published in Great Britain in 1993

ISBN 1 85782 085 1

British Library Cataloguing-in-Publication Data:
A catalogue record for this book is available from
the British Library.

Typeset by BMD Graphics, Hemel Hempstead

Printed by Cox & Wyman Ltd, Reading

1 3 5 7 9 10 8 6 4 2

Acknowledgements

I wish to thank everyone – those mentioned in the text and those not – who helped me, supported me and shared all the tough, happy and work-filled years with me.

Contents

Acknowledgements

1 Drama in Milan   9
2 Farewell to the Racket   25
3 A Penny Saved…   45
4 Ex-Tennis Player for Sale   57
5 Love Comes, Love Goes   69
6 Home Sweet Home   91
7 Mr Ambassador   115
8 From Alstaholm to Rio   131
9 'Lasse, let's go into business…'   157
10 Dangerous Games   165
11 Up at the White House, Down in Los Angeles   189
12 Business Matters   203
13 Audit by the Poolside   223
14 Family Problems   231
15 High Appraisal   241
16 Loss of Face and Empty Hands   247
17 A Polished Interviewee   267
18 The 'Predators' Ball'   281
19 'Is this a PR trip for John McEnroe Design Group?'   301
20 The BBDG Ship Sets Sail   317
21 'I'm going to bomb Stavsborg'   331
    Epilogue   353

CHAPTER ONE

Drama in Milan

The car journey from Naritas Airport to the centre of Tokyo can take up to four hours, but on the evening of Tuesday, 7 February 1989, the traffic was light and the taxi carrying Stig Sjöblom and me was making excellent time. It had been a good trip so far. In London the first audit of the Björn Borg Design Group (BBDG), which had been my idea and of which I owned 40 per cent of the shares, valued our assets at $40 million and reported that 'the company's strength lies in its professional and capable leadership, a well thought-out and executed strategy, a strong name that is known in the market-place, a unique Scandinavian image, a clear market potential in the United States, strong and developed business ties in Japan . . .' Now here we were in Tokyo to cement those ties by signing three contracts that together would be worth at least $7 million. It was a fantastic prospect for a company that was only a year and a half old, and Stig, one of our directors, and I had every reason to feel pleased. And as we checked into our hotel and agreed to meet for dinner in half an hour, that's exactly how I did feel.

I went up to my room, hung up my jacket and went to the phone to make a couple of routine calls, the first to my office in Monte Carlo. Johan Denekamp, our chief financial manager, didn't waste time on polite inquiries about the weather.

'Have you heard the rumours? They're saying in the States that Björn has got some American girl pregnant.'

'That can't be true,' I assured him. 'No, you can relax. He'd never risk anything like that. I'll bet it's Jannike spreading stories and that it's got something to do with their custody fight over Robin.'

I hoped that I had calmed Johan's fears. Of course what Björn did and what was said about him were of crucial importance to us – his was the 'strong name' that had launched the company – but there were always rumours about him, particularly in the scandal sheets. Stories about alleged romantic adventures weren't a cause for worry. Usually they were started by some girl who may not even have met him, but who seized her chance to make a little money and get fifteen minutes of attention. It seemed quite probable that the end of his relationship with Jannike Björling and the custody battle over their son had prompted the most recent tale. Nothing to worry about.

I dialled another number. My sister, Lena, had been ill for some years and I always rang her when I was abroad. As soon as she heard my voice she let out a cry. I still remember her exact words: 'Haven't you heard the news, Lasse? How can you be so calm? Radio Stockholm is reporting that Björn Borg tried to commit suicide. He was taken to hospital this morning. Lasse, don't you hear what I'm saying?'

Blood rushed to my head and I had to grip the edge of the bed to keep myself steady. Somehow I finished the conversation with Lena. I don't know how long I sat there frozen on the edge of the bed before I heard a knock at the door. It was Stig and one look at me told him something was badly wrong.

'What is it, Lasse? What's happened?'

I repeated what Lena had told me.

'Is he alive?' was Stig's response.

'I don't know. I don't know anything.'

My mind was reeling. Had Björn taken drugs? Was it an overdose? Was it really a suicide attempt? I remembered a conversation we'd had in a hotel in Los Angeles when he had told me that he didn't have anything to live for any more. But at that time he'd been depressed because his relationship with Jannike was coming apart. Was it the same problem again? Had something happened between him and Loredana? I was racking my brain while Stig bombarded me with questions. Couldn't he shut up? His voice kept me from thinking clearly. I felt like asking him to go back to his room and leave me in peace, but he had switched on the TV and turned to CNN. Björn's face appeared against a blue background. The newsreader's steady, relentless voice reported that Swedish tennis star Björn Borg had been hospitalised in Milan to have his stomach pumped after he had tried to kill himself.

I reached for the phone again and called Ingmar Alverdal, Björn's right-hand man in Stockholm. He confirmed the news report and added that Björn's parents were at their house in Cap Ferrat, on the outskirts of Nice, and didn't want to be disturbed. I hung up and looked at Stig, who was standing next to me and had heard every word.

'Never mind what Ingmar said. There's only one way to find out what's happened to Björn,' I told him. 'We *must* call Rune and Margaretha.'

Björn's mother answered the phone after a few rings.

'Hi, Margaretha, it's Lasse. I'm in Tokyo. What's this they're saying on TV? What's happened? How's Björn?'

'He's OK and he's feeling better. He called and said . . . well, he said it didn't work this time.' She sounded remarkably unconcerned.

'What do you mean "this time"? Doesn't he want to live?' I couldn't stand still and Stig was following me around to hear what was being said.

'No, it seems not,' she answered.

Stig and I just stared at each other.

'He's got to have peace and quiet,' Margaretha continued.

'Yes, of course,' I said. 'We've got to do all we can to help him recover. Business has to take a back seat. Right now we've got to support him.'

Stig looked worn out. He went over to the desk, opened a bottle of whisky and poured two generous drinks. He'd been worried about Björn for a long time and had often expressed his feelings to me. 'There's not much time, Lasse,' he would say. 'It's five to twelve, and when the clock strikes twelve the change will occur.' Like the fairy godmother in *Cinderella*, he was reminding me that Björn Borg's public image could change at a stroke. Scandals were knocking at the door. Bad publicity was the biggest threat to our business and very few people understood how thin a wire we were balancing on. I knew, of course; I'd seen so much. But I had hoped desperately – stubbornly and foolishly – that Björn would straighten out his life. Or that by the time the clock struck twelve, as Stig put it, we'd have been able to play down the importance of Björn Borg the man and build up the image of our products, making them as prestigious as Lacoste, Boss, Adidas or Yves St Laurent. Then the company wouldn't be so vulnerable to Björn's every move. To consumers, Yves St Laurent means exclusive fashions, not the real person behind that image. We hadn't made it that far. The seconds were ticking away and we hadn't reached our goal.

The first thing we had to do now was find out what really had happened. Later, after I'd spoken to Björn, with people close to him and with others in the company, and after I'd read the papers, I thought I had a very clear picture of the day's dramatic events. In my mind's eye I saw the following scenes unfold.

The telephone wakes Chino Marcese at his home in Milan about half-past seven in the morning. Marcese is the head of the Milan office of Mark McCormack's International Management Group (IMG). He's a middle-aged man with silver hair and a rough sort of charm, a typical Italian, who runs his office with a firm hand and is well-known all over Italy as a man with invaluable contacts. He answers sleepily, but wakes up completely as soon as he hears the hysterical voice on the other end of the line.

'Chino, you've got to help me! I can't wake him up! I don't know what's happened! I woke up this morning and he was lying on the sofa. He's been drinking and he's taken a lot of sleeping pills.'

Marcese immediately recognises the voice of the famous Italian pop singer Loredana Berté, so the 'he' she's talking about is Björn Borg. Marcese knows a lot about the Swede's wild parties with beautiful women and drugs.

'What did you two do last night? Did you have a fight?'

'We talked about the boy and about where we should live. You know how stubborn he is. Then he got mad, put on his jacket and ran out.'

Marcese takes a deep breath. He's had many conversations like this with the wives or girlfriends of his clients over the years. It was all a part of 'client management', which is a very strange and multifaceted occupation indeed.

'Loredana, *cara mia*, don't you think he's just sleeping off his hangover?'

'No, no, it's much worse this time. There's an empty Rohypnol bottle on the coffee table – he must have taken at least thirty pills. Oh, Chino, you've got to do something!'

Marcese thinks quickly. 'OK,' he says, 'I'll call a doctor I know who's got his own clinic and make sure he comes and gets him. Calm down and keep a close eye on him. I'll call you right back.'

He hangs up, looks up the doctor's number and dials it as fast as he can. Meanwhile Loredana watches Björn. His face is pale and his features cast dark shadows. She can't detect any breathing, but now and then she sees his eyebrows twitch and his body contort with cramps. His brow is damp with sweat. Loredana is suddenly overcome with panic.

She rushes over to him, shakes him and strikes his cheeks to wake him up.

'*Amore*! You mustn't die, you can't die!'

His only response is a weak moan that quickly fades away. Ignoring Marcese's advice, she runs to the phone and calls the emergency number.

'Hello,' she yells. 'Hurry, there's no time to waste! I need an ambulance. It's a matter of life and death!'

She listens a moment and then says, 'My name is Loredana Berté and my address is Ariosto 10. What's wrong? I'm no doctor. You heard me, he's dying. My fiancé, he's . . . he's suffering from . . . food . . . he's been poisoned by something he's eaten.'

The operator at the hospital calls the ambulance dispatcher. 'It's Loredana Berté. Her fiancé's suffering from food poisoning. Get an ambulance there as soon as possible. The address is Ariosto 10.' Then she continues her conversation with Loredana. 'What's your fiancé's name, signora?'

'What's the difference? The important thing is that you come before he dies!'

'It's the rule. I have to have his name.'

'Oh, God, what difference does it make now . . . his name is Borg.'

The operator nods her head in recognition, her thoughts racing as Loredana hangs up. In the meantime Björn has regained consciousness. He tries to get up, but falls back on the sofa. He feels violently ill, swallows and tries to pull himself together.

An ambulance siren can be heard in the distance. His fiancée, six years his elder, strokes his damp hair. 'Don't worry, *amore*, everything's going to be fine. They'll take you to the hospital and everything will be all right.'

'No, no, damn it! Not the hospital . . .'

The doorbell rings. Loredana opens the door and the paramedics come in.

'I'm fine. No problem,' says Björn from the sofa. He makes another attempt to get up, but has to sit down again so he won't fall. He no longer has the energy to argue. The paramedics stare at one another. They've recognised him.

Meanwhile Chino Marcese is sweating in his car. The traffic is horrendous and it will take him at least ten minutes to reach Loredana's place and get the situation fully under control.

The operator at the hospital is hanging up the phone after her third successful conversation. During the past half hour she has earned a nice bundle of money by tipping off the Italian press about Björn Borg's sudden and mysterious illness. Some other papers have learned what has happened via the hospital emergency room. It looks as if it's going to be a good news day in Milan. The newspapers and television stations are on the move even before the ambulance reaches the hospital. It's clear that the patient is the world-famous tennis player Björn Borg, that the illness is very serious and shrouded in secrecy, and that it has something to do with the Italian pop goddess Loredana Berté.

The whole thing's a dream for the people who craft headlines.

The emergency room staff have understood the seriousness of the situation and called the police. When the ambulance arrives, the police are on hand and do everything they can to hold back the mass of photographers and journalists. Loredana wears dark glasses and keeps close to the stretcher on which Björn is being rolled into the emergency room.

'Leave us alone,' she screams at the newshounds. 'Don't you have any feelings at all?'

Then they disappear into the building, surrounded by hospital personnel.

At that very moment Chino Marcese is leaving Loredana's empty flat, his blood boiling. He has figured out what's happend. 'Hysterical woman,' he thinks to himself angrily. 'Of course she couldn't think clearly.' Sitting in his car, he puts his hands over his face and swears vehemently.

'Have you taken sleeping pills?' asks the doctor as he carefully examines his famous patient's pupils. Björn Borg understands that he can't lie to the doctor. Moreover, he still feels violently ill. He nods his head slightly and leans back. The doctor calls to the nurse. 'Quick, bring a bowl.'

Björn throws up violently, cramps racking his body. The doctor turns to Loredana, who is pacing nervously by the bedside.

'What has he eaten lately?'

Looking away, Loredana answers. 'I think we had some fish that was bad last night, and I know he's drunk a good deal of alcohol. And he's taken some sleeping pills, too.' The doctor tells the nurse to get ready to pump Björn's stomach. When that procedure is over, the analysis of the contents reveals about twenty undissolved Rohypnol tablets and indicates that Björn has probably taken at least twenty more. After his stomach is pumped, Björn recovers surprisingly fast. The event is routinely judged as an attempted suicide and is reported as such to various agencies, including the Milan police. This titillating piece of news quickly leaks out to the press via the hospital personnel and sources close to Björn and Loredana. In his room at the hospital Björn asks Loredana to get him a telephone. Exhausted, he calls his parents.

Björn Gullström sits down at the breakfast table in his villa in Tyresö and turns on the radio. He is a tall man, nearly 55, still athletic and in good shape. He has been Björn Borg's financial manager and general adviser for nearly seventeen years. He is pouring a cup of coffee when he hears the news about Björn. Shocked, he puts down the coffee pot, looks at his wife and says quietly, 'I knew it. Somewhere inside me I knew this would happen. That poor boy. Now everything's ruined.'

At about the same time, the telephone rings in Staffan Holm's flat at Château Perigord in Monte

Carlo. Holm is president of Björn Borg Design Group SAM, the group's Monte Carlo subsidiary, and is responsible for the operations of the main office there. He is thirty-four and has moved from Stockholm to Monte Carlo the year before, leaving behind him an impressive career at Svensk Filmindustri. Johan Denekamp is on the line.

'Staffan, you'd better hurry down to the office. Something serious has happened to Björn in Milan. I just spoke with Lasse in Tokyo, but he doesn't know anything yet.'

'I'll leave right away,' replies Holm. 'Call Roffe, too.'

He throws on a jacket and forgets to say good-bye to his wife as he hurries out.

Rolf Skjöldebrand smoothes back his thinning hair and adjusts his gold-rimmed sunglasses. He is on his way to his office at the Barclay's Bank building in the middle of Monte Carlo. His bare forehead, his striking, eagle-like nose, and his jutting jaw covered with grey stubble give him a very distinctive look. He frequently improves upon the effect by combining tight jeans or fancy suits with expensive shirts and leather boots.

Skjöldebrand had worked his way up to become the guru of the Stockholm advertising world with a series of international accounts, but he hadn't hesitated long before accepting BBDG's offer to head up its development efforts. Thoughts swirl through his head as he arrives for the hastily-called meeting with Holm and Denekamp. 'Christ, the guy must have gone mad,' he thinks to himself as he parks his car.

In Stockholm, the 50-year-old dean of the Swedish advertising business, Bengt Hanser, leans back in his chair when he hears the news. He learned his trade in New York and has a long list of credits in the advertising game to his name. Hanser, too, has contributed ideas and developed some of the thinking behind BBDG. His clear, precise language has been used in most of the literature that has been sent around the world to present BBDG's business concept. Now Hanser closes his eyes and decides to leave his position as BBDG's head of information at the end of June.

It was almost eleven o'clock in Tokyo. Stig and I had discussed the situation from every angle. Why had Björn done it? After all, he had everything: a child, success, fame and plenty of money. He claimed he was in love with Loredana, and his new fashion house was on the verge of achieving international success.

'Good God, isn't that enough?' I asked Stig.

'I don't know,' sighed Stig. 'All I do know is that only Björn can solve this problem. The ball's really in his court this time.'

'Damn it, why doesn't he call? He knows why we're here. Why doesn't he contact me? After all, we're not just partners, I'm his friend too.'

Björn was not a stupid man. He knew an incident like

this could damage his image, even ruin it. The name Björn Borg stood for physical and mental strength, Swedish quality, dependability and a kind of innocence. One of the century's greatest athletes, the way he had won five straight Wimbledons, six French Masters and many other tournaments had earned him universal admiration. He was one of the the best-known people in the world, an idol, 'the gentleman of the court'. Now he lay in a public hospital in Milan while the international press speculated about his suicide attempt. My feelings towards him swung back and forth between sympathy and anger.

Stig's voice interrupted my thoughts. 'We've got to pull ourselves together, Lasse, and make the best of the situation.'

'You're right, of course. Not one more negative word. He's alive, that's the most important thing. Let's shower and meet here again in fifteen minutes. In the meantime think about what we should do. I've got a feeling that now we're going to have to do better and be more efficient than we've ever been.'

We made a list of the people we should speak to as soon as possible. Our task was to find out how much damage had been done to the company and work out a strategy for its survival. Stig went to his room with part of the list and I began to make my calls. My first conversation was with Saul Schoenberg in New York, the president of BBDG USA.

'Lars!' Like most non-Swedes, he used my given name rather than the more familiar Lasse. 'You don't know how good it is to hear your voice. This place is a complete madhouse. The news about Björn's hospitalisation has made the front pages. What's going on? Have your talked to him?'

'No, I haven't got hold of him yet. But take it easy, it can't be as bad as it sounds. You know what the papers are like. By the way, what *are* they saying there?'

'What can I tell you? There's all sorts of speculation about drugs and that he's really dead. There are articles about his difficult private life, that Loredana has left him and that he's still in love with Jannike. You know, she was interviewed on a TV show here a few days ago. This could really explode . . .'

'Saul, take it easy,' I repeated. 'It's going to be OK. Björn's going to be fine soon. We're going to issue a press release and calm down the media. I'm going to make some more calls, but give me a ring if you hear anything more.'

I wiped the sweat from my forehead and tried to stop thinking of the headlines trumpeting the story around the world. My next call was to Bob Kain, one of IMG's most cunning foxes and head of its tennis division. Bob was about 45 years old, looked like a schoolteacher, with steel-rimmed glasses and a neat parting dividing his black hair, and spoke with a discreet Midwestern twang. He was staying at a hotel just outside Anchorage, Alaska. Because of the time difference between there and Tokyo it was about five in the morning when I reached him. Bob was awake and had heard the news, so he wasn't surprised by my call.

'So, Lars, you've been saddled with a problem! Well, this is really a hot piece of news.' Kain thought for a minute before he continued. 'Björn is going to have to take the consequences and not go off and hide somewhere. He has to make an appearance, show himself in public and answer questions. That's the most important thing.'

Paul Naruse, head of our Asian operations in Singapore, sounded as if he was in shock. The only thing he could say was, 'Oh, Jesus . . . Jesus, what's happened?' Björn had promised him his last tour, the so-called Reunion Tour, in which he would play a number of exhibition matches against John McEnroe. It was scheduled to take place two months later and Paul was probably thinking how one sponsor after another would flee the field.

'Relax, Paul,' I said. 'Björn feels fine.' I made the usual reassuring noises and agreed that Stig would fly to Singapore to help him with preparations for the tour.

That's how it was all night long. We received a steady stream of faxes and phone messages, and the front desk sent up all the foreign papers with fat headlines about Borg. Journalists queued on the phone to talk to us, but we made ourselves unavailable. Sometime during the night I called my mother in Sweden, only to learn that a number of reporters were trying to get in touch with us through her. Most importantly, we conferred with the 'control centre' in Monte Carlo and talked to Ingmar Alverdal several times. He reported that Björn didn't feel up to talking to anyone at the moment, but had instructed him to say that he had suffered a bout of food poisoning and was going to Cap Ferrat to rest.

By 5 a.m. we felt that we'd done all we could. We had reassured our colleagues around the world that Björn would soon make a complete recovery and everyone agreed not to say anything to the press beyond those two magic words, 'No comment'. Bengt Hanser in Stockholm wrote the final version of the press release, which said simply that Björn Borg had been admitted to a hospital in Milan to be treated for food poisoning, that he was completely healthy and felt fine and that he was visiting his parents at Cap Ferrat together with Loredana Berté in order to get some rest.

Stig and I decided to get a few hours' rest ourselves before going to meet our new Japanese partners. I went to bed, but couldn't sleep. What was I doing? How could I have been so stupid as to put myself in this position? I had been doing so well before I took on Björn and our company. How did I end up battling all night to save my business by protecting the reputation of a man who wouldn't even talk to me during that very crisis?

CHAPTER TWO

Farewell to the Racket

Peter Worth's most challenging assignment at IMG's London office was being responsible for the affairs of Björn Borg. Negotiating and confirming Borg's schedule was a difficult job, for everyone wanted the Swede. Thanks to his early successes on both clay and grass, Borg had become the object of a tremendous amount of attention. Television coverage had ensured that his name and face were firmly imprinted in the minds of viewers everywhere. Tennis fans were impressed by his good sportsmanship as well as his brilliant tennis.

In world-class tennis each player has to participate in a certain number of tournaments each year, not all of which are well-known. Although it is against the rules of the governing body of tennis, tournament organisers pay so-called appearance money to the top players on the Grand Prix circuit. Borg's public image was amazingly positive and his drawing power was enormous. Organisers of tournaments and matches knew precisely how much his presence meant for ticket sales and advertising revenues. One aspect of Worth's job was to get them to pay as much appearance money as possible, and it was not unusual for him to arrange fees of $100,000.

As Borg's career developed, he became more and more choosy about where he played and husbanded his energies to be in top shape for the Grand Slam competitions, the

French Masters, Wimbledon and the US Open (the Australian Open is also a Grand Slam event, but Borg never cared to participate in it). Worth became a very skilful mediator between Borg and organisers who felt betrayed when the Swede withdrew because of injury or was defeated in an early round of the tournament.

Another of Worth's tasks was to sell firms the right to use Björn Borg's name, picture and endorsement, with the guarantee that Björn would make one or more personal appearances on behalf of the individual companies. These agreements were usually made for periods of three to five years and were worth a great deal of money. Björn had about five times as many endorsement contracts as any other tennis player of his time. He was Worth's and IMG's greatest source of revenue.

In 1982 Worth was in his sixth year of handling Borg's affairs. It was now late in the year, and Worth decided to take a two-week skiing holiday with his family at Val d'Isère in France. One evening soon after they arrived the phone rang as the Worth family were sitting down to dinner in their alpine lodge. Worth, who had told his secretary not to give anyone his number, looked at his wife and said, 'Who can that be?'

He knew the voice well. It was Björn Borg and after the usual exchange of pleasantries Borg got straight to the point.

'Peter,' he said, 'I've decided to quit playing the circuit. My last tournament will be Monte Carlo in April, but that's the last one.'

Worth's heart leapt. He swallowed and tried to understand.

'Did you hear what I said, Peter?'

'Yes . . . but I don't understand, Björn. You're only 26 and you've got at least another four years at the top.'

'It doesn't matter, I've made my decision,' Borg replied firmly. There wasn't any room for discussion. 'I want you to talk with the others at IMG and take care of everything. But you're not to make any public announcements yet. We'll talk about that later. And remember,' he added, 'there's no use in trying to convince me to keep playing. I've made up my mind.'

The conversation ended. Worth turned to his wife with a feeble smile on his lips. 'I'm sorry, darling, but I'm going to have to work quite a bit over the next few days.'

As it turned out, Peter Worth spent the rest of his holiday on the telephone. The first thing he did was to contact his senior colleagues at IMG. If Borg's announcement came as a shock to everyone in the world of tennis, it shook IMG to its foundations. Borg was still a superstar, although he had played only a couple of tournaments and a few exhibition matches over the course of the last year. No one had had the slightest idea that he was thinking of quitting. At a recent tournament in Montreal he had said that his goal was to return to a full schedule in 1983 in order to regain the world championship. He had appeared to be in good shape and had played excellent tennis. His decision to retire presented IMG with a disastrous prospect. Björn Borg was a profit machine. He had played more tennis matches than any other player, since he advanced very far in every tournament. Even if he were to

27

fall one or two notches in the world standings and were not to win every final, he had tremendous earnings potential left in appearance and prize monies. And his value to advertisers was still unparalleled. In 1981 he had earned over $4 million in advertising revenues, and Worth and the other IMG executives knew that his advertising earnings during his 'sabbatical year', 1982, were going to be around $3 million. The fact was that the company had earned nearly $3 million from managing Borg's affairs in 1980–82 alone, not counting what it earned from managing his investments.

The executives at IMG gathered for a war council. They decided to begin a campaign to change their star player's mind. Björn Borg's telephone was very busy in Monte Carlo. The people at IMG tried everything they could think of to get him to retract his decision. They reminded him of the long-term contracts he had signed with such firms as the tennis racket producer Donnay and the Fila sportswear company, both of which were worth millions and ran several years into the future. They reminded him that his schedule of matches had already been set and that he himself had approved it. If he were to quit, the people who were responsible for organising the tournaments he had agreed to play in would lose their biggest drawing card, and the news of his decision might mean economic ruin for many. Moreover, the IMG executives reminded Borg of the enormous amount of income he would be sacrificing by bringing his competitive career to an end, around $4 million over the next twelve months alone. But Borg was not willing to change his mind. He repeated over and over again what he told Peter

Worth: 'It's no use. I've made up my mind.'

The people at IMG knew very well what that meant. Borg had been a client of theirs since 1974 and they knew that a 'no' from Björn *was* a 'no'. Over the years it had been almost impossible to get Borg to change his mind, and after a full week of telephone conversations they were forced to admit once again that they couldn't do it. He would not continue to compete on the tennis court.

Peter Worth spent his second week at Val d'Isère calling promoters and companies around the world to break the engagements Borg had previously made. Worth hated every minute of it, for it meant that years of hard work were being destroyed.

Most of the companies demanded that their contracts with Borg be annulled or renegotiated. However, when they read through those contracts they found to their dismay that they contained nothing that made them contingent on Björn Borg's continuing to compete. Because he considered that Borg had acted unethically by signing contracts despite the fact that he had already decided not to play any more tennis, Worth promised these companies that they would be compensated in other ways, such as by Björn's making appearances for them in other contexts. Although Borg indicated rather reluctantly that he could consider accepting such arrangements, his basic attitude was that he had already performed a sufficient number of services for these companies over the years and that they would have to do what everyone else had to do, namely, accept his decision.

* * *

Björn told me that he had made his decision to quit playing at this time two and a half years earlier, but that he had kept that decision to himself. When he had arrived in New York in August 1980 he had already had a hectic season. In May he had won the French Open in a very convincing manner. It was a matter of Borg against the rest of the world, and on the red clay at Roland Garros the world didn't have a chance. He didn't lose a single set in any of his seven matches, and he had won a total of 126 games to 38, which meant that he had lost an average of only five games each match. And then on 5 July, in what has been called the finals match of the century, he had beaten his new rival, John McEnroe, on Centre Court at Wimbledon in a struggle that had lasted three hours and fifty-three minutes. The score was 1–6, 7–5, 6–3, 6–7, 8–6, but what the tennis world would remember most was the breathtaking tie-break that determined the outcome of the fourth set. Borg missed seven match balls and was forced to give up the set at 16–17. With his third set ball, McEnroe delivered a forehand that Borg, who was very close to the net, couldn't return. None of the nearly fifteen thousand fans there thought that their great hero – the man who had won the title in each of the four preceding years – would be able to accomplish the impossible yet again. Everything favoured the 'arch-rascal' from New York, who had acted scandalously on his way to the final but was now playing in exemplary fashion and with tremendous concentration against Borg.

Not having succeeded in winning the match despite seven match balls was too great a burden to bear in a fifth set, as both the fans at Wimbledon and hundreds of thousands of viewers in some forty countries around the world could sense. Borg had to be exhausted, both mentally and physically. Borg himself was probably the only person who didn't comprehend this fact. He came out on the court and continued with his usual masterly self-assurance. Even his serve was suddenly superior to McEnroe's. No one, least of all his opponent, could understand where he had found his renewed mental and physical strength. Borg lost only three points in the seven games he served, and he won five of them outright. With the set at 7–6 and the score at 40–15 in Borg's favour on McEnroe's serve, the outcome of the match was determined. Despite the fact that the American placed his serve far out on Borg's backhand side, he didn't have a chance against the Swede's return, which was a hard backhand cross that just cleared the net and caught McEnroe, who was rushing forward, off guard. Wimbledon exploded following the best and certainly most dramatic final that had ever been played, and Björn Borg sank to his knees and lifted his arms to the powers of heaven who had so generously rewarded him in this Mecca of tennis. He had won five straight Wimbledon finals. In cold tennis figures he was one of the world's greatest all-time players. Only the Australian Rod Laver, whose heyday had been in the 1950s and 1960s, could compete with him. Since 1974 Borg had won five French Opens, five Wimbledon titles, the Davis Cup, the Masters and the WCT finals, as well as about fifty other tournaments around the world. He had just turned 24, he had shoulder-length hair, and was worshipped as a god by tennis fans.

* * *

Three weeks later Borg married the Romanian tennis player Mariana Simionescu, whom he had been seeing since 1975. The couple and their two hundred invited guests participated in two weddings, one at the Bucharest city hall in the morning and the other at Bucharest's Monastery Church in the afternoon. Thus it was as a newly-wed that Björn Borg arrived in New York for the US Open a few weeks later.

The US Open was the only title of value that he had left to win. He had made it to the semi-finals in 1975 and to the finals in 1976 and 1978, but each time he had been beaten by Jimmy Connors. He felt it was necessary to win the US Open in order to achieve full recognition in the US as the best player in the world. In an interview the year before, Björn had said, 'You have to understand. The *fourth* straight title at Wimbledon meant an enormous amount, since no one [in modern times] had ever done it. But the fifth or sixth . . . no, now I want most of all to win the US Open.' It was true that he had never won the Australian Masters, but that was one competition he refused to participate in since he felt he had been badly treated in Australia in the mid-1970s. Then the Australian press had written that the young Swede hadn't cared at all about tennis, but had devoted himself only to Helena Anliot, another promising Swedish tennis player his age. Borg swore never to return. Until now he had kept his promise. But if he succeeded in his ninth attempt to win the US Open he would have won three of the four major tennis crowns in one year. In that case he might consider breaking his promise and flying to Melbourne in December in an attempt to complete the Grand Slam, which was his greatest dream.

To win enough to be remembered as the best player ever was all that really motivated him as a tennis player at this time. He was fed up with the constant travel and training required of a top tennis star. At only 24 he had played tennis full-time for nearly a decade. He was the world champion, the one everyone watched, the one everyone wanted to beat, and more and more of his opponents were now younger than he was. He wondered how much longer he would be able to stand the hard training regime. His body was the worse for wear. He had not mentioned it in public, but during the Wimbledon final he had been bothered by an injury to his stomach muscle and had been in considerable pain. He also had difficulties with a ligament in his right knee and had just been forced to leave the finals match at Toronto against the young Czech Ivan Lendl so as not to jeopardise his participation in the US Open. By the time he registered at the Drake Hotel in uptown Manhattan together with his wife, Mariana, and his trainer, Lennart Bergelin, Borg no longer felt the old thirst for competition. At the height of his career, Björn Borg longed for a life without tennis.

Björn was seeded number one in the tournament and bookmakers had set the odds at three to one. With his trademark headband in place, and with Mariana and Lennart in the stands, he went out into the heat of Louis Armstrong Stadium in Flushing Meadows, New York, which smelled of popcorn and hot dogs. Aircraft landing at LaGuardia Airport swung low over the asphalt, which sometimes nearly glowed in New York's hot summer temperatures. As usual, Borg dismissed his opponents one after the other. His strong legs held, his quick feet danced around and his surprising backhand cross scorched both the edge of the net and the sidelines. He appeared just as cool as ever in the gruelling heat.

In the quarter-finals Borg met Roscoe Tanner, the American with the remarkable serve who had defeated him in the quarter-finals the year before. Tanner won the first set, Borg the next two and Tanner the fourth. Borg dominated the fifth set, 6–3. He then met the South African Johan Kriek in the semi-finals, and Kriek shocked the Swede by taking the first two sets 6–4, 6–4. But Borg wouldn't take any more than that, winning the following sets 6–1, 6–1, 6–1. An American tennis writer wrote in one of the major New York papers: 'He's a Houdini – the first to bind himself in chains, lock himself in a trunk and allow himself to be thrown into the Atlantic – and who wears a headband and uses a two-handed backhand. And of all the people who have tried to go over Niagara Falls in a barrel Björn Borg has the longest hair.'

For his part, McEnroe had suffered through a rough semi-final with US Open specialist Jimmy Connors. McEnroe won after four and a half hours, 6–4, 5–7, 0–6, 6–3, 7–6. On the eve of the final Borg prepared himself by watching that match with Mariana at their hotel. It wasn't that he needed to study his opponent before the final – he knew McEnroe's game forward and backward – but because he suffered a bad case of the butterflies, like all finalists do.

Borg and McEnroe appeared on centre court at 4 p.m. on Sunday, 8 September 1980, to the cheers and jeers of some twenty thousand fans. It felt just like a heavyweight championship bout with Mohammed Ali in one of the corners. The crowd sensed the excitement and drama of the moment. The two players were opposites: Borg, the world champion, was a cool and merciless machine who always kept his feelings to himself; McEnroe, the second best player in the world, was a temperamental artist who frequently boiled over.

It was a repeat performance of the Wimbledon final two months earlier, a bitter struggle that lasted over four hours. But neither Borg nor McEnroe played as well as they had at Wimbledon. The real magic and the spectacular exchanges were missing this time, despite the fact that it was John McEnroe, the born artist, who won this time, 7–6, 6–1, 6–7, 5–7, 6–4. It was the first time in more than six years that Borg had lost a five-set finals match in an important competition. Some years later Björn would tell me that he drove out to his large new house at Sands Point on Long Island after the match, sat by his pool far into the night and tried to drown his sorrows in champagne. He was sad at having lost the match and at once again having failed to win the US Open, but deep down he felt something like relief. If he had won, the pressure would have been too great. He was tired of tennis and that evening by the pool he felt that his loss had given him a chance to realise his plans: to quit as soon as the right opportunity presented itself. There was no strategy behind this decision, such as quitting at the top of his career. He was just thoroughly tired of it all.

During the remainder of 1980 Borg played in only a couple of tournaments and a handful of exhibition matches. He lost a rough five-set match in the final against Ivan Lendl in Basel, but when he arrived in Sweden to play in the Stockholm Open in November his edge and his concentration had returned. Despite several attempts, Borg had never won the Stockholm Open, which is one of the most prestigious indoor titles and always attracts a number of top players. Following his loss at the US Open, Björn was determined to win this competition. His way to the finals, however, was strewn with arguments with the Swedish sportswriters. Borg had carried on feuds with a number of journalists ever since they had criticised his move from Sweden to Monte Carlo in 1974 as an attempt to avoid taxes.

The 'war' with the press had escalated in 1978, when Borg and Vitas Gerulaitis were in Israel to play an exhibition match. On one occasion some Israeli soldiers asked the two tennis stars for their autographs, and then one of the soldiers asked if they wanted to try on their uniform jackets. Borg and Gerulaitis innocently agreed. Clad in the army jackets with rifles over their shoulders, the two posed for the soldiers, who snapped their picture. The picture of these two famous 'Israeli sympathisers' was then spread around the world by the newspapers. The Swedish press characterised this innocent event as a 'political manifestation' and condemned it roundly.

The incident gave rise to considerable irritation within IMG, since politics was to be avoided at all cost in the world of sports. Matters were not improved by the fact that the PLO reacted by threatening to murder Borg for taking a stance in favour of Israel. Peter Worth spent a number of hours on the phone trying to calm the

Palestinians while a very frightened Borg sought safety at his parents' villa at Cap Ferrat, protected by machine-gun-toting guards day and night. It was not until Worth personally delivered a written apology and a guarantee from Borg that he was not against the Palestinian cause and that he did not support the Israeli cause in any way, that the matter was resolved. Borg's representatives later sought assurances from the top PLO leader that they had retracted their threat, and it was not until they gave it that Borg dispensed with his armed guards. Borg had not been able to forgive the newspapers that had made so much of the event.

A new threat to Borg's life was made on the eve of the Stockholm Open, and he was very angry that it, too, was played up in the Swedish papers. As a result Borg curbed his contacts with the press and refused to make any statements. He even went so far as to avoid the obligatory press conferences, for which the organisers fined him $2,000, a sum that had absolutely no effect on him in the circumstances. The sportswriters felt that Borg was working against them, they criticised him and the situation became even more tense.

On the court, however, Borg let his racket do the talking. He made it to the finals with the loss of only one set. In the final he once again faced John McEnroe, but this time the American didn't have a chance. Borg won in straight sets. Following his victory, he appeared at his first press conference during that year's Stockholm Open, but refused to speak Swedish, answering in English all questions put to him in Swedish. His visit to his native land thus ended in a tennis victory, but paved the way for a number of bitter comments in the Swedish papers. This was hardly a relaxed or harmonious tennis star returning home to make an appearance.

When it came to his earnings, however, Borg had every reason to be happy. His 1980 income amounted to $650,000 in prize monies from competitions, $1.1 million from exhibition matches and $2.8 million from advertising contracts. Above and beyond that were earnings of about $500,000 from Borg's investments, for a total annual income in excess of $5 million. Measured in dollars, it had been a very good year.

Borg participated in only a few tournaments in the spring of 1981, spending more of his time playing exhibition matches. He went on a long exhibition tour, first with John McEnroe in Australia (breaking his promise never to return), and then with his best friend in tennis, Vitas Gerulaitis. The trips with Vitas meant easy tennis, quick money and a lot of partying. On these occasions Borg discarded his ice-cold and apparently nonchalant demeanour, and did so to an extreme. The rumours about narcotics that had circulated before now became more persistent, and information about how the two young tennis idols used various drugs made its way into the IMG boardroom. But as long as Borg kept in shape for the important tournaments, no one raised any objections. After all, in 1981, as in 1980, these exhibitions earned him well over $1 million, and a single such match could earn him $100,000.

Borg's trainer, Lennart Bergelin, did not like these lucrative exhibition tours. He felt that in the long-run they interfered with Björn's ability to concentrate on the important competitions, and that he should instead train even harder and keep his tours to a minimum. Between tours he should schedule rest periods in order to spare his body and let the regularly occurring small injuries heal.

Borg and Bergelin were both individuals with strong personalities. Bergelin, or Labbe, as he was called, was the one who had introduced hard work into the world of tennis. Borg won, above all, because he was stronger, better trained and had more stamina than his opponents. He was the first who used strength and muscles to defeat opponents who counted on finesse and technique. It was also a matter of mental preparation. Bergelin didn't care who the opponent was or how he played. His orders were always the same: 'Get in there and fight.' This approach was perfect for Borg, who had never been one for deep analyses or explanations. The two men respected each other. Borg liked Bergelin's straightforward and simple manner, and Bergelin respected Borg for his willingness to work out very hard and for his total devotion to the sport. In their common ambition the two of them developed into the best working team in tennis. They travelled together, worked out and ate dinner together, played cards or watched TV together in the evenings and frequently shared suites in the hotels where they stayed. Nonetheless Borg always saw to it that he maintained a certain distance, particularly after Mariana came into the picture.

With the addition of Mariana, a new sort of teamwork began to emerge. Mariana took care of the laundry, packed and unpacked suitcases, arranged for the food and generally supported her husband. Bergelin booked airline tickets, arranged the training schedule, served as the masseur and amateur psychologist, and kept a sharp eye on Borg's game. Borg's job was to win his matches. But Borg was also the boss, the employer, and this was very clear when, for example, Bergelin was negotiating his salary. Borg turned the negotiation over to IMG, refusing to discuss his trainer's salary directly with him. Borg would have preferred not to have paid him at all, but to have him paid in some other manner, for example, out of IMG's own budget. Bergelin accepted every agreement without much grumbling. When it came to exhibition matches, too, he couldn't do much more than accept what his protégé decided.

It was in 1981 that John McEnroe definitely surpassed his three-year-older adversary. Borg won the French Open for the sixth time in eight years, defeating Ivan Lendl in the final 6–1, 4–6, 6–2, 3–6, 6–1, despite the fact that he had indicated on the eve of the competition that he was so tired of tennis that he could hardly stand to see a racket. This was Björn Borg's last victory in a Grand Slam championship.

He went on to London to defend his Wimbledon title. As usual, he stayed at the Holiday Inn at Swiss Cottage, took out the tennis clothes he had worn at Wimbledon since his first win in 1976 and let his thin beard grow. This time even the optimistic Bergelin was hesitant. He said that he had butterflies in his stomach, which was a new experience for him. They turned out to be well-deserved. While Borg made it to the finals against McEnroe, his serve failed him and he lost 6–4, 6–7, 6–7, 4–6. Thus ended Borg's record of forty-one straight match victories on

Wimbledon's grass courts. Borg didn't show any great disappointment at the press conference that followed, merely commenting that nothing can last for ever and that the US Open was his big goal for the year in any case.

He lost there, too, in a match that lasted four sets. Once again it was McEnroe who won, this time 4–6, 6–2, 6–4, 6–3. It was during this period that the tennis writers first began to broach the burning question, although no one dared actually ask the superstar whether he was thinking about quitting and bringing his fantastic career to an end. Nonetheless, the questions they put were new ones, as was their tone: 'Is it hard to get up for your matches?', 'Are you pursuing other interests these days?', 'Is it difficult to train all the time?' With great diplomacy, and without really answering at all, Borg said: 'Yes, I do have other interests,' and 'My style of playing requires more training than other players' styles.' There was one question, however, that he couldn't answer without revealing his feelings: 'What if you never win the US Open, which you've always wanted so badly?' His answer was: 'If I never win . . . it doesn't matter. I wouldn't mind. It wouldn't bother me.'

Following his defeat in the final, Borg showered quickly and went directly to his Saab. He drove out to his house on Long Island with a police escort and quickly closed the door behind him. He skipped both the press conference and the prize ceremony, saying, 'It's McEnroe's show, you know.'

On 27 September 1981 Borg won his last Grand Prix tournament by defeating Tomas Smid in the finals at

Geneva. Early in the competition he had had a match against a 17-year-old by the name of Mats Wilander. The curly-haired youngster was very, very nervous about playing against his famous compatriot and Borg won handily. A few weeks later Borg literally threw his racket in the cupboard and went on holiday, saying, 'Now I'm going to take time off and devote myself to things I've never had time to do. Nobody but the world's top-ranked player knows what it takes to get to the top. You have to sacrifice everything.'

When the Masters Championships took place in New York in the middle of January 1982 Borg was nowhere to be seen. This was not welcome news to the organisers, since he had won the event the previous two years in a row. As he was the champion and refused to defend his title, Borg was punished according to the rules. He lost the $60,000 that was to have been his share of the bonus pool and at least an additional $10,000, which was the size of the consolation prizes that were to be given to those who reached the final stages of the competition. Borg's desertion turned into his good friend Vitas Gerulaitis's fortune. Vitas was number nine in the Grand Prix rankings, but when Borg withdrew from the Masters he was invited to take his place. Gerulaitis turned out to be a worthy stand-in for Borg, reaching the final and defeating Ivan Lendl in a five-set match. 'That was the first time Björn ever let me win any money,' he said ironically, holding the winner's cheque for $50,000.

Meanwhile, Björn Borg was in Monte Carlo with Mariana doing absolutely nothing. He took a break from his holiday to participate in the Monte Carlo Open in

April, and the newspapers outdid one another in speculating about his 'comeback'. It wasn't a very successful one. He was defeated by Yannick Noah after having chosen a clearly suicidal tactic of continually charging the net on the slow clay court.

Mats Wilander won the French Open at the beginning of June 1982. By defeating Guillermo Vilas in a five-set match, he surpassed Borg's record as the French Open's youngest winner ever. Borg was not in Paris and it was noted that he didn't send a congratulatory telegram to his compatriot who had followed him on to the Roland Garros throne.

It was not until September that Borg made another serious appearance in the tennis world by participating in a twelve-man tournament in Montreal. There, in good conditions and in fine humour, he won match after match before falling to Jimmy Connors in the final. During his stay in Canada he announced that his goal was to be number one in the world again, that he had signed up for twelve Grand Prix competitions in 1983 and that he would show up in top shape and eager to win. It was the same Björn Borg who a few months later would pick up the phone in Monte Carlo and call Peter Worth in Val d'Isère, the same Björn Borg who would say to Worth, 'Peter, I've decided to quit playing the circuit. My last tournament will be Monte Carlo in April, but that's the last one.'

CHAPTER THREE

A Penny Saved...

The young Björn Borg had got some good advice from Björn Gullström, who had told him in 1973 that 'a penny saved is a penny earned'. Borg immediately began following that advice, so his adult life came to be characterised by a cautious attitude in money matters. Björn Gullström's task as financial adviser began at a time when Borg's income began to rocket and it became evident that his father, Rune, was not up to overseeing and conducting his son's affairs. Rune had made a number of brave attempts, however, as in the case of his negotiations with the chairman of the Swedish Davis Cup committee, Mats Hasselqvist, in the summer of 1972. Hasselqvist had decided that $2,400 a year was an appropriate level of compensation for the 16-year-old tennis player. Rune had asked for time to think the matter over and had later asked that the amount be doubled. Hasselqvist was, of course, very happy to agree, for Björn earned that much money for the Davis Cup committee in no time whatsoever. The next year the guaranteed amount was raised to $100,000.

When Björn's career went international, the small circle of people around him felt that he should have a professional agent to help him with commercial matters. Then, too, someone was going to have to help Björn on his many lengthy trips around the circuit. It finally came down to a choice between two agents, Donald Dell and Mark

McCormack, and the decision was made at lunch at Enskilda Banken in Stockholm. Björn was joined there by his parents and a number of bank officials, but it was clear that the 17-year-old Borg was the one who was going to make the decision. He chose McCormack.

When Mark McCormack played on his college golf team during the 1950s he became friends with a promising young golfer by the name of Arnold Palmer. Palmer went on to play golf professionally, which was something that McCormack's talents did not allow him to do. Instead he went to Yale Law School, and the two teammates parted ways, if only temporarily. When McCormack got a position with a law firm in Cleveland, Ohio, he offered Palmer his services as an adviser on the commercial aspects of his career on the professional golf circuit. While working as Palmer's agent in negotiating with the organisers of golf tournaments and with companies wishing to gain Palmer's endorsement of their products, and while managing Palmer's investments, McCormack came up with a new business concept that led him to found the International Management Group (IMG) in the early 1960s. McCormack's business sense and strong organisational skills formed the basis for a successful multinational company, and his ability to attract both clients and loyal, hard-working employees, usually referred to as Mark's Men, soon established IMG's reputation.

My own experience as IMG's representative for Scandinavia gave me great insights into the company, and I was not at all surprised that Björn chose IMG to represent him. He recognised the company's know-how and thus its possibilities. Borg had the ability and the patience to work with people who knew more about business and managing money than he did. But above all he liked IMG's basic philosophy: 'We are advisers – the client makes the decisions. With our help, the client will earn more money over a longer period of time.'

When Mark McCormack first met the Swedish teenager, he immediately understood that Borg was a unique athlete and saw in him the same economic potential he had once seen in Palmer. Tennis was becoming an internationally popular television sport and Björn Borg was, without question, the most interesting of all the young players. With his uniquely devised counter-slams from the base line, his lightning-quick footwork, his ability never to give up and his complete calm and concentration in difficult situations – not to mention his youth and his long hair – Borg made tennis popular with a new generation. In 1974, even before turning 18, Borg became the youngest person ever to win the French Open, and at Wimbledon he had to make his escape through a window at the back of the locker-room to avoid being overwhelmed by his fans, most of whom were radiant teenage girls who came to be known as 'Björn's gang'. That same year Björn graced the cover of *Newsweek* magazine, an indisputable sign that he had 'arrived'. Tennis had become the latest thing and its hero was Björn Borg. In that sense he was more like a rock star than a tennis player.

IMG's leadership gives its employees instructions about how they are to work with clients, so every client is treated in the same way and all of Mark's Men work the same way. The primary aspect of dealing with clients is to suggest a strategy for how best to market them and their name, how to maximise their income during their career in sports and how to manage the money they earn. When it came to the new coverboy Borg, McCormack spared no resources in putting together a suitable plan. He brought in the best tax consultants and began building up a separate sales organisation and financial management team. During the 1970s the money IMG earned on Borg financed the firm's newly-founded European operations.

In Sweden the evening paper *Expressen* had advertised its edition of 10 July 1973 with the headline: 'BJÖRN TO BE A MILLIONAIRE' and reported on his contract with Scandinavian Airlines System, better known by its initials SAS. On the advice of IMG, Borg decided to move from Sweden to Monaco in view of the former's high taxes and the latter's lack of taxes on income and capital. Björn Gullström made the arrangements for the move for Borg and his parents, who said goodbye to their old life and didn't hesitate for a moment to follow their son. Borg's move was also of great advantage to McCormack, for IMG gained indirect but very great influence over the Borg family. No one in the family spoke French, which made them very dependent on IMG's assistance. The disadvantage of living in Monaco was that Rune and Margaretha wanted to visit Sweden frequently, while Swedish tax law doesn't allow Swedish emigrants to spend more than a certain amount of time in Sweden each year. Monaco is a very small country that occupies only three-quarters of a square mile of territory. While it doesn't have income taxes, it doesn't have Sweden's space and vegetation either. It is easy for a Swede to tire of the view of the Mediterranean from a condominium on the twentieth floor in Monte Carlo's concrete desert, where the sun glares down most of the year.

These problems were not unique to the Borg family. Many people who move to Monaco eventually acquire a holiday home in France, which is right next door and has plenty of space. Sometimes these 'holiday' homes are luxury villas, and once they are purchased their owners' permanent residences in Monaco are transferred to efficiency flats. For the rich and well-known, the authorities in Monaco don't say anything about these moves, and people can maintain tax-free status without being forced to register as permanent residents of France.

When the Borg family decided to purchase a villa, IMG and Gullström put their heads together and came up with an excellent idea. They had found the perfect villa for the Borgs at St Jean Cap Ferrat, just half an hour's drive from Monaco. Gullström studied Sweden's double-taxation agreement with France and found that the best thing to do was to have Borg's parents become permanent residents of France, which would then allow them to visit Sweden more frequently. Björn gave the villa to his parents; since he was their only heir he didn't risk losing it by doing so. He himself remained a legal resident of Monaco, but could stay with his parents and use their pool as often and for as long as he wished.

With their client securely set up, IMG quickly moved on to arrange Borg's business matters: Peter Worth was given responsibility for sales, while John Webber and Julian Jakobi were put in charge of financial management. Borg immediately took to the routines they established. Worth taught him that all the decisions were his to make

49

and soon learned that Borg had a very high opinion of his own value. When Worth presented a proposal for a contract, Borg usually had a suggestion to offer, and his suggestions always pointed in the same direction – upwards, more. In addition, Jakobi's cost-conscious or even rather frugal lifestyle and cautiousness won great respect from the new tennis millionaire. Thanks to Gullström's words of wisdom, Borg also learned to consider the money he earned to be sacrosanct, untouchable. It went straight into investments and was not subsequently considered a part of his immediate assets.

This was the way in which Borg's assets were managed from the middle of the 1970s onward. Borg himself was very careful and didn't spend much money. Thanks to his contract with SAS, he had unlimited free travel. His meals and lodgings were provided by tournament organisers and firms with whom he had contracts. When he was travelling, IMG's growing network of offices around the world served as Borg's private bank. Any time he needed cash, he would simply go to one of the offices and withdraw the amount he wanted from his account.

Twice a year Borg's financial advisers, Jakobi and Webber, met with Björn's 'comptroller-in-chief', Björn Gullström, in Monte Carlo to review IMG's management of Borg's business and investments over the course of the previous six months. The record of IMG's client management was assembled in a document called the 'Blue Book', which presented the total income and total expenses for the period in question, as well as the status of Borg's investments as of 30 June and 31 December of each year. In addition, the Blue Book contained a detailed review of all transactions that had taken place during each six-month period. IMG's attitude was characterised by complete openness, which was something that was appreciated by all of their clients and their lawyers and accountants. Borg always studied the summary and the final figures that indicated his net worth and how it had increased over the past half year. After that he left it to Gullström to make sure that all the details and special transactions of any magnitude were in order. Björn Borg was soon a rich man and the division of labour was made permanent: IMG negotiated endorsement contracts, which Borg reviewed and approved; IMG managed his investments, while Gullström audited the books on Borg's behalf. IMG, Björn Borg and Björn Gullström emerged as a successful business trio with complementary talents. IMG took 10 per cent of Borg's prize monies and appearance money and a 25 per cent fee (reduced to 20 per cent in 1978) for the endorsement contracts it negotiated for him. Borg put the remainder into his inviolable investment accounts.

IMG's administration of investments constituted a source of income, but also had another purpose, namely, that of tying the client even more closely to IMG. As part of its administrative services, IMG had developed its own system for minimising taxation on income. Its flagship was European Sports Merchandising BV (ESM), a wholly-owned subsidiary in the Netherlands and it operated in the following way.

When the client began earning money, a company was set up and registered on his or her behalf in the British Virgin Islands, on Jersey or in some other tax haven. That company paid no tax in the client's home country and was usually named for the client, as in the case of Björn Borg Enterprises Ltd. ESM then was given the right to sell the client's name for endorsement purposes, in return for which it earned a commission of a maximum of 7 per cent of gross income. Since ESM was registered in the Netherlands, the firm was able to take advantage of that country's double-taxation agreements with other countries and reduce the tax on endorsement incomes, for example, from as much as 30 per cent to less than 10 per cent. Thus a Swedish company could compensate Borg for his endorsement services by paying an invoice sent to it from Monaco on behalf of a Dutch firm. It was an effective and much appreciated system, and one of IMG's top executives told me proudly that Borg paid an average of less than 5 per cent in taxes on his income. ESM paid the taxes, deducted its own and IMG's commission, and transferred the remainder to the client's company, whose assets were usually administered by the inseparable Webber and Jakobi.

If and when the assets became sufficiently large, a trust fund would be established in order to avoid taxes on capital and future inheritance taxes when, for example, the client returned home at the end of his career. These trust funds had fanciful names like Hersilia (in honour of the building in Monte Carlo where IMG had its offices) and Dracula, and were administered from Liechtenstein in order to avoid inspections by the various tax authorites. IMG also had its own investment funds in which clients purchased shares and received a portion of the profits and capital gains.

Borg liked the idea of creating a trust fund. Many

Swedes would have thought first and foremost about the tax advantages, but Borg had adopted a more international perspective and didn't consider the tax burden to be a major problem. Instead, he was attracted to the idea of a trust fund as a watertight form of asset protection. Neither creditors nor the socialist regime in Sweden would be able to take away the capital he had accumulated. Borg had found a new motto: 'Don't put your trust in money, put your money in trust.' Once money was placed in the trust fund, Björn no longer considered it available for his use. He never touched it.

At the end of 1980 Björn Borg's net worth stood at $10 million. His gross income that year was $5,050,000 and after paying his largest bill – the fees to IMG – Borg was able to add about $3 million to his capital assets, thereby increasing them by a fantastic 30 per cent. His investments were managed in the classical manner, with an optimal diversification among cash, stocks and bonds, real estate and precious metals. The cash resources were placed in various currencies. Over time IMG built up an investment fund around Borg called the Marksmen's Fund, and at one time the Swede owned 30 per cent of its assets. IMG made all the investment decisions and sought to preserve the value of the capital invested, rather than to maximise dividends.

At this time Björn Borg had about forty endorsement contracts, of which those with SAS, Saab, Donnay and Lois jeans involved worldwide rights. His contract with the sportswear firm Fila involved rights everywhere except in Scandinavia, where he played in clothes made by Jockey. He used Diadora tennis shoes everywhere except in the

US and Canada, where he wore shoes by Tretorn. Among the more exotic products for which Borg advertised were Viking sewing machines (worldwide rights), the Björn Borg doll (USA) and Björn Borg toys and soft drinks (Brazil). His income from endorsement activity amounted to $2,800,000 in 1980.

Endorsement rights were targeted geographically and according to product in order to maximise income. For the public, however, it was rather confusing to see Borg play in outfits made by Fila at Wimbledon but in outfits made by Jockey when he played in Sweden. The tennis star himself had little reason to complain. In 1981 his income from various endorsement contracts was estimated to have grown to nearly $4 million.

Even Borg's 'sabbatical year' of 1982 proved to be a great economic success. He had almost no income from matches, of course, since he competed so seldom, but that was more than offset by the easily won prize monies from exhibition matches, which brought him more than $1 million. Together with his endorsement incomes and the proceeds from his investments, 1982 was economically just as profitable as the two previous years, with a gross income of more than $5 million.

At the end of March and the beginning of April 1983 Björn Borg played against Henri Leconte in the Monte Carlo Open, losing 6–4, 5–7, 6–7 after a dramatic 136 minutes of play before a crowd of ten thousand people, television crews from all over the world and more accredited journalists than there were at Wimbledon.

'Now it's over. You've seen my last match,' said Borg, smiling. 'It's great that it's over, even if I am, as usual, disappointed about losing.'

He was 26 years old, had just retired, and had $16 million in the bank. Once again he had shown his decisiveness. He seemed to be a very enviable young man.

CHAPTER FOUR

Ex-Tennis Player for Sale

As a true lover of sports, my favourite athlete was Björn Borg. Like so many other Swedes, I had watched every Wimbledon tournament from the mid-1970s onwards, following Borg's matches, many of which were breathlessly exciting. I was impressed by his fantastic will, his winner's instincts and, perhaps most of all, by his good sportsmanship: no arrogance when he won and no excuses when he lost, which he almost never did. It seemed ironic to me that Borg endorsed Sweden's Fila sportswear and I ran the Swedish franchise for Tacchini, now famous for tennis and leisurewear. Later, I formed my own marketing company, Project House. I dreamed of bringing together the Swedish clothing industry and the name Björn Borg, not to market more tennis wear but a complete fashion line.

During a visit to London in the spring of 1982 I met Peter Worth and over lunch described my plans to him. I waited nervously for his reaction. Would he laugh at my boldness and think me a brusque opportunist? An upstart? A slightly plump Englishman in a proper City suit, he looked at me intently across the table and tried to manage a relaxed smile.

'That sounds interesting, Lars, very interesting. I'll get back to you.'

As the days and weeks passed I began to think that Peter Worth had forgotten all about my idea or that it had been rejected immediately. Then one late summer day he finally called.

'Hello, Lars! I've got good news. Björn is interested and wants to discuss your idea.'

Peter's phone call prompted me to do some more thinking about the idea of marketing clothes under Björn Borg's name. My dream project suddenly seemed to be within reach, but I had noted, along with everyone else, that Borg's name had been missing from the rankings ever since his surprisingly weak match against Yannick Noah in Monte Carlo early that spring. When I raised the point with Peter Worth, he reassured me.

'Björn will definitely not quit playing. He needs time to rest after all these hard years, but he'll return to full-time tennis next year. We've recently concluded a number of contracts, and in connection with them he has said that he has no intention of quitting. And why should he quit? He's only 26 and can earn an enormous amount of money over the next few years.'

I went into action as quickly as I could and made an appointment to see Åke Kjellman, the head of the state-owned Eiser textile and clothing company. The industry was in crisis: imported clothes from countries with cheap labour, such as Hong Kong, presented very tough competition and it was difficult to export Swedish clothes. I drew up a concept, called it Björn Borg Menswear and designed a logo. As I drove to Borås, where Eiser had its headquarters, I was nervous. My plans were very sketchy and I wasn't sure where I or my company might come into the picture. Of course, I wanted to make money with my idea; the question was how to do it.

Kjellman was a former military man in his sixties with a stern voice.

'Well, young man,' he greeted me. 'How can I be of service?'

I opened my flip chart to a picture of Björn Borg in action. Kjellman immediately asked if I was thinking about tennis clothes.

'No, sir,' I replied, 'I'm thinking of a classical line of men's fashions on the order of the Boss line, but perhaps a bit more towards the leisure side.'

'I see,' said Kjellman. 'And how does the name Björn Borg figure in? By the way, isn't it expensive to bring him into the picture?'

I had thought of an answer to that question in advance.

'You have the know-how and the machines, right? Let's say that we were to introduce a trademark on the world market – we can call it Clatch. How much would it cost to make that trademark known? How many millions would you have to invest in that effort alone? And how long would it take? But the name Björn Borg is already known everywhere and you would get a great deal of publicity around the project. This may be just what the Swedish textile and clothing industry needs!'

Kjellman acknowledged my point. He thought for a moment and then asked me to come back with a detailed proposal. He was prepared to pay $30,000 in order to proceed.

Even before going to Borås I had decided not to try to manage the whole project on my own. It would have taken too much money and would have displaced all the other plans I had for Project House. Now I began looking for an administrator whom I could trust with my dream and settled on Jimmie Ahrgren, who was known to be very good. I told him about my idea and asked if he would consider managing it for me. He said he would be very happy to do so.

Ahrgren set to work at once and after a good deal of effort succeeded in putting together a business plan that we could present to Eiser's board of directors. Meanwhile we negotiated with Borg via Peter Worth, a negotiation in which I took part and which was rather long and difficult. IMG frequently interrupted the negotiations to consult the tennis star himself, who had his own ideas about most issues. The big question was what would happen if Borg brought his tennis career to a close. IMG adamantly refused to allow the inclusion of a clause that would reduce Borg's income if he retired, while arguing forcefully that he had no such intentions. With the benefit of hindsight I know that even IMG had been misled when it came to Borg's plans for the future. In the end we signed a ten-year agreement that called for Björn Borg to receive an average of $400,000 a year for the use of his name, as well as 3 per cent of gross sales.

At its meeting on Monday, 11 October 1982, Eiser's board of directors decided to launch the Björn Borg line of clothing. This decision immediately produced head-lines, like this one in the Stockholm evening paper *Expressen*: 'Borg to save 200 Swedish jobs – sells leisure clothes for millions.' This was the positive launch the company needed and that I had predicted to Åke Kjellman at our first meeting.

A presentation was to be made to Björn Borg and selected members of Eiser's board of directors, and I was among those invited to the newly-opened office in Stockholm. I had met Björn once or twice before, but only very briefly. He was a pleasant, modest and good-natured fellow who laughed and smiled very easily. Dressed in leisure clothes and looking very healthy, he seemed relaxed as he greeted us politely, introduced himself and made small talk with everyone. I was immediately impressed by how professionally he conducted himself at this first meeting with his future principals. However, despite the fact that the idea was mine and that I had taken the initiative with both Eiser and IMG, neither my services nor those of Project House, aside from a few small assignments, were welcome any longer. I naturally felt hurt and slighted.

I followed the project more or less from afar over the course of the next year. I thought that a number of mistakes were made, the first of which was hiring the Swede Rohdi Heintz to design the line. He was known as a clever designer, but his clothes were expensive to manufacture and the cut was far from the classical look I had had in mind. Although the Björn Borg trademark appealed to lots of people, the clothes Heintz designed were too extreme to capture a very broad market. Moreover, they were not top quality. Eiser invested millions in promoting the line. Didn't they understand that the marketing was practically all done by virtue of the name Björn Borg? Instead of investing in marketing, the company should have put all its resources in the quality and manufacturing of the product.

My ties with IMG were reinforced during this period. We had come to know each other better during the negotiations for the Eiser contract, and Project House became IMG's agent in Scandinavia, receiving commissions for the contracts we negotiated. I absorbed all the information I could about how IMG functioned and attempted to apply that know-how to Project House Ltd. I did not, however, have any plans for us to become especially involved with Björn Borg. He was IMG's 'property' and we had our hands full of exciting projects. We began to work with Borg only because his name fit in with some of our projects, including one for a twenty-seven-hole golf course in Vallentuna, north of Stockholm.

Kullenbergs, a Swedish construction company, had purchased the land and financed the construction of the golf course. A lot of time had been spent looking for a good way to market the course and we were given the assignment. After considering a number of ideas, my partner, Egon Håkanson, and I came up with a plan to create Sweden's first corporate club, a club that would provide conference facilities, tennis, a health spa, a restaurant and a hotel in addition to golf. We proposed that companies in the Stockholm area would purchase shares in the club for purposes of representation and programmes for their employees. The problem was that we couldn't find a good name for the club, and that put everything on hold. And then we thought of Björn Borg.

Furnished with a new flip chart, I visited Kullenbergs' main office in Gothenburg to present our proposal to the firm's chief executives. This time I was hardly nervous at all and looked forward to the reactions the proposal would provoke. I wasn't disappointed. As I presented the business concept I could see that the idea was being received very well, but it was also clear that Kullenbergs' leadership felt something was missing. Then I showed the last page of my flip chart, which once again was graced by a picture of Björn Borg in action. Everyone immediately understood what I was about to say, and for the first and probably only time in my life I was greeted by spontaneous applause.

Later that day I contacted Peter Worth and told him the whole story. He liked the idea immediately and thought it would be great for Björn. Not only would he earn money, but having a golf course and corporate club named for him would contribute to keeping his name 'alive' now that he had retired. I emphasised that there was no time to waste, and a preliminary contract proposal arrived by courier a couple of days later.

Kullenbergs accepted the conditions that IMG presented on Borg's behalf: $100,000 for the use of his name and $10,000 plus expenses for making personal appearances at the club. The contract was initially to run for ten years and these amounts were to be increased by a certain percentage each year. The contract also guaranteed Borg an annual share of the profits.

Nor was Project House left out. We got $500,000 for the work we had done, and Kullenbergs asked us to manage the sales memberships in the club in return for a commission of 30 per cent. We had already drawn up a budget concerning sales to various companies, based on the premise of 500 member companies each paying $6,000 annual membership dues. Kullenbergs decided to invest another $5 million in the construction of a luxurious clubhouse.

Meanwhile Björn Borg Menswear had shown its first autumn collection. The place that Eiser International AB, as the subsidiary formed to manage the new clothing line was called, had chosen was Paris and, more specifically, Roland Garros Tennis Stadium, where Borg had won the French Open in 1974, 1975, 1978, 1979, 1980 and 1981. As Eiser president Per-Axel Eriksson put it, 'You have to get ahead in a variety of ways. Renting Roland Garros was the right setting for this. We at Swedish Eiser have to make ourselves known in Paris when we compete with well-known giants like Yves St Laurent.'

In Paris with the Eiser people, I realised for the first time the adulation Björn Borg enjoyed abroad. When he appeared at the stadium in his new line of clothing it seemed as if the cheers would never end, and afterwards people literally fought to get close to him. There were an enormous number of people from the media. Everyone wanted to talk to Borg, but even the designer, Rohdi Heintz, received his modest portion of attention, and I had to admit that his collection really made an impression in this special setting. That evening the entire Swedish entourage had dinner together, and I couldn't help asking Borg, 'What is it like for a regular guy from Södertälje to become so well-known out in the big world?'

He only laughed. The next day one of the Stockholm evening papers, *Aftonbladet*, wrote: 'Yesterday Björn Borg won his seventh victory at the venerable old Roland Garros Tennis Stadium – without a tennis racket in his hand. This time he could relax and leave both hands in his pockets.

Borg, the king of clay, took his first step into the world of fashion.'

The successful première gave rise to great expectations for Björn Borg Menswear and orders quickly began coming in. Then something happened that simply must not happen: Eiser was unable to meet the orders. In the summer of 1983 Eiser International AB had orders to the value of around $20 million, but was able to deliver only $2.6 million worth of clothes because it wasn't able to manufacture them any faster. It was a catastrophe. A large number of stores had set up special Björn Borg departments and in the autumn of 1983 their shelves were embarrassingly empty. The success of Björn Borg Menswear at the Paris showing had led Eiser to feel very optimistic about the venture; after this débâcle that optimism turned to pessimism and no one seemed prepared to repair the market's loss of confidence in the company. The parent firm was dissatisfied, and in desperation Eiser International's leadership team put together a consortium to buy the company from the Eiser conglomerate. Björn Borg was invited to participate in the buy-out, but both IMG and Björn Gullström were vehemently opposed to the idea.

Gullström discussed the matter with me and I agreed with him. I was going to the Far East in 1984 and met Björn Borg in Tokyo. He was there on a visit and was staying with his father at the same hotel into which I had booked. I gathered up my courage and phoned him, and we agreed to meet in his suite. It was early in the morning and when I arrived Björn was having breakfast in his bathrobe. He didn't say very much, instead listening to what I had to say about the purchase of the company. This was the first time I had had a real opportunity to talk about business alone with Björn. He didn't reveal where he stood during the conversation and we didn't talk about it afterwards. I had no idea whether he had even listened to what I said. In the end, however, there was no buy-out and Eiser International AB remained the property of the Swedish state.

As was my habit, I spent my summer holiday in 1984 with my wife and two daughters on Gotland. One of the things I most enjoyed doing there was playing golf at Kronholmen Golf Course, a lovely and rather windy course on the coast with a lighthouse as a landmark behind the eighteenth hole. As I was enjoying a beer on the clubhouse veranda after my round one day in July, a man in his forties with a great head of curly hair sat down next to me and said hello. I recognised him from Stockholm. His name was Jack Rothschild and I knew that he owned a company called Romella, which marketed perfume. We began chatting and soon found ourselves starting a new round at the first tee. As we played, Rothschild began talking business and asked whether we had any plans to sell perfume under Björn Borg's name. I replied that we had discussed the idea and that we had several options. Rothschild said that he had just introduced a line of perfume under the name of Björn Axén, the hairdresser to the Swedish court, and that it appeared to be a very promising venture. He indicated that he was more than interested in doing something similar in collaboration with Björn Borg. I thought it was an interesting prospect and, since there was no obstacle to my making proposals and taking initiatives for new ideas involving Björn, we ended the day by making a date for lunch in Stockholm a month later.

Rothschild was well prepared. He had already developed detailed plans for how to market the product and when to introduce it. For his part, Björn liked the idea and gave it his approval. Peter Worth joined us for our next meeting and a few months later the Björn Borg perfume for men was a reality. The fragrance was composed by the renowned perfume manufacturer Givaudan and the bottle was designed by the guru of the business, the Frenchman Pierre Dinand. The contract was signed and would eventually pay Björn Borg another $400,000 a year.

CHAPTER FIVE

Love Comes, Love Goes

On Friday, 15 June 1984, the phone rang in Christer Gustafsson's small and unpretentious flat in Stockholm. As he used to say, the place was 'just big enough to turn around in'. Gustafsson was 35, called himself a public relations consultant and made part of his living as a night-club host at Alexandra, one of Stockholm's chicest clubs. He was tall and blond, and it wasn't solely because of his position at the nightclub that he was popular with women; he was also very nice and easy-going. Gustafsson didn't take life any more seriously than he had to, and this particular afternoon he reached for the phone hoping that he'd hear a bright young female voice.

'Hi, this is Björn,' said the energetic voice on the other end of the line. 'How are things?'

Gustafsson immediately forgot what he had just been thinking about and laughed happily.

'Well, hello! Are you in town, when did you arrive and what's up?'

'Just about an hour ago. Thought I'd spend some time in Stockholm. Would you like to go out and eat this evening and have some fun?'

'Sure! Come over to my place and then we'll go down to Cecil's this evening.'

* * *

Christer Gustafsson and Björn Borg had met in the mid-1970s in connection with one of Borg's endorsement assignments and had ended up at a discothèque, where they had met girls and had a good time. After that they got together once in a while when Björn was in Stockholm. Since Björn had first reduced his tennis schedule and then quit, his visits had become much more frequent and the two friends had seen a lot more of each other. Christer was the type of person Björn liked to be around. He was quick-witted, didn't have a care in the world, had a voracious appetite for life and moved in all the best circles in Stockholm. Theirs was an easy-going friendship; tennis, business and money were among the topics banned from their discussions. Gustafsson knew very well that Björn expected of him nothing more than relaxation and entertainment. There weren't to be any problematical discussions.

The two men shared an interest in music. Christer did some work for a recording company, primarily arranging parties for artists visiting Stockholm and looking for fun. He and Björn went around with a number of the leading artists in the music industry, such as Rod Stewart, Elton John, Eric Clapton, Olivia Newton-John, Liza Minnelli, Bruce Springsteen and Prince. Björn knew some of them before they came to Stockholm, and they were anxious to get together with him when they were in Sweden. But the main interest he and Christer had in common was girls. As Christer put it, 'We are both healthily fixated on sex.'

Björn and Christer liked to hang out at the various popular nightspots, where they usually picked up some girls – sometimes two each – and took them to Christer's little flat or to the Sheraton or the Grand Hotel, where Björn often rented a suite during his visits to Stockholm. The nights were long, hot and uninhibited. The two friends were very potent young men and nobody cared that Björn was married.

As an active tennis star, Björn had lived a highly structured life. He had always played tennis with Bergelin for a short time each evening, then watched television with Mariana and gone to bed early. But he always knew what life outside of tennis had to offer. Sometimes he and Lennart would take a couple of days off from tennis life and live it up. Especially Björn. Once, for example, they had spent a few days in New York. One evening they ended up at Studio 54, where they ran into Mick Jagger, whom Björn knew. Jagger sat down with Bergelin to ask his advice about a problem he was having with his leg muscles. He was concerned that he wouldn't be able to carry out his next tour. From Studio 54 they had gone to Jagger's flat with some girls they had picked up. It was Björn's job to enjoy himself with the girls in Jagger's bedroom while Jagger and Bergelin looked more closely at Jagger's leg-muscle problems in the living room. While Björn merrily made love, Bergelin had been treated to a private audience of a life-time while Jagger went through his paces for the next Rolling Stones world tour.

Björn could pick up girls any night or day of the week, and Bergelin was amazed that he could so easily pass up on an opportunity to have a private audience with Mick Jagger. But then Björn is a man of simple tastes. He'd never craved culture or refinement. His tennis fans thought him mysterious, 'the ice-man', but there was a lot less to Björn than that. His libido always ruled his brains.

Björn was more than happy to participate in the sweet life with Christer, but I seldom joined them. I simply didn't have the time, since I was almost always working. Sometimes I asked how things had been and usually Gustafsson would smile and say, 'Oh yeah, we got them out of their clothes ... good Lord, Lasse, I've died and gone to heaven!' Björn would just smile.

Mariana had accompanied Björn on his last trip to Stockholm, in April 1984. It had been a short visit and Björn had had a number of engagements. He had offered to lend his person to the opening of the newly renovated nightclub Alexandra, where the autumn collection of Björn Borg Menswear was going to be shown. Björn and Mariana were also to christen the *Lady of Stockholm*, an 80-foot torpedo boat that had been renovated for use as a luxury charter boat in the Stockholm archipelago. The boat belonged to Tom Maxi, a friend of Christer, and Björn had promised to perform the christening in return for being able to use the boat for free on a weekend of his choice.

Mariana was a very warm and energetic person who was usually in a good humour, but something was obviously wrong. At the opening of the nightclub Mariana stayed close to Björn all the time and tried to keep his attention focused on her, but without any success. Björn was polite, but rather chilly towards her. The party continued afterwards in a private flat, but came to an abrupt end when Mariana suddenly began crying hysterically. The next day both the Borgs were present at the launching of the *Lady of Stockholm* together with a select group of Stockholm's social élite, including Princess Christina's husband, Tord Magnusson, and the new pop singing star Carola, on whom Björn was keeping an interested eye. Mariana swung the bottle of champagne against the bow of the boat and then she and Björn left immediately for the airport to catch a flight to Monte Carlo. It was the last time they were seen together in Stockholm.

Björn and Mariana had been together since June 1976. The then 19-year-old Romanian was a promising tennis player, and Björn, who had just been knocked out of the quarter-finals of the French Open, had invited her to join him, his father and Lennart for dinner. Mariana had been very happy, but also surprised at the invitation, since she and Björn did not know each other very well. Her mother was in Paris with her and gave her permission to accept the invitation. After dinner the two young people were left on their own and went straight to the nearest bar. They didn't stay long before going to Björn's hotel room, where they spent the night together. After that they were a couple and were married a little more than four years later.

The relationship was never a completely happy one. Mariana gave up her own tennis career soon after she and Björn met. The couple lived out of suitcases in hotel rooms around the world, trying to create a life for themselves in which everything focused on Björn's tennis game, and there were more and more exhibition matches and more and more endorsement contracts. Conflicts and tensions between young married people are not unusual in any circumstances, but the Borgs' were exacerbated by Björn's very close relationship with his mother, Margaretha. When problems arose between Mariana and Björn, his parents always took Björn's side, no matter what the issue. Mariana also had problems of her own. She suffered from kidney stones for many years, but some papers speculated that she had other illnesses too. Thus the *Daily Express* ran a headline in 1981 proclaiming 'Mariana Borg – Cancer'. There was no truth to the story, but the rumours caused a great deal of suffering.

Life in Monte Carlo did not turn out as Björn and Mariana had dreamed. Mariana told some people within IMG that things were not altogether as they should be, especially in their conjugal bed, in which Björn was showing less and less interest. Earlier on they had tried unsuccessfully to have children, but now they weren't even trying. Their fights over Björn's visits to Stockholm and his intense participation in the night-life there became more and more frequent. Björn would often go to the airport intending to fly home to Mariana in Monte Carlo and then change his mind and take a taxi back into Stockholm to continue partying with Christer. By April 1984 he could no longer hide his lack of feelings for Mariana. The relationship was over. For all practical purposes it had been over for a long time. Neither I nor anyone else could understand Björn's indifference, but, then, it really wasn't our business.

When Björn and Christer sat down for dinner at Cecil's on this particular Friday evening in June, the place was full. Summer had arrived and with its arrival the temperature of Stockholm's night-life had increased. The two friends ate a quiet meal, talked about this and that, and tried to ignore the curious glances that were directed at them. After a while well-known designer and modelling agent Sighsten Herrgårdh approached their table. The usual formalites over, Herrgårdh turned to Christer.

'You haven't forgotten about being on the jury this evening, have you? Remember, half-past nine at Boulevard.'

A puzzled Gustafsson just stared at him.

'What? Sit on a jury?'

'Sure, Christer, just like last year. You know, the beauty contest at the discothèque.'

'Oh, damn!' he exclaimed. 'Is that tonight? What do you say, Björn, do you have anything against going over there for a while and looking at girls?'

Björn laughed. 'No, that sounds great.'

'Excellent,' said Herrgårdh. 'By the way, Björn, would you be willing to serve on the jury, too?'

Björn didn't need much convincing to agree to that suggestion. So the small group, which also included night-club queen Alexandra Charles, the third member of the jury, drove the short distance to Sturegatan, where the Boulevard discothèque was located.

Jannike Björling went to that same discothèque that evening with her sister Suzette. Jannike, who was about to turn 18, had been raised in a rather simple home in Stockholm, where she lived with her divorced mother, Ilse, and her sisters Suzette, 16, and Nadja, 6. She had quit school two years earlier, because of her lack of interest and, as she put it herself, her laziness, and during the past winter she had turned down an offer to become a photo model in Paris. She had just ended a relationship with a man with whom she had lived while she supported herself as an au pair, and returned to her mother's house. Now Jannike was unemployed and unattached.

At the Boulevard that evening Jannike was asked by the owner to take part in the beauty contest since they were one girl short. She thought it sounded like fun, but also thought it a bit embarrassing, since a number of her friends were there. At first she said 'no', but then let herself be talked into it.

Björn was immediately attracted to Jannike when he saw her on stage clad only in a white T-shirt and a bikini bottom. He didn't say a word, but he didn't stop looking at her for a second. Afterwards he asked Christer to invite a few of the girls to a party at the Alexandra and was very careful to point out that Jannike should come along. Jannike didn't win the contest, but was finally convinced to accept the invitation to the party that followed.

Once at Alexandra, Björn immediately reserved a suite at the nearby Stockholm Plaza Hotel and the party soon moved there. Björn smoked cigarettes, drank beer and was in a great mood, laughing and talking much, much more than usual, but he had eyes only for the beautiful 17-year-old at his side. Hours went by, and one person after another left to go home. Finally, in the early hours of the morning, everyone had left, everyone, that is, except Jannike. Björn had talked her into staying. He had fallen head over heels in love.

Midsummer's eve, which is always celebrated in Sweden, fell the next week and Björn took advantage of his free weekend on the *Lady of Stockholm*. The boat left its moorings on Friday and headed out for the thirty thousand or so islands that make up the Stockholm archipelago. Captaining the boat was Ingmar Alverdal. The others on board were Björn, Jimmie Ahrgren, Christer Gustafsson, some of their friends and their friends' wives and girlfriends and Jannike Björling with one of her best friends, Monica Eriksson.

Björn had begun trying to talk Jannike into going on the two-day cruise the night they met. Feeling uncharacteristically unsure of himself and not really knowing what Jannike thought of him, Björn had Christer carry on the negotiations. For her part, Jannike had been shy and hesitant, and had not accepted the invitation until her friend Monica had promised to join her. Once on board, Björn made no secret of his feelings. He courted Jannike throughout the midsummer holiday, fawned over her and sent her small notes. He couldn't think about anything else and both nights forgot to arrange where he himself was to sleep. Each time he wanted to go to sleep he found all the beds taken. Jannike didn't dare share her bed with him with such a crowd on board and with the boat's thin walls. Björn chose to sleep on a blanket on the deck outside the cabin where Jannike and Monica were sleeping. That way he at least knew that no one else was with them.

The weekend after the cruise Björn went to his summer paradise on Kättilö, in the Gryts archipelago on the border between the two Swedish provinces of Östergötland and Småland. This retreat, which he had bought for $400,000 in 1978, comprised sixty acres, about ten small islands, a large house and several other buildings.

Earlier that June Björn had sold the complex for $580,000 because he felt it was too far away from Stockholm and too difficult to maintain, but he did not have to move out yet and planned to spend a few days there with his parents. It wasn't very long, however, before he missed Jannike so much that he called Christer and asked him to pick up Jannike and Monica and come out to Kättilö that Saturday.

'Sure,' said Christer, 'but how should we get there?'

'Don't worry,' replied Björn, 'I'll order a helicopter and have it pick you up in Stockholm.'

Jannike was terribly impressed that her new boyfriend had sent a helicopter to fetch her. Neither she nor Monica had flown in one before, so they were nervous, curious and rather giggly when they got on board. They talked about the flight the whole way and Gustafsson thought to himself, 'Good Lord, they really *are* only 17.'

The visit to Kättilö was a short one. Just a few hours after they arrived Björn and Christer took a ride in Björn's motorboat. Sweden's summer holiday season was in full swing and one of the sights for tourists was Björn Borg's summer residence. Looking out over the water, the two friends could see boats drop anchor at a suitable distance and their occupants try to catch sight of the former tennis player through their binoculars. But this was not the kind of attention Björn wanted. He liked to use the newspapers to drum up the publicity he wanted and for a number of reasons he was ready to show off Jannike. He decided that the four of them would take the motorboat out to the sailing port of Sandhamn the next day for the start of the annual Gotland Round sailing regatta. There were sure to be a number of willing journalists there and this appearance would be his first move in the process of breaking off with Mariana.

Provided with sea charts and a picnic basket, the quartet left Kättilö for Sandhamn early Sunday morning, arriving at their destination late that afternoon. Björn loved this exotic part of Sweden. He often said to me, 'Lasse, being in the archipelago is the greatest freedom there is.' It was a feeling he had inherited from his father, who had taken him on boat trips in the archipelago at an early age and taught him his way around the nearly infinite number of islands. In Sandhamn they found a big regatta party at the main hotel. The organisers quickly arranged a room for Björn and his party, and invited them to participate in the celebrations. Among the party-goers were two journalists from the women's magazine *Svensk Damtidning*, who followed Björn and Jannike around hardly able to believe their eyes. Björn and Jannike didn't leave each other's side all evening, hugging frequently without any inhibitions. Having studied this behaviour carefully, the journalists excused themselves and left for Stockholm as soon as they could. After a couple of days of partying, Björn and Christer and the girls also said goodbye to Sandhamn and took Björn's boat to Stockholm.

The first thing the four of them saw when they docked in the centre of Stockholm were posters advertising *Svensk Damtidning*. The blazing headline read: 'Björn Borg's new girlfriend – JANNIKA.' Contrary to what one might expect, the quartet got a great kick out of the headline. Jannike and Monica laughed about the misspelling of her name, while Björn and Christer were impressed that the magazine had produced the posters so fast. It was only a couple of days since the reporters had seen the new lovebirds at Sandhamn. Björn had succeeded in his main purpose: getting the news out. Now he went underground again.

As the summer wore on Björn practically moved into Jannike's room in her mother's flat. I saw them on occasion, but Björn seemed most comfortable when he was alone with Jannike and her family. Having broadcast the news, he was now trying to keep his new relationship as secret as he could, but Jannike couldn't always keep quiet. To a friend she said innocently, 'He's tremendously rich! He must have tens of thousands of dollars in the bank.' Nor could Jannike's mother, Ilse, always keep things to herself. She was flattered by the attention she received from the newspapers, which led to a bitter feud between Björn and her. Björn insisted that in this matter, as in all others, he was the one who was to deal with the press.

When the Wimbledon championship rolled around that year, the four friends went to the Stockholm archipelago again, this time visiting friends on Skarpö Island. Björn refused to watch the televised final between John McEnroe and Jimmy Connors and even asked that the volume be turned down, since he couldn't stand hearing the noise of the balls being hit back and forth. Then he and Jannike disappeared into one of the other rooms in the spacious summer-house. Thus, the five-time Wimbledon winner missed one of the century's outstanding matches in the tradition-rich tournament. John McEnroe defeated Jimmy Connors 6–1, 6–1, 6–2 in eighty minutes, delivering thirty-one serve aces.

There was still to be tennis in Björn's life that summer. Before announcing his retirement in January 1983, Björn had promised to play the ATP tournament in Stuttgart that summer. As he put it to me, he had 'already been paid to play'. Quite understandably, the organisers had demanded that he play despite his announced retirement, but Björn had no desire to participate, preferring instead to repay the appearance money he had received. IMG had succeeded in convincing both the organisers and Björn that he should instead play in the 1984 tournament. The date for that planned 'comeback' was now set for 17 July, fifteen months after Björn's farewell match in the Monte Carlo Open. Ironically, his opponent was to be Henri Leconte, who had beat him there. Björn had not got himself in shape prior to the tournament, being far more concerned with Jannike. Travelling to Stuttgart, his mind was occupied with another matter. Afterwards he told me that it was then that he realised he had to do something about his private life and made his decision to divorce Mariana as soon as possible.

There was a hushed silence when Björn went out to centre court at Weissenhofen tennis stadium a few minutes after four on the afternoon of 17 July 1984. The German papers had wondered: 'With just ten days' training under his belt, does Björn have the stamina to defeat Leconte, who just recently beat the clay master from Paris, the Czech Ivan Lendl, away from home in the Davis Cup?' But Björn had not even had ten days' training for the match; he had hardly hit a ball. Later he told me that he hadn't had the slightest interest in the outcome of the match. It was something of a fiasco, with Henri

Leconte winning 6–3, 6–1 in forty-seven minutes. The Swedish evening paper *Aftonbladet* wrote, 'Björn showed undertones of disappointment in himself when he talked about his impressions afterwards. But he remained calm and left the arena with a broad smile on his lips.'

What no one knew was that his thoughts during the match had not been on tennis. How, he was wondering, was he to get a divorce from Mariana? How much would it cost? How should it be arranged? That he smiled despite this was understandable. Björn was very much in love and very happy. He called Jannike frequently from Stuttgart, and for the first time he told her that he wanted to divorce Mariana. He also decided to tell IMG his plans; after much thought he had decided to let the firm make the necessary arrangements with Mariana.

Back in Sweden there were some people who were beginning to worry, including Björn Gullström. He feared that Björn was visiting Sweden too often and that the tax authorities would soon decide to do something about it. Sweden's levels of taxation were then the world's highest, which had led many top business executives and several well-paid athletes to leave the country, and the tax officials were merciless in checking up on them.

I often wondered what Björn's plans really were. Would he take Jannike to Monte Carlo, a city that he himself described as being 'ice-cold and boring'? Or would he move back to Sweden? What did he plan to do with his life?

Björn spent 24 July, his and Mariana's fourth wedding anniversary, in Sweden. The couple had not seen one another for nearly two months. About two weeks later

Björn boarded an SAS flight in Stockholm on his way to Hawaii, with stops in New York and Los Angeles. Mark McCormack had lent Björn his holiday house on the island of Maui, as he had done several times in the past. During this 'honeymoon' in Hawaii, with no journalists or photographers able to reach Björn and Jannike, IMG made the announcement that Björn and Mariana were to divorce. It was 22 August. Mariana was in Monte Carlo and confirmed for the press that the marriage was over and that the divorce papers were to be submitted the following week. She had no idea where Björn was. In the divorce settlement Mariana received a luxury flat in the Monte Carlo Sun, a fashionable address next to the Monte Carlo Country Club, and a one-time payment of $2 million.

When the news of the divorce became public, rumours about Björn's girlfriend began to run rampant and the search for the couple began in earnest. Both Christer and I had been contacted numerous times by newspaper reporters wanting help in getting pictures and various bits of information. We had, of course, kept quiet about what we knew, but this time the journalists' level of interest beat all past records. The couple were to land at Stockholm's Arlanda Airport on 25 August, and after talking to Björn by phone in Hawaii Christer and I had planned a small coup to protect them from the rather hysterical press corps. We couldn't prevent a number of papers from booking journalists on the same flight Björn and Jannike were taking from New York; one of them even succeeded in getting a seat in first class just a few yards from the couple. Björn and Jannike refused to give any interviews.

Nonetheless, during a stopover at Copenhagen's Kastrup Airport a number of photographers succeeded in gaining entry to the airline's VIP lounge and taking pictures of them.

SAS Flight 410 landed at 3.15 on Saturday afternoon. Christer and I waited with Jannike's mother, maternal grandmother and little sister in the VIP lounge while hordes of international journalists and photographers hovered in the arrivals hall. Björn and Jannike entered the lounge tanned and happy, but tired. Björn beamed like the sun; I have never seen him happier, before or since. Jannike hugged her relatives and began to describe their fantastic stay in Hawaii. Christer and I had arranged for Björn and Jannike's passports to be checked in the VIP lounge and for their bags to be brought there. When the formalities were out of the way, we left by the back door, where our cars were waiting, and drove off as quickly as we could. The photographers and journalists waiting fruitlessly in the arrivals hall cursed us once they learned what we had done. Some of the journalists caught up with us as we drove into Stockholm and followed us to Jannike's home. Jannike disappeared into the building and up to her flat, but Björn waited on the street until the photographers arrived. As proud as a peacock and in the best of moods, he let them take pictures of him before following Jannike upstairs.

The pictures that all the papers were crying for, pictures of Björn and Jannike together, would be taken two days later. Monday, 27 August, was the date for the elaborate opening of the Björn Borg Sports Club in Vallentuna. The futuristic clubhouse had been completed and Project House had sold 260 corporate memberships. It looked as Kullenbergs' hopes would be more than fulfilled. All the corporate members were invited to the opening, as were the media. The sensitive question for us was how we were to handle the Jannike issue. It was obvious that the papers would make the assumption that she would be at the opening and would thus send teams of reporters and photographers to cover it. Project House and Kullenbergs were jointly in charge of the event, but it was Björn who made the final decision. For the first time in our relationship I realised that it was Björn and only Björn who made the decisions when it came to the media. That was his area. 'I know how to do this. I know precisely how the papers should be handled. I'll take care of it.' I was to hear him say the same thing many times in the future. Björn decided that Jannike should go to the opening. I felt he was wrong and was uneasy about the outcome.

Björn, Jannike, Christer and I drove to the opening in my car. Jannike, who was naturally so attractive that she didn't need to use cosmetics, had rather overdone her make-up and looked provocative. I wondered how the corporate members of the club would react when a heavily made-up teenager stole the show. And what would Kullenbergs' management say? Whatever happened, there wasn't much I could do about it.

At noon Björn was sitting next to Göran Gahnström, the president of Kullenbergs, on the podium we had arranged in the clubhouse restaurant, which was jam-packed with members, journalists and photographers. One reporter had come all the way from Japan to report on the Björn Borg Sports Club. Gahnström opened the proceedings by talking about the club and its purpose, and the efforts that lay behind it. Björn added a few words, and then the press was given the opportunity to ask questions. Meanwhile, Christer and Jannike remained on the floor below the restaurant. After a while they quietly ascended the spiral staircase between the two floors, and Jannike took a seat some distance from the podium. The minute the photographers caught sight of her they went crazy, throwing themselves over her and bathing the restaurant in the milky white light from their flashbulbs. I had never seen such a fuss made over anyone, including Björn. It was now my task to tell the press that they were free to put questions to Björn and Jannike. Björn looked proud, as he always did when he was with Jannike, but his answers were evasive and superficial. Nonetheless, the journalists seemed happy, especially after Björn and Jannike posed for them in front of the clubhouse. There was no question as to how the opening of the club would be presented in the papers the next day. And sure enough, one of them commented, 'What did [the opening] count against the year's hottest romance?', while another declared, 'Jannike's debut – she didn't say a word, but stole the whole show.'

Both Kullenbergs and Project House refrained from commenting, but in private my partner, Egon Håkanson, gave me a dressing-down. He thought it was scandalous that I had allowed Björn to take Jannike to the opening. Egon didn't understand that Björn refused to listen to advice once he made up his mind. I could understand very well that the corporate members might be unhappy with the way the club had been inaugurated. For that matter, I had begun to wonder about Björn's commitment. Early in the spring of that same year Göran Gahnström and I had flown to Verbier, the French winter sports resort where Björn was to play an exhibition match. We went there so that Gahnström could get to know Björn and so that the two of them could come to an agreement about how the club was to be run. We had agreed to have dinner together after the match. We watched Björn play in a cold and draughty hall against the rather corpulent Adriano Panatta, and afterwards we went to meet him. Björn came over and greeted us, but after a very brief conversation he excused himself and said that he had promised to spend the evening with another party. We felt slighted that we were not going to have dinner with him as arranged, and the only thing we could do was take the first available flight home. We had travelled all the way to France in vain. Björn had more important things to do.

Autumn arrived and Björn found himself increasingly rooted in Stockholm. He lived at Jannike's, spent his days with Christer and his evenings with the four Björling women unless he was at a party. Björn in love was a very different character, so easy to deal with, just like a pussy-cat. He used to tell me, 'To be in love is the greatest thing on earth.' He said it was the most fantastic thing that had ever happened to him in his entire life. He was captivated by Jannike's beauty, and youth, and was quite content to spend endless nights at home with her watching TV and videos. He wanted to do everything within his power to please Jannike, even to the extent of hiring her sister Suzette to be his secretary.

Björn didn't touch a tennis racket during this period, but Christer and he often went running. Occasionally they called me at the office and asked if I wanted to join them, and sometimes I did. Björn was in superb physical condition. He never showed any trace of his partying when he was out running, and neither Christer nor I understood where he got his strength. It just seemed to come naturally, as if he were virtually made of steel. Björn and Christer would begin by running at a pace that I could manage, but then they would pick up speed and tease me loudly: 'Come on, fats! Get the lead out!' Christer was in excellent condition and could usually keep up with Björn. I ran until my chest ached, but as soon as I caught up with them they would change speed again and disappear with a laugh. After that I wouldn't see them again. Nonetheless, those were pleasant times and we always had a good laugh afterwards.

Another popular way of exercising was with Christer's Thursday Gang. Björn and I were invited to join this group of a dozen friends who played soccer in the summer and hockey-bockey in the winter. After every match we went to a pub to eat and have a couple of beers. Only one person in the group was in a hurry to get home those evenings, and that was Björn. He would begin to get impatient after an hour or so, longing to be with Jannike, but he was happy and seemed adjusted to a normal everyday life. Christer and I were pleased, too, that Björn had met people who didn't care that he was a celebrity and who treated him as one of the lads. Having fun with other people in informal settings was something he had missed over the years.

One day in the autumn of 1984 Björn called me at my office and said he wanted to see me. He arrived about an hour later, sat down and got right to the point.

'I've made up my mind,' he said, 'and you are the first person I'm telling. I'm moving back to Sweden.'

CHAPTER SIX

Home Sweet Home

Björn and Jannike were looking for somewhere to live. Because of the tax laws, Björn himself could not be listed as the owner of a property, since that would mean that he would automatically be considered resident in Sweden. It was for this reason that I, or rather Project House, was serving as a front for him. We had checked out a number of places and were about to look at a large, airy, turn-of-the-century-style flat with four rooms and a kitchen. I pressed the entry phone and after a few seconds we were let in to the building. I was a bit concerned as we took the old-fashioned lift up four floors. Would this be the flat, finally? I had found it at an agent's and, on paper at least, it met Björn's demands. All my previous suggestions had been rejected for one reason or another.

The sturdy oak door opened and a woman in her fifties appeared.

'Hello,' I said. 'I'm Lars Skarke, and I'm here to look at the flat. By the way, I have two friends along with me . . .'

Björn and Jannike stepped forward, and the woman raised her eyebrows, but didn't say anything. Björn and Jannike said hello politely and introduced themselves. The woman smiled and nodded.

'You see, Björn is going to be in Sweden quite a bit in the future,' I explained, 'and the idea is that he should have a flat while he's here. So we thought it would be a good idea for him and Jannike to come along and take a look.'

Björn and Jannike looked around the flat, inspecting it, measuring the rooms with their eyes, discussing various points with one another and thinking things over. Fifteen minutes later Björn looked at me and shook his head lightly, as if to say, 'Sorry, Lasse. It's not quite the right thing, not *exactly* the kind of place we're looking for.'

The search for a flat continued. Earlier that autumn Björn had finally found a replacement for Kättilö, and I had been involved in that deal, too.

'I want you to help me find a summer house for Mama and Papa,' he had told me. 'It has to be in the archipelago.'

By this time we had known each other for about two years and had become much closer. I thought it was fun to be with him and, of course, I have to admit that I was flattered that Björn Borg was one of my best friends. I was noticing, too, that Björn was increasingly turning to me first when it came to a number of issues and that he had more and more confidence in me. But sometimes I resented the fact that he never *asked* for anything; his practice was simply to give orders. He expected that the services he required would be given the highest priority and be performed immediately. Sometimes I couldn't help feeling like a substitute for IMG.

Moreover, I couldn't help wondering about Björn's eager attempts to settle down and live a 'normal' life, with a wife and children, a flat and a summer home, and a fine car and a motorboat. Would he be able to realise his dream without really working at it? Did he think he could buy a secure, normal life? That ideal is not just one more product on the market, but something you create for yourself through hard work, failures, experience and patience.

As for the summer house, I looked round Stockholm and made a number of suggestions, but in the end the agent who had found Kättilö for Björn now found him a place called Alstaholm on Värmdö Island. Björn loved it as soon as he saw it. It had a manor house, two secondary buildings flanking its courtyard, a guest-house, a tennis court and acres of land. What was more, the main building was only about 160 feet from the water and just half an hour from the centre of Stockholm by car. Fully furnished and ready for occupancy, the asking price was $620,000. Björn paid cash and gave the place to his parents.

In October we finally had some success in our search for a flat. A friend tipped me off that a flat was being renovated on the top floor of his building, under the eves. By that time I had a very good idea what Björn and Jannike were looking for and I went to see it. They wanted a flat that was out of the ordinary, preferably with a sloping ceiling and large, open surfaces, but not too ostentatious. It was also important that it be cosy and homey. The flat satisfied these conditions and when I took Björn and Jannike to see it they thought it was perfect. They looked around the large three-room flat and were as happy as two small children on Christmas morning.

'This is it! We'll take it!' whispered Björn.

But it wasn't that simple. There were many twists and turns before all the papers were signed. The cooperative building society was a small one and had its rules. When the board learned that the flat was to be bought by our company, it put its foot down, since it was only willing to sell the place to someone who was going to live there. I eventually got to know the treasurer of the society quite well and begged and pleaded him to help us. In the end I was forced to tell him the truth, that is, that Björn Borg was planning to use the flat during his visits to Sweden. This news spread quickly among the people who already had flats in the building, and many of them feared that if Björn moved in, there would be an endless stream of journalists and photographers in the building. Somehow my friend the treasurer succeeded in getting the deal approved. The price was $180,000, which was expensive but hardly unreasonable.

The purchase was sealed at a meeting in the offices of the stockbrokers Hägglöf & Ponsbach, where Björn Gullström was then working. We had agreed to meet Gullström in order to inform him about Björn's plans to move home and to get the $30,000 in cash for the down payment. It turned out to be a short and rather confused meeting. Björn arrived nearly half an hour late and acted rather strangely. He said almost nothing, and when I asked him what was wrong, he seemed distant and said he felt a bit dizzy. He claimed to have taken a couple of strong sleeping pills the night before and said that they were apparently still having an effect on him, which seemed a bit strange. We concluded the meeting quickly, and Björn and I went to the bank to take $30,000 out of his account. Björn didn't say anything. He filled out the necessary forms at the bank, was given the money and handed it to me. With the $30,000 in cash in an envelope, I then went straight to the estate agent, made the down payment, and was given the keys to the flat at Vegagatan 7, which now belonged officially to Project House and unofficially to Björn Borg.

Very happy and very much in love, Björn and Jannike spent the next day buying furniture for their new flat. First they bought a large, flashy, grey leather corner sofa, then the dining-room table and chairs and then the bedroom furniture. They decided to leave the third room unfurnished for the time being.

One person who definitely opposed the purchase was Björn Gullström, who advised Björn against moving into a residence of his own in Sweden. Again and again he warned his client about the tax authorities. Since he was registered as living abroad, Björn was not allowed to be in Sweden more than six months a year. If he stayed longer, he would be forced to pay taxes in Sweden just like any other citizen. Given Björn's income, that would mean a disastrous combined tax burden of 85 per cent in Sweden, as opposed to 0 per cent in Monte Carlo. None of these warnings had any effect. Björn was in love and happy, and he had decided to live with Jannike in Stockholm. And that, of course, was the way it was to be. He just said, 'Take care of it!'

At that time I was doing a lot of work with the Swedish Skiing Federation and became acquainted with Gert Karlsson. He was short, energetic and more or less addicted to his work, but he was also considerate, friendly and caring. Gert had a number of projects under way and was generally known as one of Sweden's most powerful lobbyists. At the time he was the chairman of the Swedish Tourist Council, but once had been the Minister for the

Future and Deputy Prime Minister Ingvar Carlsson's boss. Ever since that time the two men had been very close to one another.

At one of our meetings I indicated to Gert that Björn might be moving back to Sweden and asked whether anything could be done concerning taxes for athletes like Borg, who had large incomes and large fortunes and didn't want to be forced to live abroad for economic reasons. It so happened that Gert had been thinking of the same issue for some time. We agreed that we would both think about it further but not discuss it with others, and that we would keep in touch.

'We'll come up with something,' Gert said, with a glimmer in his eye.

I often went to visit Björn and Jannike in their new home. Björn had put up an enormous stereo system in the living-room and hard rock blasted from the speakers. We spent days listening to music and watching films we rented from the video shop around the corner. Björn and Jannike also spent a good deal of time reading what the papers wrote about them. They studied every detail, and Björn was frequently engaged in trying to discover who had leaked this or that piece of information to the press. Many times it turned out that Jannike's mother or sisters had said something, but never anything important. Of course, the situation was difficult for them, since they weren't used to dealing with clever reporters who knew how to uncover the information they wanted. Jannike's mother must have been very relieved when Björn and Jannike moved across town, taking their media coverage with them.

* * *

I continued to think about how Björn's return to Sweden could be facilitated, and came up with what seemed a pretty good idea. At first it had been just a vague thought of somehow involving Björn with the Tourist Council. Then it hit me: why not give Björn, the world's best-known Swede, a senior position with the Tourist Council? In fact, why not make him Sweden's ambassador for tourism and charge him with representing Sweden at home and abroad, speaking about Sweden enthusiastically, and participating in various advertising efforts on behalf of the country? In short, his task would be to attract tourists to Sweden, in return, of course, for a not insignificant honorarium. This plan would be good for Björn, good for Sweden and good for the Tourist Council!

I discussed the idea with Gert and then consulted Björn. At this time, in early 1985, he was floating on light, fluffy clouds. He had visited me at Project House one day in February, sat down in my office and, with a triumphant smile on his face, told me he was going to become a father in September. I congratulated him and said that it was going to be a boy. Somehow I always know about these things. Björn was coming to my office almost daily during that period, and a couple of weeks later I told him about my idea.

'Björn, what would you say about being Sweden's ambassador for tourism?'

I explained further, and he looked rather hesitant.

'Is it true?'

'No, but it can be. If we play our cards right, you can earn a pretty sum for moving home to Sweden.'

'No, no . . . it'll never happen.'

'If I know Gert Karlsson the way I think I do, it's not at all impossible. In any case it's worth a try,' I said.

We talked some more, and it soon became clear that for once in his life Björn was not thinking first and foremost about money. He saw it more as a mark of recognition and a possible ticket to a new life in Sweden. For my part, I thought Björn should receive $200,000 a year, that the contract should run for five years and that Project House should receive a certain amount of compensation. When I mentioned the amount I thought Björn should receive, he still looked hesitant. At the same time, however, he couldn't hide the fact that he liked the idea.

'That would be wonderful! Damn, how nice!' he said.

Gert felt that the matter would have to be discussed by the cabinet if we were going to succeed. His old friend Ingvar Carlsson was now Minister for the Future, and wasn't it the future we were discussing? Any appointment would have to be confirmed at that level, and since it was an election year, Gert, an old Social Democrat, was not above seeing Björn Borg as an election-year boon to his party. In order to understand the context one must remember that Björn's decision to leave Sweden in 1974 had raised a real storm. It had been severely criticised and he had been accused – in the press, in several phone calls and in numerous letters – of tax evasion, one of the very worst accusations one could make against a Swede. The general feeling was 'Björn Borg is a brilliant tennis player, but a terrible Swede.'

Now, ten years later, public opinion had shifted in the wake of the tax authorities' scandalous treatment of

Ingmar Bergman, which had driven him into exile. When
Astrid Lindgren later rebelled against a court order to pay
more in taxes than she earned, she won everyone's
sympathy. The Social Democrats had lost the election in
1976 and had found themselves outside government for
the first time in forty-four years. At the time when Björn
wanted to move home again, they were again in power,
but it was an election year and they were not doing well
in the polls. Every bit of help was welcome, even if it came
from a fabulously rich, retired tennis player who had
earlier been accused of tax evasion, but who wanted to be
'reconciled' with his native land and start a family there.

'Yes, it would be right on target,' repeated the chairman of the board of the Tourist Council in yet another
phone conversation. 'There's no question but that it could
contribute to creating a new and more positive image of
Sweden. But,' he said 'what will it cost?'

Gert and I had not discussed any figures, but when I
told him the amount I had in mind he did not seem at all
surprised. What he did give me to understand, however,
was that the Tourist Council didn't have that kind of
money. I went on to say that Björn could not officially
move back to Sweden before January 1986. He had to
remain an official resident of Monte Carlo during the 1985
tax year, and it was important that the Swedish tax
officials did not raise any problems with this arrangement.

'It shouldn't be any problem,' I suggested. 'Björn
hasn't, in fact, been in Sweden very much.'

'No, no, of course not,' said Gert with a short laugh.
'Things will work out. And when it comes to the contract
with the Tourist Council, you'll have to talk with our

president. But as far as I can see there shouldn't be any problem.'

Björn continued to be sceptical that these plans could be realised, so I arranged for Gert to meet him and me at the Mornington Hotel in Stockholm. Gert told us he had made an appointment to see Ingvar Carlsson to get backing for the plan inside the cabinet. Björn smiled and looked pleased. When we were about to leave, Gert cleared his throat and looked at Björn.

'Oh, Björn,' he said, 'perhaps you can now help *me* with something.'

'Sure, what is it?'

'Well, you know that we're trying to land the 1992 Olympic Games for Åre and Falun. A delegation from the International Olympic Committee will be coming to Falun in the beginning of June and we thought that we would try to charm them a bit. It would be great if you would agree to help us out.'

'I'm free in early June, so of course I'll help!'

As we left the hotel, I thought to myself how cleverly Gert had put his question to Björn, as an aside. For his part, Björn looked at me with a sly little smile on his face.

'That wasn't bad, Lasse,' he said. 'I didn't know you had contacts with the Social Democrats.'

The fact was that I didn't have such contacts, but I soon would.

The meeting with Ingvar Carlsson – the man who would become prime minister following the assassination of Olof Palme a little over a year later – was held in his office in the complex of government offices in downtown

Stockholm early one spring day. I put on a dark suit, a white shirt and a discreet tie in honour of the occasion. As I was in the habit of doing when it came to presenting my ideas, I had put together a flip chart to take to the meeting. I had butterflies in my stomach, but at the same time it was a fantastic feeling.

Carlsson's secretary, Christina Eklöf, greeted Gert and me and showed us into his office. I immediately took a liking to the tall, lanky politician. His smile was broad and friendly, and he seemed to be a good, down-to-earth person. My nervousness disappeared.

The office was large and light. To the left was Carlsson's desk, with its neat piles of paper; to the right, a group of sofas. We sat down. In addition to Gert, Ingvar Carlsson and me, Olof Palme's press secretary, Marita Ulvskog, also took part in the meeting. Her task was to note down everything that was said so that a transcript could be produced for Olof Palme in case he wanted to know more about the meeting. According to what I had heard, Palme did not wish to know about matters that might later prove to be embarrassing to him in any way, and I figured that it was probably Marita Ulvskog's job to determine if this was such a matter.

The meeting began with a rather informal discussion about the situation of athletes in general. Ingvar Carlsson was very interested in sports. He had played quite a bit of soccer in his youth and thought it was a shame that more and more athletes were leaving Sweden, although he also expressed a certain understanding for their situation. Then we came to the real point of the meeting and I was given the floor. With the help of my dear old flip chart, I

101

presented my idea about Björn Borg and the Tourist Council, as well as the further elaborations of the idea that Gert and I had worked on together. I emphasised that Björn Borg's moving back to Sweden would offer an opportunity for reversing the trend. If a man as wealthy as Björn could move home, surely many others might follow in his tracks. Carlsson seemed to like the idea of having Björn serve as Sweden's ambassador for tourism. Gert made the point that it would be important for the Tourist Council to receive the funds that would be required to put this idea into practice. Carlsson looked at him and nodded in agreement.

About a month later, Ingvar Carlsson invited us to lunch with several senior civil servants and members of the cabinet, including the Minister for Sports, Ulf Lönnqvist, to discuss the matter further. Björn, of course, was the guest of honour. That morning, however, Björn called to say that he wouldn't be able to make it. It was the first in a long series of last-minute cancellations.

On Friday, 7 June 1985, the time had come for Björn to fulfil his promise to Gert Karlsson in connection with the efforts to land the Olympic Games. Björn, Jannike and I drove to Falun in my car. We were not faced with an especially difficult job, for our main task was to join the delegates from the International Olympic Committee (IOC) that evening for a dinner at which the King and Queen of Sweden were to be the guests of honour. In addition, Björn was to participate in a press conference the next day. Beyond that, we were simply to be pleasant and generally upbeat in conversations with the members of the IOC.

We checked in at the Grand Hotel in Falun and changed clothes for the dinner. The host for the evening was Falun's largest, and Sweden's oldest, industrial firm, Stora. Björn and Jannike attracted a great deal of attention as we went from the hotel to Stora's banquet hall. In ninety-nine cases out of a hundred people took a look and perhaps whispered a bit to one another. But on this occasion a rather drunk local resident caught sight of the couple and called out to Björn, 'You should pay taxes, you bastard!'

Björn didn't miss a step, just stared straight ahead and walked on, but Jannike couldn't restrain herself. She yelled back, 'We pay more taxes than you do!'

As it turned out, however, Jannike was not right, especially not that year, when, for all practical purposes, Björn lived in Sweden but avoided paying any taxes there.

When we arrived at the dinner, the local press immediately went after Björn and asked him why he was in Falun.

'Jannike and I have been in Stockholm a few days and we were invited by the Tourist Council to come here. I think it's fun to show up on Falun's behalf. I don't know if I can influence the decision in any way, but it would be great if Falun and Åre were to host the Winter Olympics in 1992,' said Björn professionally, with a smile on his face.

Before dinner the delegates came up to Björn and Jannike couple by couple to say hello, and all of them wanted Björn's autograph. He chatted with them, laughed and signed autographs, a practised professional in action. King Carl Gustaf and Queen Silvia, who was dressed in a lovely folk costume, also had their hands full. It was around these two couples that the elegantly-clad dinner guests assembled. After dinner we stood talking with the King and with financier Peter Wallenberg about tennis, tourism and the effort to land the Olympic Games. We were continually interrupted by people who wanted to say hello to Björn. The King, who is a very pleasant man, broke off the conversation after a while, clapped his hands and said, 'No, boys, this just won't do. Now we must get to work!' We began our charm offensive among the IOC delegates.

I was impressed by how professionally Björn operated on occasions such as this, but I also saw another side of him in Falun. Behind his calm mask, he was impatient. Nothing was to take too much time. It was as if he figured out his schedule by the second. I realised during the course of that evening that he got very little out of meeting people and that he wanted to get away from the dinner and the guests as quickly as possible. It couldn't simply be explained by the fact that he smoked a lot and didn't want to let people know it, could it? When he needed a cigarette, he always left the room. I wondered if there were other reasons for his impatience.

The contract with the Tourist Council was signed two weeks later. In fact, there were two contracts, one with Björn Borg himself, under which he was to work for the Tourist Council without reimbursement, and the other with Björn's new company, Björn Borg Enterprises Ltd, which was registered on Jersey, the true tax paradise. Björn Borg Enterprises was much better about seeing to it that it was paid. The company was to receive $200,000 a year for five years in return for 'renting' Björn Borg to the Tourist Council. The money was to be paid directly to the company's bank in Liechtenstein. No one from the Tourist Council questioned the reasonableness of the arrangements. It was a good deal for both parties. Björn avoided paying taxes on his honorarium in Sweden, and the Tourist Council avoided having to pay any fringe benefits or employer's tax on the fee. In return for coming up with the idea and coordinating the progress to contract, Project House was to receive $200,000 over the course of the five-year contract. I had been informed that the Tourist Council had no money with which to pay these sums, and although I don't know where the money came from, it was probably public money that had come from tax revenues.

Björn had promised me that he would hand out the prizes at Tennis Legends, an event that was to be held in Visby on Gotland in July 1985. Project House organised the event, and the list of participants included Ilie Nastase, Fred Stolle, Stan Smith and Tom Okker. Björn came to Gotland with Jannike, who was seven months pregnant, Christer and Jannike's best friend, Ann. My wife and I put up the whole party at our summer home on the eastern side of the island. Björn made himself at home right away, and on a couple of mornings, he, Christer and I put on our jogging shoes and ran along the long, sandy beaches. The only things you could hear were the waves, the wind and our heavy breathing. Life was not as peaceful between Björn and Jannike. They bickered all the time. The weather was very hot and Jannike was very large with child, which naturally made it difficult for her, but I could not really understand Björn's irritation. Christer and I both noticed that he frequently had difficulty relaxing, despite the fact that he was having a good time, and showed signs of wanting to escape. This was especially difficult to understand in view of the fact that he was in love and apparently very happy. As far as I knew, he had not looked at another woman since meeting Jannike.

Several days before the tennis competition was to begin, Björn and I went to see Ingvar Carlsson, who also had a summer house on the island. He had said several times that it would be nice if we could come and visit him and his family. First and foremost, of course, he wanted to get to know Björn better. The visit was easily arranged and Ingvar, his wife, Ingrid, and his daughter, Pia, greeted us with a freshly baked cake and coffee, which they served outside. After the cake and coffee – Björn refrained as always from such treats, fearing that he would put on weight – Carlsson took us on a walk and showed us around the neighbourhood.

Björn and I both liked Carlsson right from the start. We talked a bit about the Tourist Council and about Björn's upcoming appointment as ambassador for tourism, but Carlsson wasn't interested in discussing the details about that or about Björn's moving home from Monte Carlo. Ingvar Carlsson simply said that he thought it was great that Björn wanted to move home, and that he welcomed him back and wished him luck. We concluded that Carlsson was most interested in talking about old sports memories, and in that relaxed mood we spent a couple of pleasant hours with him and his family.

On Monday, 8 July 1985, two days before Tennis

Legends was to begin, we held a press conference in Visby for the four tennis veterans who were participating in the tournament. It was not a great success. Fred Stolle made the mistake of putting a bottle of beer on the podium in front of him, which gave rise to several bitter comments in the papers the next day. It soon became apparent that a seriously sports-minded Sweden was not fully prepared for a show like Tennis Legends, in which the participants joked and had fun. The journalists did their best to dismiss it as a 'gimmick', which was rather sad, not least because Visby Tennis Club did an excellent job.

Then Björn stole the show. I can honestly say that I had never been more surprised in my life. After the official press conference Björn walked on to the podium and took the microphone. He cleared his throat and looked out over the very large crowd of assembled journalists. Silence fell and Björn said, 'As most of you probably know, I am in the process of forming a family and I want to do it in my native land. Therefore, I have decided to move back to Sweden. That's all I wanted to say.'

This statement provoked a blizzard of questions and comments. Björn gave a number of brief answers, but soon brought his impromptu press conference to a close. The response in the newspapers the next day was enormous. *Expressen*'s front-page headline was 'Welcome home, Björn!' Inside was an interview with Björn's mother, Margaretha, in which she was quoted as saying, among other things, 'He's a man of surprises, our son.' Some papers jumped to the wrong conclusion. *Aftonbladet* claimed: 'Björn must pay millions of kronor to become a Swede', and *Dagens Nyheter* speculated that Björn's annual

107

income was about $6 million, which would produce a little over $5 million a year in taxes for the Swedish state and the municipality in which Björn chose to live. The paper pointed out that it would be a good deal for Sweden, but its statements were, of course, far from accurate. In fact, moving home was not going to cost Björn very much at all.

On the drive home after the press conference, the road was lined with cars filled with reporters, all of whom wanted exclusive statements from, and pictures of, the 'returning son'. Björn cursed and complained about the press persecuting us, but what had he expected after making that announcement? I wondered why Björn didn't simply talk with the journalists about his plans for moving home instead of giving them his initial statement to nibble on. If he could say 'a', he could certainly say 'b' as well. That way the reporters would not have chased after him, and he would have had peace and quiet. Did he perhaps consciously do things to ensure his being pursued by the press? Did he want to impress someone? Whatever the answers to those questions might be, with a good deal of cunning and hard work, we succeeded in making it through Björn's remaining days on the island without too much disturbance. Of course, a number of journalists and photographers did sneak around our house, but none of them was allowed very close or given any information.

The Tennis Legends final was between Stan Smith and Ilie Nastase. It was a fantastically beautiful summer day and the stands at the Botairlund tennis court in Visby were overflowing. Among the three thousand souls who had come to see this match between the veterans was Ingvar Carlsson, who sat one row behind Björn and Jannike.

As agreed, Björn handed out the prizes. He wore a suit and tie, had his hair cut short, was suntanned and looked healthy and relaxed. When he went out on the tennis court to award the first prize to Stan Smith, the crowd cheered wildly. Inspired by that, Björn made a long speech in which he said how happy he was to be moving home again. In his victory speech Stan Smith said that he had never before seen Björn as happy as he was then – nor ever heard him say as much at one time. Nastase joked as usual and said that it wouldn't be long before Björn himself would be making his debut in Tennis Legends. Björn answered with a laugh that it would be another six years, but that he looked forward to the day.

The day after the final our guests left Gotland for Sweden's other holiday island, Öland. I stayed on to enjoy a couple of weeks of holiday. A day or so later I had a call from a reporter who wanted to know more about Björn and his business dealings. Among other things, I was asked to estimate Björn's market value. That was an impossible question, of course, but I answered in the same way that Mark McCormack usually did: 'Björn Borg will always be a name that will sell well. I expect that we're talking about hundreds of millions of dollars if we take the long view.'

My answer was printed in the paper, and I didn't give it much thought until Björn phoned me. He had read the article and was calling from Öland. He was hopping mad and let me know it. He said that I was not to mention any figures when talking with reporters. I didn't understand him. My comment in the paper was harmless, and similar things had been said on many other occasions by other people. I heard Jannike's voice in the background and figured that they had once again been sitting around checking out what the papers were writing about them, had got each other all upset and then appointed me as scapegoat of the day. But this was the first time I had been given that particular role and I was hurt and unhappy.

'Quite frankly, I don't understand what you're trying to say. You should be proud that I have such a high opinion of your market value.'

'You're not to make statements about such things! I take care of the press and don't you forget it.'

I stopped feeling hurt and suddenly became very angry. Here I had got a flat for him, found him the post as ambassador for tourism, developed the idea behind Björn Borg Menswear and done many other things. Admittedly, Project House had earned a good deal from our joint ventures, but it would have been nice to have been given some small thanks. If Björn didn't think there was any reason to thank me, then there was no reason for me to take his dressing me down. Moreover, I had recently witnessed a good deal of his erratic behaviour, which worried me.

'If that's the way you want things, it's OK with me,' I said with considerable anger in my voice, meaning every word. 'We don't need to have anything to do with each other any more. If you think what I do is so wrong, then it's just as well we don't do anything together in the future.'

It was quiet at the other end of the line, and I realised that he wasn't used to being spoken to like that. When he spoke again, his voice sounded altogether different.

'No, no, Lasse, that wasn't at all what I meant. I just

want you to think about what you say so nothing will go wrong. You know how journalists are.'

The Tourist Council decided to present its new ambassador on 28 August, just eighteen days before the election, despite the fact the matter had been arranged much earlier. Now that the news of Björn's appointment was to be released, the public relations drums were beaten vigorously.

'It is a great honour for me to represent Sweden,' said Björn. I'm being paid for this – just how much is a private matter. But I will pay taxes like every other Swede.'

On 15 September the Social Democrats got just under 44 per cent of the votes and were able to remain in government with the support of the Communists. There are many factors that determine the results of any election, but I am convinced that Björn Borg played a certain role in the outcome of the 1985 elections.

Björn himself wasn't thinking at all about politics or business. Three days after the election, at 8:55 p.m. on 18 September, his son, Robin, was born. A day or so later Björn and I were out eating dinner and having a few beers in Stockholm. He was, of course, very happy and looked forward to bringing Jannike and Robin home from the hospital. After a while he fell silent and it was obvious that he was thinking about something special. He looked at me, smiled slightly and said, 'Don't think that we are going to get involved in a lot of contracts and other deals now. I want to concentrate entirely on my private life. Everything else will have to wait. It's just as well that I say it straight away.'

The fact was that I didn't have any plans to involve myself with his affairs to any great extent. He had a job with the Tourist Council, the Björn Borg Sports Club and the perfume series with Romella, and a clothing contract with the Japanese firm Seibu. Nor had his endorsement contracts with Fila, Donnay and Diadora expired. I myself had more than enough to do at Project House, which had grown enormously during this period. Moreover, I was part owner of two other companies and owned real estate in Stockholm and London. Those commitments were sufficient to keep me busy and it was enough for me that Björn and I were close friends. I thought I had showed him by way of what I had done for him how much I valued our friendship. Spontaneously, I replied, 'That's great, Björn. You're doing exactly the right thing and it's worth it. Arrange things in your private life so that they work out, for that's more important than anything else. Each of us needs his castle.'

Björn's comment that he would pay taxes 'like any other Swede' was inaccurate. There was, of course, a tax strategy in connection with his moving back to Sweden; it was simple, effective and even legal. Björn's advisers figured out that he needed $14 million in liquid assets to live in Sweden without any worries for the rest of his life. Investments in real estate, boats and cars were to be taken from that capital. The dividends from investing the remainder in Sweden would cover taxes and normal expenses. When this calculation was presented to Björn, he decided not to bring more than $9.4 million with him, which was the amount he declared as his total wealth when he moved to Sweden in March 1986. These funds were taken from Björn's companies and trust funds. On 18 April 1985 IMG formed Björn Borg Enterprises Ltd for Björn's Swedish and foreign revenues. Björn owned all the shares in the company. With this move IMG stopped using companies owned by Björn's trust funds so there would be no evidence of the existence of the trust funds after that date in the event of a future Swedish tax audit.

Björn's remaining assets of some $50 million were left in foreign trust funds, for which Björn's father served as protector. It was important that Björn no longer had access to those funds. Since he was now officially a resident of Sweden, if Björn were to touch those assets after his return to Sweden, they would be considered part of his personal capital and he would risk paying on the order of $41 million in tax. In other words, Björn relinquished to his father all control over the bulk of his fortune for as long as he was to live in Sweden.

In terms of paying taxes, then, Björn's move back to Sweden was not burdensome. According to the tax regulations, he was allowed to declare as little earned income as he could in order to limit taxes on his capital and on the income it produced. For the 1986 tax year, therefore, Björn reported an earned income of slightly more than $2,000, and his total tax came to just over $200,000. For the 1987 tax year his earned income was about $50,000 in salary from Björn Borg Enterprises Ltd, and his total taxes amounted to around $128,000. In 1988 Björn paid exactly as much in taxes as he had in 1987, which meant that he paid a grand total of $460,000 over the course of those first three years. During the same period his income from serving as ambassador for tourism amounted to $600,000 tax-free. In other words, instead of having to 'pay millions of kroner to become a Swede', one could say that Björn received about $140,000 more from the Tourist Council than he paid in taxes. It is very surprising that the Swedish tax authorities never questioned the fact that Björn declared his total wealth to be $9.4 million at the time of his return to Sweden. For that matter, no one seemed to question anything when it came to his money.

The only hiccup occurred late in the autumn of 1985. The tax authorities in the Stockholm district sent a letter to Björn at the flat at Vegagatan 7, urging him to report his immigration from abroad immediately. He brought this communication over to Project House with a distressed look on his face. Were the tax authorities 'on to him'? Did he now run the risk of having to pay Swedish taxes on his 1985 income, which would amount to a minor catastrophe? At the suggestion of Gert Karlsson, Björn Gullström and I responded with a long letter on Björn's behalf in which I confirmed that Björn had been in Sweden no more than precisely 131 days that year. In addition, I confirmed that Björn did not own the flat, but that he would have a residence of his own available to him when he moved back to Sweden in 1986. We did not hear anything more from the tax authorities.

CHAPTER SEVEN

Mr Ambassador

Christer parked his bronze Golden Eagle Jeep in front of Vegagatan 7 and waited. It was early autumn 1985 and he and Björn were going to work out with the Thursday Gang. After a while Christer began drumming his fingers on the steering wheel. Björn was almost never this late. On the contrary, he was usually on time, especially on Thursdays. Christer looked up and down the short street, which is only about a hundred yards long. Suddenly he caught sight of something moving between two parked cars ahead of him. It was someone with a sort of kerchief over his head. Whoever it was hunched down behind one of the cars, then snuck forwards still hunched down and suddenly ducked in behind another car. Gustafsson chuckled to himself, thinking that it was probably some kid playing. He continued to watch, however, and saw that the figure was working his way towards the Jeep. The person's head was still covered, but Christer could see that he was carefully peering out through a gap in the kerchief. Now the man was right next to Christer's Jeep on the passenger side and, much to Christer's surprise, opened the door, hopped in, threw off the kerchief and hissed: 'Drive, damn it! Jannike mustn't see me! I've taken at least a G.'

Gustafsson looked at the figure beside him. Björn Borg looked worn, haggard and exhausted. His hair stood on end, his eyes were glazed, pearls of sweat stood out on his forehead and he looked very scared. As usual, he was wearing a tracksuit and a pair of tennis shoes. He sank back in the seat with a sigh.

'What do you mean, a gramme?' asked Christer, although you didn't have to be a professor of chemistry to figure out what Björn was talking about.

'You know, coke . . . cocaine,' answered his very tired friend. 'We've got to get out of here. Jannike might show up any minute and she'll be furious.'

There was no get-together with the Thursday Gang that day. Instead, Gustafsson stepped on the accelerator and headed out toward the parks of Djurgården. It was the first time he'd seen Björn in this state and he was shocked. Christer might very well go on a binge once in a while, but he considered himself to be a pretty healthy athlete and he certainly didn't have any patience with narcotics. He drew the line there and he had no plans to cross it. He didn't quite know what to say as he drove the big Jeep through Stockholm, so he kept his mouth shut. Once the first shock subsided he figured that it must have been a one-time event, an accident. But at the same time . . . in the middle of the day? And so close to Robin's birth? No, something was clearly wrong. Christer swore quietly under his breath. He liked Björn and had been very pleased when Björn had finally seemed happy and at peace with himself. Christer thought that he had some part in this change, since he'd been the one who'd brought Björn and Jannike together. But now . . . this shit? He hadn't thought any further by the time they reached Djurgården. A few minutes later Gustafsson turned on to a small gravel road and parked. He and Björn sat down on a bench and let the time pass. A little over an hour later Christer got up.

'OK, Björn,' he said in a determined voice. 'Let's jog a little bit so you'll feel better. Then you can tell me whatever you want to. It's up to you.'

Björn got up without saying anything. He hadn't said much since he'd flung himself into the Jeep. He looked pale and miserable, and Christer felt sorry for him.

'Come on, Björn,' he said, trying to smile. 'We're going to solve this! There's nothing to worry about.'

They began to run along Djurgården's many trails. Christer kept up quite a tempo, while Björn ran along behind him. Björn was breathing heavily and began coughing and sniffling badly after just a few minutes, but he never tried to get Gustafsson to slow down the pace. After about twenty minutes they were back at the car. Björn coughed and tried to catch his breath. Jogging probably hadn't been all that good for him, since his heart-beat had already been accelerated by the cocaine, but his body was in great shape and he'd at least overcome the worst of his anxiety. They sat down on the grass and caught their breath, but neither said a word. The situation was very sensitive and Gustafsson didn't want to be pushy. If Björn wanted to talk, he would listen. If not, he still planned to do something about the matter. But not right now.

After spending half an hour almost asleep on the grass, Björn pulled himself together. He shook off the worst of his exhaustion – he probably hadn't slept for the last twenty-four hours – and in a thin voice said he wanted to go home. After that Björn did something he'd never done before. He went up to Christer and gave him a big hug.

'You've saved my life, Christer. I'll never forget this.'

'That's something of an exaggeration,' thought Gustafsson. 'It's not that easy to bump Borg off.' He got in the Jeep, started it up and drove Björn home.

A few days later Christer called me at Project House and said he wanted to see me. It was important. I told him he was welcome to come over and he showed up half an hour later. He was tense and nervous and he had a hard time telling me what he had come to say. It came out soon enough.

'I'm terribly worried about Björn,' he said. 'I think he's taking drugs. We've got to help him.'

He told me the whole story. I didn't say very much, but I thought about the conversation I'd had with a journalist a few years earlier. The journalist had told me about persistent rumours that Björn and Vitas Gerulaitis partied heavily when they travelled around the world on their exhibition tours. He'd said that drugs – usually cocaine – and women were often involved. An article I'd read in a Swedish magazine had hinted at the same thing.

I told Christer that we had to keep the story quiet, but that I would find out as much as I could. When Christer left, I phoned IMG in London, but that call did nothing to reassure me. I began trying to convince myself that perhaps the situation wasn't as bad as I feared. I didn't know much about cocaine, only what I'd heard and read in the newspapers. 'Maybe that's the way things are in international circles,' I thought. 'People just snort a little cocaine instead of drinking booze.' Just as if it really wasn't all that dangerous and people could control their use of it. But, damn it, it was still dope. I made up my mind to ask Björn about it myself.

As it happened, Björn and I were to travel to Tranås together the following week. Björn had said no to all new proposals for a contract, but after a good deal of thought he had made one exception. He'd agreed to sign a contract with Stiga, which was known not only for its ping-pong products, but also for its lawn-mowers. Björn was to take part in an advertising campaign for the company that would involve about two days of work and pay about $50,000. Even more important, Björn had liked the advertising concept. He would pose with Stiga's most advanced lawn-mower for a picture whose caption would read 'a master on grass'. We were going to the factory to sign the contract.

As I drove, I tried to think of a way to pose the question. I knew I had to ask him and several times I took a deep breath in anticipation, but I couldn't get the words past my lips. Björn simply gave me a questioning look. A chance finally presented itself about twelve miles from Tranås. We had stopped to get petrol and Björn caught sight of a newspaper headline with his name in it. He asked me to buy him the paper to see who was talking about him now. I got behind the wheel again, gave Björn the paper and started up the car. By this time I'd prepared myself and I simply asked, 'Björn, is it true that you use drugs?'

He looked up from the paper, sat there without saying anything and thought about how to reply. I knew right away that it was true and I could see that he knew I did.

'Where have you heard that?'

I certainly didn't want to mention Christer's name in this connection, so I said, 'I've heard it from different sources. Is it true?'

'Aw, it's just something that happens now and then. But there's no problem. I'm not an addict, if that's what you're thinking.'

Björn looked straight ahead and didn't say anything else. I felt uncomfortable and kept quiet. I cast a glance at him and thought he couldn't possibly be an addict. He looked much too healthy and wholesome for that. No, there couldn't be any danger. Not with Björn Borg. That would be impossible.

Twenty minutes later we turned into the car park outside Stiga's factory. I was still mulling over the conversation we'd had in the car, but Björn seemed entirely unperturbed. Inside we were greeted by a special welcoming committee headed by the company's managing director. The company had gone out of its way for Björn's visit. A platform had been built in the courtyard so that Björn could be shown off to all the employees. First, however, the contract was to be signed. This was done with great ceremony. Then everyone except Björn and I went out into the courtyard. There the managing director addressed the employees, and finished by saying: 'And, my friends, we're now going to mount another massive campaign. Here he is, the "master on grass" himself!'

Björn went out and climbed astride a large lawn-mower. The employees, entirely unprepared for this, gave a cheer that must have been heard all over Tranås. Then they literally stormed the lawnmower to get Björn's autograph.

* * *

The question of narcotics hung heavy in the air as we drove back to Stockholm, but by mutual, yet unstated agreement, the topic was taboo. It was hardly appropriate to raise the matter again right after our successful visit to Stiga. On the way home, however, Björn said, 'This simply doesn't pay enough to bother with. You're not to make any deals like this any more. We've got to do better, Lasse.'

'Well, maybe so,' I answered, not forgetting that, as always, Björn himself had approved the contract. 'But I'm learning, Björn.'

In the autumn Björn did just as he'd said he would: he concentrated on his family life. During the week he participated in his training programme at the Swedish Tourist Council. He wandered from one office to another at Sweden House, appeared in films designed to sell Sweden abroad and in photos that were to appear in brochures. Aside from get-togethers with the Thursday Gang, he spent the rest of his time with Jannike and Robin. One of his main tasks in caring for his family was to protect it from the press, which had become even more persistent after Robin was born. Both Swedish and foreign reporters and photographers were constantly on the hunt for news titbits and pictures. An American magazine had offered $200,000 to get a few photos of Robin with Jannike and Björn, but Björn wouldn't give an inch when it came to his son. He was a devoted father, and whenever I visited his flat I found him with Robin. He seemed happy and at ease with his life.

* * *

Björn's first official mission as Sweden's ambassador of tourism included visits to Cologne and Berlin. Björn and I flew to Cologne together with a couple of other representatives of the Tourist Council on Wednesday, 26 February. Our job was to visit a travel agency that specialised in trips to Sweden, but when we arrived it turned out that the owner was simply interested in promoting his own business. He had put up lots of pictures of Björn together with information on when the great tennis star would be at the agency. He was taking gross advantage of Björn's and the Tourist Council's services, and we didn't stay long.

Björn and I agreed that we'd take the night off before our trip to Berlin the next day. We sat around Björn's hotel room drinking whisky and talking business, agreeing, after the incident at the travel agency, to evaluate all future assignments very carefully to be sure they were legitimate. The level of the whisky in the bottle fell rapidly, and the same was probably true of our conversation, but, as I mentioned before, Björn was made of steel. That evening I found I had definitely met my match when it came to alcohol. Björn could drink almost as much as he wanted without it really showing; he only became a bit more talkative.

Eventually we ordered dinner from room service, ate and were ready to go out on the town. Before leaving the hotel we asked the head porter to recommend some clubs we should visit, and he gave us what he called several 'promising' addresses, with a meaningful look. We took a taxi to the first club on the list, went in, sat down at the bar and each ordered a gin and tonic. The place was nicely decorated, with the bar running along the narrow end of the large, dimly-lit room and several comfortable sofas placed around the room on oriental carpets. Sitting at the bar was a long line of beautiful young women. We noticed how they looked at us and how some of them snickered and whispered, 'Oh, look! It's Borg.'

'Hey, Lasse,' said Björn with a laugh after a moment or two, 'don't you feel a little dirty? Maybe we should see if there's a sauna. For that matter, I feel a little stiff. Who knows, maybe we can find a masseuse, too.'

It was a great idea. Sure enough, the place had a sauna and, indeed, we found we could certainly have a massage. We quickly took off our clothes, showered and sat down in the steamy sauna. In a few seconds we were joined by two extremely attractive and, of course, totally nude women. They said hello and sat down very, very close to us. After a while Björn looked at me, smiled again and said, 'I think we should close the sauna part of the club for the evening. Surely it's enough if *we're* the only ones here?'

After a brief negotiation the manager of the club put a notice on the door saying that the place was 'reserved'. It turned out to be quite a night! Whenever we were thirsty we ran boisterously to the bar for more refreshments and to see what else was on offer. During the course of the night I had to admit to myself that I was second to Björn, and not only when it came to holding my booze. Björn had a big appetite for the girls. He recovered very quickly from each and every one of his 'private conversations' with one of our 'therapists' and he smiled all night long. He *was* made of steel. I have to admit I did pretty well myself, but after a couple of hours I was completely worn out. I went to the bar, had a beer and sat there in something like a trance. About three in the morning Björn sat down next to me and ordered a beer. He seemed to be in top shape. Tired as I was – and almost unconscious – I wondered where in blazes he got all his energy. Then Björn looked around the room and discovered two girls he hadn't seen before.

'Look,' he said with surprise, 'there's two more! Come on, Lasse!'

I staggered off with Björn, while the bartender muttered, 'You guys must be crazy.'

When I got my wake-up call around ten the next morning, I didn't just have a hangover, I was *ill*. I dragged myself out of bed, shambled into the bathroom and was shocked by how swollen my face looked in the mirror. 'God,' I thought, 'I'm going to die.' I was soaking with sweat, my hair was terribly damp and my eyes looked like narrow red slits. I looked bloated, pale and sick, but I decided I was going to tough it out and get ready to face what was surely going to be one of the worst days of my life. The car that was to take us to the airport had been ordered for eleven o'clock. I stood under the shower and then ordered a glass of apple juice and a pot of coffee. I couldn't even think of eating!

I went down to the lobby just before eleven to check out. Björn and our travelling companions were waiting for me.

'Good morning!' said Björn, appearing energetic and fully rested. He looked at me more closely and asked, 'Hey, what's wrong? You look terrible! Have you been out on a spree?'

I muttered something about probably having caught a bit of flu and said I was planning to go to bed as soon as we arrived in Berlin and would be fine the next day. Björn gave me an ironic look – and a really rough time for the rest of the day, which seemed to please him a great deal. On the plane I sank down in my seat and leaned back. I longed intensely for a warm and comfortable hotel bed to creep into so I could lick my wounds in peace. Björn, however, was in the best of moods. He sat next to me and tried to get me to drink a beer. He told me that it was what I needed, but I protested loudly.

We landed in West Berlin in the afternoon and took a taxi to our hotel. Once in my room I took the phone off the hook, hung out the 'do not disturb' sign, threw myself into bed and slept like a log until the next morning. I woke up feeling like a completely new man, full of spirit, fully refreshed and firmly resolved that the next time I partied with Björn I'd definitely avoid trying to keep up with him.

The West Berlin tourism fair is by far the most important event of its type held anywhere. Countries from all over the world put up displays, each one more imaginative than the other, and the whole place positively bubbles with life. We were really impressed when we arrived there in the morning. Hawaii had girls dancing the hula-hula on sandy beaches surrounded by palm trees, Australia had coral reefs and koala bears, and Egypt had pyramids. The Swedish display was not one of the more imaginative ones. It was dominated by a huge, wooden horse, while several blonde hostesses did their best to attract attention to the blue and yellow displays. But Sweden had one thing that none of the other countries had: Sweden had Björn Borg. I'd been with Björn so much that I had come to view him as just another regular friend of mine, but in situations like this I was quickly reminded of how tremendously famous he was. Most activity came to a halt when Björn stepped on to the Swedish display. He was a fantastic attraction. No one passed by without noticing him and stopping, and Sweden's soon became one of the fair's most visited displays. Björn seemed to be enjoying himself. He made small talk with as many visitors as possible, wrote autographs, passed out brochures, told people about Sweden's unbeatable nature and wonderful summers, and was an ideal representative for his country. He smiled all the time, just as if he had been born to the role of ambassador for tourism.

The mayor of West Berlin wanted to meet Björn and came to the Swedish display surrounded by his prominent guests and a number of television cameramen. Björn was then interviewed in his role as Sweden's ambassador of tourism and took the opportunity to brag about all of Sweden's virtues. Later that evening, when the interview was broadcast at prime time, I thought to myself that $200,000, tax-free or not, was actually much too little compensation for the publicity Björn was giving Sweden.

That afternoon Björn and I had a look at the other displays at the fair. It was interesting to see how the various countries made the most of their special features in their efforts to attract visitors. The display I remember best was Peru's. It was designed like a jungle landscape, with thick vegetation, lianas, colourful flowers and bubbling waterfalls, and the recorded voices of various animals. A very realistic hut had been built in a clearing in the trees and in front of it sat a dark-skinned Inca, bare from the waist up. The Peruvian hostesses told us that the Inca had lived his whole life in a similar setting in one of Peru's jungles without any real contact with the outside world. We watched him with considerable curiosity and tried to determine his age, but without success. All of a sudden I got an idea. I asked one of the hostesses to ask the man whether or not he knew who my companion was. She said something to the Indian, who squinted carefully at Björn, smiled and slowly said: 'Borg.' The Peruvian girls cheered and applauded, I began to laugh and Björn suddenly seemed embarrassed. After that incident I was never again surprised at how well-known Björn was everywhere.

Early that evening the Swedish Tourist Council arranged a large reception in the ballroom of our hotel. Our job was simply to be pleasant, and Björn set a fine example. Although he didn't like surprises or programmes that went on and on, he was always the happy and polite tennis star when people were watching. If we later felt like sharing a bottle of whisky up in our room, that was our business, but we never did it in public. We both agreed that when we were working, we were working.

The reception began to taper off after an hour or so. Björn and I retreated to our hotel room and had our whiskys. We had eaten a hefty dinner before the reception and decided that that was enough food for one evening. We were feeling good. We had done a good day's work, weren't scheduled to return to Sweden until the next day and didn't have any other obligations, so . . . after a couple of whiskys, one of us asked the other, 'What do you say? Should we take a look at Berlin's night life?'

'Sounds like an excellent idea,' the other answered.

And off we went. I remembered clearly the way I'd felt Thursday morning in Cologne, and I was determined that I was going to maintain a much slower pace this time round.

'We want to go to a very good club,' we told the taxi driver. 'A super club.'

He dropped us off in front of a small building.

'*Sehr, sehr gut!*' he said, smiling from ear to ear.

'Oh, well,' said Björn, 'we're going to have a drink in any case, so we can certainly check this place out for a while.'

It *was* a great place. Eventually, a young woman dressed in a short, tight-fitting black dress and wearing a charming, chalk-white smile, came over to us.

'Would you like to take a swim in the pool?' she asked in English with a trace of a German accent.

Half an hour later we had closed the entire pool area so that we'd have it to ourselves. The floor and the pool were covered with marble, the walls with Italian tiles. There were a number of waterbeds in the room and a large group of sofas in one corner. Soft music was playing from discreet speakers. The two of us were soon splashing in the water stark naked. I rechristened Björn 'Arne' in honour of an old Swedish swimming champion whose last name was also Borg. After a while we noticed that we were no longer alone. Some girls in bikinis had sat down on the edge of the pool. Björn was like a fish in the water, swimming back and forth between the girls, who by this time had taken off the little they had been wearing.

The evening spilled over into the night, and time flew

by with some swimming, some massage and some relaxing exercises on the waterbeds. Sometime after midnight Björn told me to follow him to the locker-room, where he went into one of the toilet stalls and signalled me to join him. He closed the door, took out a small, rolled-up piece of paper and opened it on the washbasin. He turned his back to me and leaned over the white powder. I heard how he inhaled deeply through his nose. Then he turned to me and said: 'Here, you take the rest.'

'Isn't it dangerous?' I asked nervously. It was the first time in my life I had had contact with any narcotics.

'No, not at all,' Björn said irritably. 'Don't be silly. This isn't anything, see for yourself. You'll just feel a bit more alert and you'll be able to do more, that's all. Trust me! It *isn't* dangerous, I promise.'

He returned to the pool, leaving me alone with the powder on the washbasin. I mulled over whether I should try it just once. Maybe it wasn't dangerous; it certainly was exciting. In the end I decided against it and rinsed away the soft white powder.

We stayed another couple of hours before going back to the hotel. I didn't tell anyone about the incident and, if the truth be known, I didn't give it much thought either. I didn't notice that it had had any effect on Björn and thought to myself that perhaps cocaine wasn't really all that dangerous when you got right down to it.

The next morning I woke up about eight, feeling quite rested after five hours' sleep. Normally I didn't need any more than that. I dressed quickly, packed my things and left the room. Björn opened his door almost as soon as I knocked and we agreed to have a quick breakfast in the restaurant before going to the airport. One of our travelling companions was sitting in the lobby. We could see that something seemed to be terribly, terribly wrong.

'Have you heard what's happened?' he asked. His face was grey and he looked very sad, almost crushed.

'No,' I answered with some hesitation, feeling rather sheepishly that it might have had to do with one of our nocturnal escapades. Björn didn't say anything, but just looked at the man's face.

'Olof Palme was murdered last night,' he said quietly. 'He was shot to death on a street in Stockholm.'

We stood there silently for a long time, none of us able to say anything. Could something like that really happen in our little, peaceful and innocent Sweden? Impossible! That sort of thing just didn't happen in our country.

'Is it true?' I was finally able to say. 'I mean, are you sure . . . that it isn't just a rumour or something like that?'

'Unfortunately, it's entirely true,' he said distractedly. 'I just spoke with Stockholm. He apparently died instantly.'

Björn took the news harder than the rest of us. He talked about the shooting all the way to the airport, repeatedly saying with a great deal of concern: 'The main thing is that they catch the murderer as soon as possible. We've got to know who it is. What if it's a madman who's out after famous people?'

CHAPTER EIGHT

From Alstaholm to Rio

The waves lapped at the bow of the large motorboat as Ingmar Alverdal steered away from the pier on Djurgården with a practised hand. It was eleven o'clock in the morning on 6 June 1986, the Swedish national holiday and Björn Borg's thirtieth birthday, and the sun was shining in a cloudless sky. I took off my clothes, changed into my swimming trunks and leaned back comfortably in a lounge chair with a beer close at hand. In addition to Ingmar and myself, his future wife, Liselotte, and my wife, Birgitta, were on board. Unfortunately, my relationship with Birgitta was rather strained, but now we were all on our way to Alstaholm, the small estate that Björn had bought for his parents and where we were going to celebrate his birthday with a big party. I looked forward to the party and felt proud and privileged.

Earlier that year Björn had bought a place of his own, called Viking's Hill, in Nacka, a short distance from Stockholm. He and Jannike had moved in officially on 11 March, which was the date from which Björn once again was a registered resident of Sweden. The purchase of Björn's house reminded me of the purchase of his flat a year and a half earlier. We must have inspected at least ten places in the Stockholm area, but none of them had fulfilled Björn and Jannike's desires. In the end Björn had heard about Viking's Hill and had quickly decided to buy it for $600,000. I found it strange that Björn chose that particular villa, since I thought many of the others we had looked at were much nicer. Viking's Hill faced north and the three-storey building seemed to me to lack a warm and comfortable atmosphere despite the gingerbread work that graced its façade. The house that originally stood here had burned down and an exact copy was built in its place. It was too new and had not been lived in, and I was struck by a cold and rather desolate feeling when I entered it. I decided that it was Viking's Hill's proximity at Alstaholm and to his parents that had convinced Björn to decide on a place that was so isolated. He also liked the shoreline and the pier, where he could keep his boat, the much written about *Dunderburken*, or *Thunder Can*. On this day, however, not everything was as it should be at Viking's Hill, and Björn had decided to have his party at Alstaholm.

Ingmar skilfully navigated through the narrow waters at Skurusund and out towards the archipelago. We had borrowed the boat, which had plenty of sleeping space where we could spend the night. Two hours later we had laid the foundation for our summer tans and were approaching Alstaholm. A large number of boats lay in the waters offshore, some of which had cast anchor just a couple of hundred yards from Alstaholm. We could see reflections of the sun dancing off binoculars and cameras, and knew that the press had begun its coverage of Björn's thirtieth birthday party.

At Alstaholm's pier we were greeted by Rune and Margaretha. A large, yellow marquee had been put up on the lawn. The birthday boy himself was having fun playing in the grass and laughing with Robin. We interrupted their play, gave them both hugs and congratulated Björn on his birthday. I had two presents with me, one from Project House and one from me personally, and I gave Björn my gift first. Björn loved dogs and had wanted to have one for a long time. His favourite breed was the golden retriever, and I had originally planned to surprise him with a puppy. I had even gone to look at a new litter. But then I thought about Björn's many trips, on which he took his family, and decided instead to give him a gift certificate that he could present in return for a dog at a time he thought suitable. His face lit up when he saw the card, and I knew that he appreciated the fact that I had remembered this interest of his. The present from Project House was even more appreciated, and not just by Björn. It was a jet-ski, a sort of water moped, and most of the people at the party tested it out that afternoon, especially Jannike, who loved it.

Björn had taken care of most of the details in putting the party together, including choosing the food and the caterer. He had also sent out the invitations. We were about twenty people in all, which was rather few for a thirtieth birthday party, but Björn didn't have that many friends in Stockholm. In addition to the four of us who had come together, the others included Björn Gullström and his wife, Björn's first tennis coach, Percy Rosberg, and his wife, Björn's maternal grandparents, and some of the members of the Thursday Gang and their female guests. It was a happy and noisy afternoon, with tennis, rounders and jet-skiing. Later in the afternoon the skies clouded over and a soft summer rain began to fall. It was time to eat and we hurried into the tent.

The buffet was fantastic. There were all the foods you

could think of, as well as the best of wines. I gave a speech, as did Jannike, and Björn thanked everyone for coming and for the presents he had received. Alverdal proved to be a past master not only at navigation, but also at singing drinking songs. Laughter and song emanated from the tent and floated out over the bay, where the boats bobbed at anchor. The rain disappeared and gave way to the sun, which painted a rainbow arching across the water in the early summer evening.

After a couple of hours we began to spread out in the garden in small groups. Some of us took a walk along the water, while others sat in the garden drinking whisky. But two people simply disappeared. We couldn't find Björn or Jannike anywhere. It was clear that they had decided to go off by themselves for a while, but the minutes were becoming hours and still the host couple did not return. Rune and Margaretha tried hard to smile, but no one wanted to ask where Björn and Jannike had gone. Everyone knew that something was wrong. I figured that they had had a fight and were trying to solve the problem. Their absence put a damper on the festivities, of course, but Ingmar stepped in and soon had people singing and laughing again.

Björn and Jannike finally reappeared a few hours later, and with them they had a number of other people, including the wrestler Frank Andersson. By this time, around eleven in the evening, the birthday party was winding down. Björn acted as if nothing were wrong. He talked and laughed, but at regular intervals he and Frank and someone else would go off to the boathouse. We all wondered what was going on, and Björn Gullström's wife,

Anna-Stina, finally said, 'What's going on there? Are they taking drugs? Damn it, I'm going home now!'

She went up to the house, called a taxi and left. Several other people soon followed her example. Those of us who stayed tried to enjoy ourselves as best we could. Christer and I finally went to the boat and had a nightcap. It was then that he told me what had happened, which he in turn had learned from Jannike.

After the buffet Björn and Jannike had snuck away and called a taxi. They had gone to a nearby hotel to meet Frank Andersson, who was there with some of his friends. Björn had begun flirting with a woman in Frank's party and Jannike had returned in tears to Alstaholm, where Margaretha, Rune and Christer had taken turns trying to console her. An hour or so later Björn, Frank and the others had arrived. Björn made up with Jannike and then they all came out to the tent to join the rest of us. Christer didn't know what they had been doing in the boathouse.

I sighed, shook my head and went down to the cabin to sleep. I could hear Björn and Ingmar up on deck, talking and laughing. Björn seemed as full of energy and as carefree as could be. Lying there in the dark, I thought about him and his total power over his environment. No one questioned what he did, least of all his parents. They backed him up no matter what happened. I had never heard them even criticise him; it seemed unnatural.

Björn was definitely a man with two faces and his abrupt changes of mood and shifts in personality were causing uncertainty among those around him. When he arrived at Alstaholm he had been the world's most charming fellow, happy, thoughtful and open. Later the same day he had changed into a restless, unpredictable character who had gone off and ignored his guests. He became inarticulate and mysterious. I didn't understand him at all.

I got divorced that summer. Birgitta and I had been together for seventeen years, since I was 19, and had grown increasingly apart. Not long afterwards I met Maria Bohlin, who everyone called Mia and who was blonde and very sweet. Mia notwithstanding, Project House took practically all of my time. Among other things, we had purchased the Scandinavian Enterprise Open Golf Tournament on the European circuit from its founder and fiery promoter, Sven Tumba, one of the greatest entrepreneurs I have ever met. Unfortunately, the golf tournament didn't turn out to be good business for Project House, but it still meant a tremendous amount of work.

Björn and I got together almost every day, and Jannike and Mia also became good friends. We had dinner together, went to the cinema and played parlour games. Björn's favourite game was Trivial Pursuit, and he usually won. Most of the time we would go out to Viking's Hill, where Björn began to put down deep roots. In contrast, I don't think that Jannike ever really felt at home there. I can imagine that the place, which was rather isolated, was *too* quiet and calm for a young girl who had grown up in the city. It was almost twelve miles from Viking's Hill to the centre of Stockholm, and even though Björn had given Jannike a Mercedes – and bought himself a Ferrari at the same time – she couldn't just take the car and drive into town whenever she wanted. Jannike had her hands full with Robin, even though he had a daytime nanny. For his part, Björn loved the shoreline and the view out over the water. He built a large pier with a boathouse. His *Dunderburken* lay moored near the beach, a veritable monster of a boat. It had cost about $600,000 to build and between $120,000 and $140,000 a year to operate. It was extremely fast, making almost 80 knots an hour, and Björn loved speeding along the waves in it.

One early autumn day in 1986, as we were sitting in a traffic jam, Björn looked at me and suddenly asked, 'What are you and Mia doing at the end of November?'

'I haven't any idea. Working, I suppose. Why do you ask?'

'Well,' he said, grinning, 'would you like to come to Brazil with me? I'll pay all the expenses.'

Björn was serious. He was to be the guest of honour at a Grand Prix tennis tournament and wanted to take a few friends with him to have a little fun, as he put it. I had always dreamed of going to South America, especially to Rio de Janeiro. I had worked most of the summer, so it wouldn't be hard to take an extra week of holiday, and Mia also wanted to go.

The long-awaited November day came. There were seven people in our party, including Björn and Jannike, their two friends Ann and Christos, Christer Gustafsson, Mia and me. The flight was a fabulous experience. We had nearly the entire first-class cabin to ourselves and the service was absolutely fantastic. The airline was one of the sponsors of the GP tournament and treated us like royalty; we felt almost embarrassingly spoiled. Ahead of us was more than a week in the sun, with swimming, tennis, deep-sea diving and sightseeing. To put it succinctly, we felt marvellous.

A large committee of representatives of the organisers and various sponsors welcomed us to Rio. It soon became clear that our trip and our expenses were being paid for by the organisers and some of the sponsors of the tournament, and that Björn had made that a condition of his accepting the invitation. I smiled slightly to myself. It's easy to offer to pay for your friends with other people's money. Well, there was nothing to be upset about – the thought was still a good one.

The Grand Prix Sul America Open was to be played on the holiday island of Itaparica, a minute point on the map roughly six hundred miles north of Rio, just outside the coastal city of Salvador. We flew on and arrived at this most delightful little island paradise a couple of hours later. Palm trees swayed in the breeze, the Atlantic was blue-green and the waves rolled in over the long sandy beach. The dominant institution on the island is Club Med's great holiday centre, with its hotel, bungalows, restaurants, night club, swimming pools and private beach. The tennis facility where Sul America Open was to be played was within the Club Med complex. It consisted of a few rubber asphalt courts laid out among the palms and something that was meant to approximate a centre court, with low benches covered by roofs and room for about a thousand spectators. This very different and rather exotic tennis stadium was to see, among others, Emilio Sanchez from Spain, Jean Fleurian from France, Victor Pecci from Paraguay and Andres Gomez from Ecuador participate in the tournament. In addition, the Swede Peter Lundgren was also to play, and was accompanied on the trip by his coach, Per Hjertqvist.

Lundgren was one of the players with whom Björn sometimes practised in Stockholm and it was thanks to Björn's efforts that Peter had succeeded in recruiting Hjertqvist as his personal coach. Earlier in the year Björn had agreed to play an exhibition match to help his young colleague. The match, of course, was to be played between the two of them, and part of the revenues were to go towards paying Hjertqvist's salary. Björn had set two conditions: that the match was not to be played before a paying audience and that Björn himself was to determine how the proceeds were to be divided. I sold the exhibition match to a company in Stockholm called Ahlsells, which paid $100,000 to have access to the two tennis stars for the day. Ahlsells invited their employees and their most important customers to the match, which was a popular thing to do at a time when business was booming and there were funds for such things. When it came to divide the $100,000, Björn thought for a long time. 'Well, Peter shouldn't get too much . . .,' he mumbled to himself, deciding to give Lundgren half the money. We also made a private deal with Ahlsells, which was in the electrical business. They agreed to install outdoor lighting worth about $12,000 at Viking's Hill at no charge. Björn was very proud of that deal. He didn't care very much about the $100,000, but the outdoor lighting in return for an insignificant tennis match . . . now that was something! This was one of Björn's peculiarities. He was sometimes extremely rigid with his own time when it came to the big jobs and sometimes overjoyed by rather insignificant extra earnings. The distinctions were not always entirely clear.

On the whole, Björn really liked 'in kind' deals. I will never forget the time he and Christer came to Project House with a large bag. They emptied its contents – thirty or forty compact discs – on my desk with great pride. It turned out that they had worked out a contract with a record company in Stockholm all on their own. Kim Wilde was in Sweden to promote her latest record and the president of the record company, a good friend of Christer, had pleaded and begged for Björn to pose for a promotional photo with the beautiful English singer. Free records for Björn and Christer were to be the reward. Björn thought it was an excellent idea and went to the photo session.

'Not too bad, free records,' he smiled contentedly, adding generously, 'We can get some for you, too.'

'Great,' I said, groaning silently to myself. First of all, Björn probably could afford to buy every record shop in Stockholm if he wanted to, and, second, I knew that the record company executives and Kim Wilde were congratulating themselves on their unexpected jackpot. They used the picture of the happy Björn Borg with the English beauty in different promotional contexts and the record sold fabulously. If I am not totally mistaken, Björn once made a similar deal with a sausage manufacturer. 'You filter out mosquitoes and swallow camels,' I used to tell him.

It was hot on Itaparica but the Atlantic breezes were pleasantly refreshing. We sunbathed, swam and got a tan in a couple of days. In the evenings we ate fabulously. Everything was free and of the highest quality. Afterwards we went off to the nightclub, watched some fine shows, danced and drank champagne. All Björn had to do was to spend some time with the organisers now and again and to play doubles with one of the most important sponsors in a so-called pro-am tournament, which was played alongside the Grand Prix tournament. Unfortunately, Peter Lundgren was forced to withdraw from the main competition at the last minute, having succeeded in injuring his foot in the swimming pool! He could hardly have chosen a better spot to recuperate in than Itaparica.

The days went by at a quiet, relaxed pace without anything really happening. We all simply got tanner and lazier in the blazing sunshine. Björn advanced in the pro-am tournament with his delighted partner. They went on to the finals, which were telecast all over Brazil and which they won. On the last day of the tournament there was a masquerade ball at the nightclub. Christer went as Rambo, decked out with ammunition belts and camouflage. Jannike was Cleopatra, I was Julius Caesar and Björn dressed up as Robin Hood. When I saw him in his costume I couldn't help saying, 'So, you're the one who steals from the rich and gives to the poor!'

It turned out to be quite an evening. Many of the Grand Prix players had stayed on for the party. The champagne flowed, everyone danced, Christer won second prize for his costume and none of us really remembers just when we fell into bed.

The next day we left Itaparica by helicopter, headed for a day's stay at a hotel right on the sea outside Salvador.

141

After checking in we took a little tour around the hotel, where there were a number of shops. Jannike and Mia had the itch to shop, while Björn and I followed them about, walking slowly and talking tennis. I told him that I had once played against Terje Larsen, who had hopped around on one leg throughout the match and that it had been difficult.

'You'll never beat me,' Björn grinned.

'I can beat you easily,' I replied cockily.

'OK, we'll play a best-of-three match this afternoon,' said Björn. 'But it will be just like a real match.'

'Of course,' I said. 'And we have to play for something.'

'A hundred dollars to the winner!' said Björn.

We said goodbye to the girls and left. It was no problem getting the use of one of the courts. It was somewhat off to the side, which suited me just fine. I didn't need any spectators. This was about honour and pride, and I was a little nervous. Sure, I had played tennis regularly for many years and kept myself in pretty good shape, but I had volleyed with Björn a number of times and knew what it was like. He was usually kind and half-lobbed the ball back, but sometimes he couldn't resist really slamming it. His forehand was especially hard and he could place it precisely where he wanted. Going down to the court in our tennis clothes, we teased each other mercilessly – God help the one who lost!

The rule, then, was that Björn would hop around on one leg, but that he would switch legs between balls. Try it yourself and see what it's like! And remember that I had played at least once a week for the past ten years, had good control of the ball and was in pretty good shape. There was

142

no question about it, I was the favourite against the five-time Wimbledon champion! My tactic, of course, was to get Björn to hop around as much as possible, so I alternated between short and long balls, and between playing against his forehand and his backhand. I did everything I could to wear him down and to beat him. Our competitive juices were really flowing and we stared at each other icily between balls.

My tactic succeeded perfectly. I soon got the upper hand and drove Björn from one side to the other without mercy. I won the first set 6–3, and the second set continued in the same style. I heard Björn breathing more and more heavily and saw how he shook his head in resignation after I hit yet another untouchable backhand cross. At 5–3 I figured I could break his serve and win the match. I had even begun to think about the ribbing I would give him afterwards . . .

Then a problem arose. A number of people began to gather around the court. The rumour had spread that Björn Borg was playing tennis on one leg! People laughed and cheered, and it was immediately clear to me that I wasn't the favourite in their eyes. Suddenly my arm turned to rubber. I returned one serve way outside the court and the next into the bottom of the net. Björn looked at me questioningly, smiled and shook his head a little as if to tease me. He won three straight games and took the set 7–5. The decisive set was just a matter of routine for him. As usual, Björn Borg turned yet another threatening defeat into victory, winning 6–3. Then he sank to his knees and raised his arms to the heavens in his famous Wimbledon pose. That evening I really learned what it is to be given a hard time.

* * *

The next day we went deep-sea diving – that is, I was seasick and miserable in the boat and admired the diving feats performed by Björn and others. We returned to Rio de Janeiro that evening, having booked rooms in a fancy hotel on the Copacabana in advance. The organisers and sponsors of the Grand Prix tournament paid all our expenses in Rio, too. When we went out in the crowds to shop we were even supplied with broad-shouldered, gun-toting bodyguards, who looked like they had escaped from a detective story.

Rio is a fantastic city, framed by the sea on one side and the mountains on the other. I was told that in the summer of 1501 three ships sailed from Lisbon to explore South America. In January 1502 the explorers reached a bay and thought it was the mouth of a river *(rio)*. They called the place Rio de Janeiro, or January River. Now, nearly 500 years later, the city has more than five million inhabitants. Once night falls, spotlights light up the mountain tops and the famous statue of Christ casts its light out to sea in the east. Buildings lie crowded very, very close together along the narrow strip of land between the sea and the forested mountainside. The Copacabana, the site of most of the luxury hotels, skyscrapers and casinos, is the very heart of the city and at night when the lanterns shine brightly, Rio looks like an endless, glittering promenade.

One of the reasons for the Rio visit was that Björn was to participate in an exhibition match as a promotional event on behalf of Tretorn, the Swedish tennis-ball maker. When the limousine arrived at the hotel to pick up Björn, Christer and I went along. The tennis club was about half

Top: Björn weds his first wife Mariana. He was 24.

Above: Björn with his second wife, Italian pop singer Lorendana Berte, whom he married in 1989. They have since parted.

Opposite: Björn with ex-girlfriend Jannike Bjorlin and their son Robin, now seven.

Top: Björn with an armed Secret Service agent during our visit to the USA in 1987.

Above: On our way to the tennis match played during the official visit to the United States in September 1987. The match was played between Björn Borg with George Bush and Vitas Gerulaites with Swedish Ambassador, Wilhelm Wachtmeister. The Swedish Prime Minister, Ingvar Carlsson, is pictured in the middle.

Top: A tennis match to remember. On court and ready to go Björn Borg, Vitas Gerulaites and George Bush.

Above: Björn challenged me to a tennis match. Even though he agreed to handicap himself by hopping on one leg he still won!

Above & Below: The private racer boat competition in the Stockholm Archipelago. Ingmar Alverdal and I assisted Björn in his monster of a boat Dunderburken (Thunderbox). But, sadly, we never reached the finish line. At the banquet which followed, Björn gave a speech and King Carl Gustaf listened.

Top: The only way to travel when island hopping in Brazil.
Above: Lazy days on Itaparica - an island off the coast of Brazil.

Top: On the way to Brazil, autumn 1986.

Above: Still more globe trotting. Björn was sent to Dubai in February 1988 by the Swedish Tourist Board. I was attempting to sell BBDG in the Middle East.

an hour by car from the Copacabana. After the welcoming ceremonies, a very athletic man approached Björn and they greeted each other heartily. They stepped aside and chatted briefly, after which Björn went into the locker-room to change for the match. Then Björn's friend, who, it turned out was a well-known former soccer player for Brazil, came up to Christer and me.

'Do you want some, too?' he asked, smiling at us.

We didn't know what he meant, so we laughed rather weakly without answering. He didn't repeat the question and we began talking about something else.

Björn played his exhibition match against one of Brazil's best prospects. He was in good tennis form that day and cleaned up the court with his young opponent. After having a bite to eat with Tretorn's representatives we returned to Rio and the Copacabana.

That evening, while Mia took a nap, I went up to Björn and Jannike's suite for a drink. I was in great spirits. I had really been able to relax while we were in Brazil and felt strong and healthy. I entered the suite and noticed the strange, charged atmosphere immediately. Björn looked secretive and rather mysterious, while Jannike seemed evasive and irritated. Neither of them said a word and I felt that I had come at a bad time.

'What's wrong?' I asked in surprise. 'Aren't we going to have something to drink before we go out? You look like you need it.'

Björn looked at me for a minute and then at Jannike. 'Should we tell him?'

'No!' she barked. 'Please, Björn, don't do it!'

But he had already made up his mind.

'Oh, it doesn't matter. He already knows anyhow.'

He lifted a large ashtray on the coffee table. Under its convex bottom were a number of neat lines of white powder. I looked at Björn sitting next to Jannike on the sofa.

'Have a line,' Björn said with a smile. He seemed in the best of moods.

Just as in Berlin, I was again torn by my conflicting feelings, on the one hand spontaneously rejecting the idea and on the other being curious.

'How do you do it?' I asked, embarrassed.

Björn began giving me careful instructions.

'The most important thing is that you trust me entirely and do exactly as I say. Then it's not at all dangerous . . . so trust me.'

I nodded and looked at Jannike. It was clear that she didn't like the situation at all. She shrugged her shoulders and muttered something under her breath, while she shook her head as if there wasn't anything she could do about it. Björn continued his lesson without paying any attention to her. He made me feel like a little boy who was about to sneak his first smoke.

'Whatever you do, for God's sake don't say anything about this to Mia,' I said. 'She'll go crazy.'

'No, no, don't worry,' said Björn, continuing his instructions. 'When you inhale the coke, take a long, deep breath. Otherwise it can get caught in your nose and it doesn't do any good there, if you know what I mean.'

'Good heavens,' I said with a nervous laugh. 'This must be the first time it has snowed in Brazil.'

Björn responded with a broad grin and even Jannike

146

started to smile before catching herself. The silly joke cut through the worst of the tension. Björn took a banknote out of his pocket and rolled it into a thin tube.

'Watch how I do it,' he said, 'and then do it precisely the same way.'

He leaned over the table, put the tube up to one of his nostrils and held the other nostril with his finger. Then he moved the tube to the end of one line and inhaled vigorously while moving the tube along the line. In two or three seconds the line was gone. He inhaled deeply a few more times and then snorted a couple of times to be sure that nothing had got caught in his nose. For a moment I again felt scared about what I was about to do, but then my curiosity got the upper hand and, so as not to change my mind, I quickly put my rolled-up banknote to the little line that Björn had set up for me.

'Hold your other nostril so you'll be able to inhale better. But first take a few deep breaths to clear your nostrils,' urged Björn in the background.

I practised a few deep breaths before putting the tube to the powder. Then I closed my eyes and breathed in as deeply and as hard as I could, and I didn't stop until the whole thin line was gone. Thus it was that I took off on my virgin trip with cocaine. I shook my head a little and sucked in air.

'It takes about twenty minutes to take effect,' said Björn. 'Take it easy. There's no danger.'

I leaned back in the easy chair and waited for the effect to hit me. I didn't have any idea what would happen. Would there just be a jolt in my brain? Would I get high, go crazy and lose control? I began to think about what the expression 'high' actually meant. When I swallowed I felt a sort of bitter roughness way back on the roof of my mouth. I told Björn about it.

'That's good. That means you did it the right way.'

The minutes went by. Björn snorted another line, this time with his other nostril. In the end Jannike finally sat down at the table and seemed ready to participate in the 'party'. Björn gave me more instructions, this time about how to hide the fact that you've been snorting.

'Look in your nose very carefully and rinse it with water so that you don't have a lot of powder left. Check in the mirror,' he lectured. 'When you go out, make sure not to blow your nose when people can see you. And never sit around snuffling, because that will make people suspicious. Don't go to the WC too often. Just behave normally and no one will have any idea. Keep a whisky or some other drink nearby and people will think you've just drunk too much.'

'You really know a lot about this, Björn,' I joked.

He looked at me and shrugged his shoulders.

'Oh well, you learn from life.'

I still didn't feel the least effect. In fact I was much more clear-headed and sober than I had been for a very long time. I wanted to tell Björn and Jannike about my feelings, and so I did. Why didn't I get high? Wasn't that what was supposed to happen? I must have gone on a long time about that, because Björn started laughing at me.

'Do you feel good?' he asked.

'Sure, I feel great, but why doesn't anything happen?'

'You don't know it,' he said, 'but you are actually quite high right now. That's the way cocaine works. You become as clear as crystal and you get a lot of ideas. You want to talk about everything under the sun and you can't sleep. You can be awake several days in a row.'

After the first half-hour I was no longer afraid or nervous. I thought to myself that this wasn't any worse than alcohol, and I didn't know whether to be relieved or disappointed. I asked Björn to put up a little more for me and he carefully raked together a small line. I could see that he was being careful that I didn't take too much.

'Be careful with the granules,' said Jannike. 'It's expensive.'

I snorted the second line the same way as the first one, although I used my other nostril just as Björn had done. Once again I waited for some kind of a kick, but it never came. I realised that what Björn had told me was true. My thoughts became very clear and I felt very sharp and gifted. Above all, I didn't feel intoxicated. To my surprise, I wasn't hungry and I didn't know how I would be able to bring myself to eat that evening. On the other hand, I drank a great deal of water. An hour or two passed and we discussed everything between heaven and earth.

Eventually we picked up Mia, went to a discothèque and had a great evening. There were some Swedish tourists there who were excited about meeting Björn Borg. After a while I drank a few glasses of champagne, but without very much enthusiasm. The feeling I had had in the suite – the positive and sharp one – disappeared more and more, but I was still in top condition. I concentrated on behaving normally and I must have succeeded, since Mia didn't make any comment. I explained my lack of appetite by saying it was too hot to eat.

At three in the morning we returned to the hotel, aware that we had to get up early that day. Björn's doubles partner from Itaparica, a rich and influential businessman who was our host and was paying for some of our expenses during the trip, had invited us to spend a day on his yacht. He was to pick us up at the hotel at eight and had promised us a day we would not soon forget. I lay in bed and tried to sleep. I usually didn't have any problem falling asleep after a few minutes, but that night I tossed and turned and couldn't relax. My brain was like an anthill full of ideas. I lay next to Mia and listened to her deep, long breaths.

When the alarm clock rang four hours later, I was still wide awake. I hadn't slept a second and didn't feel at all well. It was impossible to relax, my mouth was dry and my nose felt as if I were coming down with a cold. It wasn't hard to figure out that these were the after-effects of the cocaine, and I understood what Björn meant when he said that you could be awake for days at a time. I got out of bed with some effort, greedily grabbed a bottle of mineral water and emptied it in long, thirsty gulps. I opened the window as wide as I could and saw that the weather was as beautiful as usual. I woke Mia just as the phone rang. Björn sounded tired.

'Hi,' he said, 'how are things going?'

'As well as can be expected. I've got something of a hangover, you know,' I replied. 'How are you?'

'Oh, just fine. But . . . Jannike and I can't go on that boat ride today.' He didn't give any reason, and after a short pause continued, 'You two go ahead and go along! It doesn't matter if we back out.'

Back out on the person who had paid for our lovely stay? I couldn't believe he could even think of it.

'I'll bet our host doesn't think so,' I ventured. 'I really think it's a pretty bad idea to cancel at the last minute. After all, you're the guest of honour.'

But I could hear from his voice that he had already made up his mind and I knew what that meant. We agreed that we would meet when we returned to the hotel. When Mia heard that Björn and Jannike had backed out, she was terribly angry.

'That's pretty damn bold! What happens if we back out, too? Have they thought about that? Here we have to be good soldiers and save their reputations. What's the matter? Can't they climb out of bed? Shit!'

Mia couldn't contain herself. She dialled the number for the suite and Jannike answered. Their conversation was pretty strong, with some harsh words flying in both directions, and it ended by Mia hanging up.

Our host was waiting for us in the lobby. When he heard that Björn and Jannike had backed out, his eyes seemed to turn even darker. There was an uncomfortable silence. I tried to explain that Björn was feeling ill. He made some sarcastic comments and then off we went.

It turned out to be a wonderful day. Our new friend had recovered his good spirits by the time we arrived at the harbour. We headed out to the open sea and had the wonderful day we'd been promised, I even succeeded in sleeping for about an hour.

Our host, who had also invited us all to dinner that evening, returned to the hotel with us late in the afternoon. The others were lying around the pool sunning

themselves. Everything was just fine. Björn said hello
politely and acted as if nothing had happened. He didn't
even apologise for not joining us that morning and, as
usual, no one said a thing. No one was ever angry with
Björn for any length of time. Maybe it was partly because
he was so famous and no one wanted to risk offending
him, but it was certainly also because he acted so
boldly and easily in such situations. He had such a strong
sense of himself that he allowed himself to act any
way he pleased and that made it difficult for others
to react.

That evening there was another cancellation, but this
time it was only Jannike who stayed at the hotel. Björn
was evasive when he was asked what had happened and I
assumed that they had had one of their many arguments.
During dinner, Björn was quiet and restless. I could see
that he wanted to leave as soon as possible, and when the
rest of us decided to go to a discothèque he said to me,
'I'm going back to Jannike. Do you want anything?' 'No,'
I replied rather acidly. I could see that he wanted to
appease me after having backed out of the boat trip that
morning and now that he was leaving the rest of us so
early, but I wanted him to know that I disapproved.

One of the first people I saw at the discothèque was
the soccer player we had met the day before. He smiled
and waved.

'Where's Björn?' he asked.

I said that Björn had been forced to go back to the hotel
to take care of Jannike, who wasn't feeling well. Once
again I was defending what Björn had done.

'What the hell does he mean by that?' the man

complained loudly. 'We agreed that we would meet here and make an evening of it.'

From what the man said, I understood that he had met Björn at the hotel earlier in the day – it wasn't very hard to figure out what sort of business they had conducted there – and Björn had promised to meet him and his expectant friends at the discothèque that evening. In the meanwhile, Björn had found other things to think about. The awkward moment passed, and we joined the man's party. Once again it was very late before we got back to the hotel, but still early enough that Christer and I decided to have a nightcap on his balcony.

We found a surprise waiting for us. Björn was sitting alone on the balcony and cocaine was strewn all over the bathroom. He had obviously been snorting by himself. We went out and sat down with him. Björn wasn't his usual self. He looked worried and tired and had black rings under his eyes. He didn't seem to see us and sat there as if he were off in his own world.

'Have you guys seen?' he hissed. 'Check out the chick in the window over there . . . yes, over there, I say! I've sat here watching her half the night.'

We looked in the direction he was pointing, but we didn't see what he was talking about. The nearest window must have been at least a hundred yards away and it was physically impossible to see anything through it. This was a terrible situation and I was really frightened. Was Björn hallucinating? There simply wasn't any girl in any window. I immediately decided to go to bed. I wanted to get away from there as quickly as I could.

The next day Christer told me that Jannike had come

in a few minutes after I had left. She had been beside herself and had sworn up and down at Björn, who was still sitting on the balcony and spying.

Mia was going hang-gliding the next morning. I accompanied her without any idea of taking part, but when I saw her jump from the cliff and the hang-glider sail slowly out over Rio, I knew that I couldn't resist. I thought to myself that if I were dumb enough to try cocaine, I could certainly try other ways of achieving a high. It was a two-person hang-glider, and the instructor gave me extensive instructions before the jump.

'You can't hesitate on the cliff,' he said, 'for if you do, we won't get enough air under the wings and we might fall straight down . . . and then it's, well . . . *kaput, finito.*'

I wasn't sure that he trusted me completely, but we got ready to jump. I aimed for the cliff and ran as fast as I could, and then we jumped out into infinity. It was a powerful feeling to be up in the clouds and look down over the city, the sea and the mountains. Unfortunately, I was a little too heavy, so we began to sink right away, and our landing was quick and uncontrolled. I sprained my ankle in the process, which gave me a good reason to take it very easy during our last day in Rio. I lay in bed and Mia, who had made a brilliant landing, took care of me.

Our ten days of holiday had come to an end, and on 6 December we said goodbye to Rio. I longed for home. After all that had happened, I had thought a great deal about Björn. I was frightened and shocked by what I had seen of him on this trip. It was a burden being one of the few people who knew how things really stood with him. He had said that he wasn't a drug addict, but was that really true? It was one thing to have stayed at the hotel and missed an insignificant cruise if he didn't feel well, but he had *continued* that evening and even escalated his intake. The image of Björn on the balcony wouldn't go away. It was too much – he needed help.

Or did he?

I turned around and looked at him as he sat in the row behind me on the other side of the aisle. Björn winked and flashed his usual, happy smile.

CHAPTER NINE

'Lasse, let's go into business...'

In 1987 Björn found himself in a new situation. Four years had passed since he had retired from competitive tennis. He had established himself in Sweden with a family and a home, but he was unused to having so much free time. His contractual responsibilities with Eiser, Romella, the Tourist Council and the Björn Borg Sports Club sometimes gave him a good deal to do, but they hardly created a nine-to-five routine for him and his old contracts through IMG required less and less of him. There were financial repercussions too. Björn Borg Enterprises Ltd had revenues of just over $2.1 million in 1986, but we could see that those revenues would fall to around $1 million in 1987, and endorsement incomes from tennis manufacturers would fall dramatically from $573,000 in 1986 to $211,000 in 1987. Many other contracts were about to expire and IMG didn't appear to be doing very much to renew them or to negotiate new ones. Simply put, IMG didn't think it was possible to sell a retired tennis player, even if his name was Björn Borg.

Björn was unaccustomed to not being in demand and he began to think that IMG had let him down; the company wasn't showing him the loyalty he expected from it. The way Björn saw it, IMG was only interested in other, younger Swedish tennis players.

I tried to get Björn involved in Project House, but at

the same time I didn't want to be accused of trying to take advantage of his name. Nonetheless, through our dealings I had shown Björn both that I believed in him and that I could negotiate new contracts for him. As a result he turned to me more and more and began to suggest that we should go into business together, just the two of us, without any interference from either IMG or Project House. True to his old habits, Björn started demanding an increasing amount of my time and attention. It was obvious that he had something in the back of his mind, and in February 1987 he put forward his proposal.

'Shouldn't you and I buy some real estate?'

I looked at him, waiting for more details.

'Everyone else is investing in real estate, so why shouldn't we do it, too?'

I was taken by surprise. I had expected him to raise the question of my assuming part-ownership in Björn Borg Enterprises Ltd, which was something he had mentioned in the past. Still, there was a good deal to be said for what he was suggesting. I knew from my own experience that real estate speculation was the key to making fast money in the 1980s. At the time, I was half-owner of a company called Cassatoria, which owned properties in Stockholm and London and gave me access to some very good contacts in the business.

Björn's proposal was attractive, and while it did not solve the question of finding something for him to do, it might be a step in the right direction. I decided to accept. Now Björn Borg and Lars Skarke would join the real estate carousel of the 1980s – we were going to be real estate sharks.

Real estate prices were rising steadily. All you had to do was to avoid paying too much for a property and to have sufficient funds to pay for the deficit that arose after the purchase. The deficit was the difference between rental incomes and the cost of maintaining the property, most of which consisted of interest payments on the loan taken out to make the purchase. If you were able to do that, you would soon see a rise in the value of the property, which you could cash in on either by selling it or borrowing money against it to make new purchases. We found a block of properties in Solna and Hågersten that cost $15 million and calculated that we needed another $1.2 million a year to make a go of it.

We then acquired a company that was expected to make approximately that much profit each year for about five years. The shares in the company cost us $2.6 million. Björn borrowed the entire amount from the bank, while I borrowed my share – 40 per cent of the total or $1.04 million – from him in return for a promissory note. He was then able to pay the interest on the bank loan from his income from capital. The owners naturally made a nice profit by selling their shares, but Björn and I knew that we had made a fantastic deal. This company was in the business of buying real estate and was thus able to deduct losses from administering properties from the profits earned from its other activities. We bought the company on 9 March 1987 and the company bought the properties in Solna and Hågersten the very next day. (Somewhat later we could even afford to buy another piece of real estate – this time in Malmö – for $3 million.) Abracadabra, the pieces of the puzzle had fallen in place. If this sounds strange, it is because the 1980s *were* strange. Transactions like these took place all the time and the investors were cheered on by the banks.

We renamed the company Stronghold Invest AB, 'stronghold' being the English translation of the Swedish *borg*. We thought that was better than using Björn's name. The newspapers got hold of the story anyway, since the name of the buyer had to be registered with the municipality, and you can imagine the printer's ink spilled over that transaction.

Björn thought we could go further and take on other business dealings along with our real estate purchases. Now he revived the idea of my joining him as part-owner of Björn Borg Enterprises Ltd and proposed, via Björn Gullström, that I buy into his company abroad for a small amount of money in return for assuming responsibility for the operation. By this time Björn and I had developed a deep and very close relationship, not only through our business dealings, but also because of our personal experiences together, and I was moved by this show of confidence in me. I also thought that such an arrangement might give me an opportunity to help Björn find himself and become a more harmonious human being. Nevertheless, I was very busy with Project House, and my interest in real estate had led me into a number of other commitments. Then, too, I hadn't been able to erase the unpleasant memories from our trip to Brazil.

I explained my situation to Björn Gullström as best as I could without burdening him with what I had experienced in Rio. I didn't want to seem negative by rejecting the offer, so Gullström and I agreed that he would discuss with Björn the possibility of giving me a time-specific option to purchase stock in his company for a specified amount of money. Gullström came back to me with a ten-year option to purchase 40 per cent of the shares in Björn Borg Enterprises Ltd for $100,000. The price was very advantageous, since the company had exclusive rights to the use of the name Björn Borg and to the compensation Björn received from his old agreements and from new ones I negotiated for him. On the other hand, the assets and revenues were to be invested in developing companies using the name Björn Borg. We were both to be active in the company for the duration of the agreement and were to receive equal salaries and benefits. Yet, while the price was a carrot for me to achieve good results and to devote myself fully to doing business with Björn, the option agreement in some ways confirmed the nature of our relationship.

Signing the agreement would not mean anything revolutionary or dramatic for me. After all, it was only an option agreement and didn't commit me to any binding responsibilities. Nonetheless, it made me feel as if I were cornered. I was forced to make a decision. Björn wanted to do business and needed me as a friend and a partner. Moreover, I liked him very much. The agreement was like a hand reaching out to me.

But I had other people to think about, too. In addition to Project House and my partnership with Egon, there was also my commitment to Harry Westelius, my partner in Cassatoria. We had agreed to sell Cassatoria and had negotiated a deal with Convector, a real estate firm owned by Per Arwidson. Aside from being paid handsomely for our company, we were offered the chance to work with Arwidson in his venture into the consulting business and foreign real estate. I was to be paid a very large salary as well as a one-time bonus of $1 million on signing the contract. It was a fantastic offer.

One day as we were driving to an appointment I raised the question of cooperation with Björn.

'I've got to know,' I said. 'You were going to concentrate on your private life and put things right. What's happened? Do you want to begin working now?'

He looked at me. 'You know very well that love has its ups and downs. Even it gets to be a matter of habit. You have to have other things to do. Sometimes I hate them all. Women, that is. The worst thing is that we need them.'

I couldn't help laughing out loud. 'Yes, you sure are right there.'

He laughed too, then answered my question. 'Yes, I'm serious. I've made up my mind. But I don't want to stand around department stores signing autographs and things like that. I want to have some other role where I can feel free.' He thought for a minute and then went on, 'I don't want to be at the centre of attention in the same way. And I'm not up to travelling around the world any more. But of course I'm going to work!'

I listened carefully, thinking over what he said, and then I asked, 'But . . . can you behave?'

'No problem, Lasse, trust me.'

There were no reservations in his voice.

'Yes, but as you know,' I said, 'I've got a very good

offer from Per Arwidson to make a decision about. I've almost made up my mind. Moreover, I've got to try to reduce the profits from my sale of shares to him. He's promised to help me with a short-term tax-planning loan for $2 million.'

Björn looked at me and smiled slightly.

'Those millions are pennies in this context. We can earn unlimited amounts and have a great time together! And a loan is no problem. I can guarantee it.'

For the rest of the trip I drove in silence, weighing the pros and cons of his offer. Project House was going to be dealing only with sponsoring in the future and there was hardly room there for both Egon and me. He was 'Mr Sponsoring', so it was appropriate for me to resign. Being the entrepreneur that I am, I was very tempted to put together a company around Björn Borg. Not least of all, it would give me the opportunity to complete what I had once started with Eiser. It was a challenge and I have always had difficulty resisting challenges.

Against making this choice was the fact that Per Arwidson would be disappointed if I didn't accept his offer and my own lingering worries about Björn and his lifestyle. Did he really want to do business, or was he just trying to cement our close friendship? Björn had given me plenty to think about.

CHAPTER TEN

Dangerous Games

It's about forty miles by car from Viking's Hill, which lies south-east of Stockholm, to Stavsborg, the beautiful eighteenth-century home on Ekerö Island, north-west of the city, that I had bought in 1986, and it can take as long as two hours to drive the distance during rush hour. Therefore Björn usually chose to take a helicopter when he came to visit. That wasn't anything out of the ordinary for him; he was used to travelling by the quickest and most comfortable means available. It wasn't quite as natural to me, but I certainly didn't have anything against it. On this particular Saturday afternoon in the late spring of 1987 the helicopter landed at the usual place down by the lake. Björn climbed out, waved at the pilot and then walked up towards my house.

We sat on the veranda drinking cold beer. I had thought about our conversation in the car a good deal, and a business concept had slowly but surely taken shape in my mind. It was partly based on what Björn himself had said.

'Björn,' I said, 'I've got an idea I want you to think about. But first I have to ask you once again: are you 100 per cent sure you don't want to be the centre of attention in the same way you used to be?'

'Yes, absolutely,' he replied without hesitation.

'OK, then listen. My idea is that we should change the

165

way people think of you. Instead of being a person, you would become an image. Think of Lacoste, for example. My daughters buy Lacoste sweaters because they are very nice and of very high quality. They don't have any idea that there was once a tennis player of that name. An image, a trademark, call it what you like. You know, Lacoste wouldn't sell any more sweaters even if old Henri did stand around a department store signing autographs.'

Björn looked at me and listened intently.

'I think we should do something like that,' I continued. 'Clothes, of course, and maybe some other things, too. Everything of the very best quality. Then we can use your name to sell them, but *you* wouldn't have to be at the centre of attention. You could stay in the background as a kind of guarantor of the quality of our products.'

I had worked hard to find the right words, and Björn understood immediately. He nodded thoughtfully.

'At the end of the day,' I said, 'the name Björn Borg will stand for quality and be a positive image. When people hear the name Björn Borg they will immediately think of our fine products, not about the person who gave them his name. Just like Lacoste. Quite simply, Björn, you will be a trademark.'

Björn looked out towards the lake and was quiet for a long time. Then he began to smile.

'This is really great,' he said, looking approvingly at me. 'Yes, it's exactly what I want.'

'So we agree! Then let's get going.'

We shook hands. Now we were partners. I informed the board of directors of Project House of my decision and then said 'no, thank you' to a surprised and indignant Per Arwidson.

Our business concept had many advantages. His role would allow Björn the time to straighten out his untidy private life, while still giving him something worthwhile to do during the day. It would give him the motivation to keep going, which I was convinced he needed, and make me feel more secure because our business would not depend on his personal contributions. In addition, Björn's name had the rare aura needed to launch a company and trademark. Off the top of my head I couldn't think of any other name with the same business possibilities – *everyone* knew who he was, and his name was associated with victory and success.

Even as this thought passed through my mind I remembered an incident during one of Björn's earlier visits to Stavsborg. Björn, Mia and I had been sitting at the kitchen table when one of my cousins came over to 'inspect' my new home. My mother had told her about Stavsborg and had mentioned my priceless gardener, Bengt, who was one of my mother's favourites.

My cousin sat down with us in the kitchen and had a cup of coffee. Our conversation turned to sports, in which we were all interested, and we began quizzing one another. Björn asked who had invented the current high-jumping style known as the 'flop'.

'Fosbury,' answered my cousin.

'Very good,' said Björn.

She enjoyed the praise and then said to him, 'You must be the Bengt I've heard so much about, Lasse's gardener.'

Björn stared at her in amazement. No one said a word while the truth dawned on my cousin.

'But . . .,' she said, blushing deeply, 'you're . . . Björn Borg!'

Björn and I burst out laughing. It must have been the first time in many years that anything like that had happened. In an effort to cover her embarrassment, my cousin then asked, 'Well . . . are you playing any tennis these days?'

Björn gave her his standard answer between his fits of laughter: 'Oh yes, I love tennis. And I'll always love tennis.'

Smiling at the past, I returned to the present. 'So you agree that we should try to get somewhere with my business idea?'

'Of course,' answered Björn.

'Good! Then I think we should do the following. I know a man in the advertising business who is very good at developing business concepts. I'll present the idea to him and see what he has to say.'

'That sounds perfect.'

During the spring and the summer Björn seemed to be on an emotional and behavioural roller-coaster, with his peaks and troughs more sharply defined than ever. At times he would be the proud and happy family man who took Jannike and Robin with him in the helicopter or in one of their cars and visited us at Stavsborg. During this period Björn did what he was supposed to do. He showed up on time for his appointments and was frequently at Project House, where he read his mail and discussed upcoming meetings and trips.

At other times Björn would fight with Jannike about the most insignificant things, and I could see how fragile their relationship was. In fact, they had fought and quarrelled ever since their visit to Gotland almost two years before. Björn wasn't used to a girl like Jannike, who had definite ideas and a will of her own. He had been used to having his smallest wish fulfilled and all his conditions met by others. Now he had to accept someone else's conditions on occasion and it wasn't easy for him. I think this was the first time in his entire life that Björn had become emotionally dependent on another human being. It made him sensitive and vulnerable, but also angry and sometimes really furious. He wasn't completely in control any longer, and that was an entirely new experience for him.

Christer Gustafsson had noticed the cracks in Björn and Jannike's fragile relationship early on. He told me: 'At first they seemed to make a dynamic combination, but we soon learned that if they were together for long enough they would explode.

'Initially, Björn had rejoiced at being in love, but then he realised how vulnerable it made him too. They were like the blind leading the blind. Their strong temperaments were so alike that they were unable to complement each other in the way that some couples can make up for each other's inadequacies. They were unable to cope with minor problems together, and trivial difficulties would result in a fierce argument.

'Dining out with them as a couple became a nightmare as their relationship became embroiled with jealousy and suspicions. They didn't think twice about having a screaming row in a restaurant, making life extremely uncomfortable for all their guests.

'They both rejoiced in being mean to each other in the most childish fashion. Their love had turned sour, and they were like two kids in a sandbunker both trying to out-nasty the other. There was constantly a bad atmosphere around them and they would often drag me in as some kind of referee.

'Björn wanted people to adore him and he was used to getting what he wanted. Jannike didn't want to be another "yes" person in his life, and deliberately set out to be difficult. If she angered him too much he would become very angry, then soon replace this heated emotion with sheer ice. A naturally passionate person, she found his coldness towards her intolerable.'

Bjorn had different ways of reacting to his problems with Jannike. Sometimes he started vehement arguments, during which he would call Margaretha and Rune in the middle of the night and ask them to come over and help 'put things back together again'. They always helped out, even if they would later complain about how difficult it was. Sometimes, to ease the tension, I would joke about it with Rune, saying things like, 'I'm going to buy you a fireman's helmet so you'll have it in time for the next alarm.' He would smile, but it wasn't an amusing situation and, as always, Margaretha took Björn's side.

Sometimes Björn simply threw Jannike out of the house, not by being physically violent, but by hounding her and swearing at her. She would take the white Mercedes and drive home to her mother or to the flat in Vegagatan. After a while Björn and Jannike would make up, and she would move back to Viking's Hill. And when things between them were fine again, then things would be fine between Jannike and Rune and Margaretha, just as if nothing had happened.

Matters didn't improve when Jannike began to go out dancing with her girlfriends. Björn would pace up and down at Viking's Hill and imagine all sorts of things. Then he'd phone me at Stavsborg and say he was coming over. Soon we'd hear the sound of a helicopter beating its way through the air.

I was always there for Björn, although sometimes I felt more like a therapist than a friend. But he didn't have anyone else to talk to and I felt sorry for him. On the whole we were together a great deal that summer. Mia was increasingly unhappy about Björn's visits, since it was almost always a question of trying to help him with his personal problems.

One night, after Björn had sat around discussing his problems until long after midnight, I made up a bed for him in one of the guest rooms. Just as I was about to fall asleep, Björn appeared by my bed with a pillow and a blanket in his arms. He had heard noises and thought he had seen a door open, so he thought there were ghosts in the eighteenth-century house. He was afraid and asked to sleep in my room. Mia was in Stockholm at the time and came home about an hour later. She got quite a shock when she found Björn lying asleep on the thick carpet at the foot of our bed.

During his visits Björn would sometimes embark on long, bitter monologues about Jannike. He told us, for example, that she had gone into Stockholm one evening and he had sat alone in front of the TV in his dreary Viking's Hill. She wasn't home at one, or two or even three in the morning. Finally, as he lay in bed unable to sleep, he heard the lock turn. It was about 6 a.m. and he pretended to be asleep when Jannike crawled into bed. When they got up he had tried not to say anything or to reveal his jealousy or suspicions. But the same thing happened again. And again.

One night, he said, he had called Rune and Margaretha and asked them to come over to take care of Robin. He had then driven into Stockholm and found Jannike at one of the fashionable nightclubs. Björn had stood in the queue and hoped that, for once, people wouldn't recognise him, but of course someone did, and he had been ushered past the queue and into the club. Inside he had caught sight of Jannike on the dance floor. Who was she dancing with? Who was his rival? He watched her for a long time in order to find out, but she was dancing quite innocently with one of her friends. Finally he had gone up to her. Jannike had been furious and had accused him of spying on her. In situations like that five Wimbledon titles didn't mean very much.

Björn *was* terribly jealous and his suspicions led him to take other, even stranger measures. For a while he spent a good deal of money having private detectives keep an eye on Jannike when she went into Stockholm.

Björn told me that he was going to break up with Jannike once and for all, but that he hadn't decided when he would do it. It sounded absurd to me.

'How can you live with her if you've already decided to break up?' I asked. 'Isn't it a good idea to do it right away and get it over with?'

172

'No, not yet!' was all that he said.

'I hope you never treat me that way,' I said to him.

He shook his head. 'No, don't worry. I won't.'

At one point, Björn suspected that Viking's Hill was bugged. He got Ingmar to bring out electronic surveillance experts to inspect the phones and check for other listening devices. Although the experts found nothing, Björn continued to speak in a very low voice around the house for some time thereafter. On occasion he was also convinced that the police were watching him. He said that he had clear indications that they were doing so.

During these periods of upheaval with Jannike, Björn often showed up late for various appointments or backed out altogether. On these occasions he would phone our secretary, Mary Ahl, in the morning and ask her to 'cancel'. The worst case was when he called her at home early one Saturday morning and told her to cancel his participation in the filming of a promotional video for the Tourist Council in Lappland later that day. The plane was to leave Stockholm at nine to fly to Kiruna, where a helicopter would be waiting for him.

'You've got to call and cancel,' Björn ordered her. 'I'm not going.'

'But Björn, you have to! They've hired a helicopter and the film team is already up there. Everyone's waiting for you! You can't just back out now!'

'I can't go. I've got a fever and my temperature is 104°F.'

Mary called me at home immediately and told me what had happened, but I knew there was no hope of doing anything about it. Björn had probably been up the whole night. So Mary had to call the Tourist Council and pass along the news. Björn Borg wasn't popular with the film team in Lappland and it took Gert Karlsson and his colleagues plenty of time to forget that cancellation.

Björn liked to escape to a room in the central part of Stockholm owned by an acquaintance of his who was always able to supply him with drugs. Björn's companion was boundlessly proud of the fact that he knew the former tennis star, and Björn thought it a very practical way to get drugs. Sometimes Björn would start fights at Viking's Hill for no other reason than to give himself an excuse to slam the door behind him and drive to this particular address in Stockholm.

Then, suddenly, the roller-coaster would climb out of its decline and Björn would be the loving family man again. And everyone forgave him, believed him and thought, 'It's not so bad after all. There's nothing wrong with Björn Borg, anyone can see that. Just think how wholesome he looks!'

I was one of these optimists. At the same time, I still carried with me memories of Björn sitting on that hotel balcony in Rio, and in similar situations many times since. I wanted to help him, but I wasn't sure how I could and I made a lot of mistakes. The worst mistake I made was that I took cocaine with him on many occasions. It may be that I was, like the partner of an alcoholic, doing it initially in order to be able to diminish the dimensions of the problem in my own eyes, or to help him 'control' his misuse or perhaps simply to participate in some way. I just don't know, but I do know that I underestimated the danger of cocaine and that it could have ended very badly for me.

Cocaine is an infernal drug. The feelings of euphoria, alertness and strength it initially induces can turn into irritability, restlessness, anxiety and agitation. It increases the pulse rate, raises the blood pressure, causes sweating and can result in feelings of persecution, apathy and confusion. Dependency on cocaine sneaks up on its victims mercilessly. The brief, intense feeling of well-being quickly creates a craving for more . . . and more. Nonetheless, I was stupid enough to join Björn in visits to his special hideaway, where we used the drug together. In my own defence, I can at least say that I sensed the dangers of the drug and began discussing them with Björn. Cocaine was pleasant in small doses and on isolated occasions, but was it possible to keep one's use at that level? When did the poison begin to control the person?

I could see that Björn was approaching the borderline of addiction, if he had not already crossed it. He used narcotics almost every day for long periods of time at a stretch in the summer of 1987. Finally I said to him, 'Promise me one thing: don't take drugs in Sweden any more. If you have to do it, at least don't do it here at home.'

This was not a matter of a double standard. I thought that if Björn stopped using drugs in Sweden, he might get to the point where he'd stop using them when he was travelling. It would be a special sort of 'de-escalation'. I was also thinking about myself, for if Björn didn't use drugs in Sweden, then I wouldn't feel pressure to do so or risk being tempted.

'Yes, you're right,' Björn said. 'Sometimes I almost think I'm going a little nuts.'

I also suggested that he seek medical help and enter therapy. I raised the possibility with his mother, and it was one point on which we agreed. Margaretha told me that she had seen Björn with Vitas Gerulaitis during a visit to Gerulaitis's tennis school in Florida. She suspected that they were using cocaine: 'They went around there and "snuffled" all the time.' I introduced Björn to a psychologist and he began therapy. He also went to a doctor who knew about his problem.

But the drugs already had too strong a grip on him. He was so paranoid that he refused to trust any of the doctors, accusing them of spying on him and interfering in his life.

Nobody in Björn's life – including myself, Jannike or his parents – had a strong enough influence to force him to stay the treatment. We were all too beholden to him in one way or another actually to stand by our convictions. I suppose what it boils down to is that we were all on his payroll.

Björn would financially have cut any of us off if we persisted too much. He had created a luxurious life for his parents and yet he was capable of cutting off their income in an instant if they made life too difficult for him. We were all guilty in that respect.

If things continued in the way they were going Björn could have ended up facing a prison sentence – or much worse. I believed his debauched behaviour and increasing dependency on drugs were leading him to an early grave.

Christer Gustafsson became Björn's 'playmate' in the twilight hours and, when he recounted to me the sordidness of the situation, I was both shocked and saddened.

Christer told me how he had rubbed his eyes in disbelief as he once watched Björn weeping and sobbing naked in the corner of a room. Tennis fans would barely have recognised him as he writhed with his hands crudely tied behind his back. Above him stood a 6-foot tall woman dressed in a black leather peep-hole bra, pants and thigh-high leather boots brandishing a thick leather belt.

'You are guilty and now I am going to punish you', she screamed at him as the belt came lashing down on his bare buttocks.

Life had changed dramatically since the early days when Björn and Christer had made a handsome pair as they held court at Stockholm's fashionable hang-outs like Café Opera or Alexandra's.

'Björn could have his pick of women, it was so easy for him,' Christer told me. 'I think it was the very availability of women which gave him such a warped attitude towards sex. He simply didn't need to try.'

Christer told me that Björn could make women to do absolutely anything for him, and it all became another game to him. Previously normal, heterosexual women would perform graphic acts of lesbianism for him to satisfy his lusts. Christer believes that Björn had grown up in a world where people would do absolutely anything for him – where he was the boss – and sometimes he liked to escape into a world where he was the servant.

'Games of dominance and bondage fascinated him,' remembers Christer. 'He loved to be punished and discuss out loud his wildest fantasies. When he was high, Björn liked to make love anywhere and everywhere: upright against the wall, across a coffee table, in the sauna, in the shower, on the floor, upside down and inside out. You name it and Björn Borg has done it.

'Björn loved to take drugs – especially cocaine – which would relieve him of his self-consciousness. After a few lines of cocaine his sex urges would come straight to the surface. If we were with a couple of girls, the polite conversation was soon over as Björn began his familiar sleazy sexual patter. He was very proud of the size of his manhood and he loved to discuss what he would like to do with it and what he wanted the girls to do with it.

'He loved to parade naked, and he once said to me, "You know Christer, the world is my sauna!"

'We creased up laughing about that one.

'He always wanted the girls to praise him and would frequently demand during sex, "Do you like it?"'

Christer told me he would tease him about it afterwards, and Borg would grin proudly. They were two guys having a great time.

But the more the drugs took a hold on his life, the more his tastes became depraved. Instead of dressing up and being seen in the smart places, he liked to pull on some sloppy clothes and go to a basement flat owned by a friend of his in town.

'There were mirrors on the walls, with black carpets and matching sofas. The lighting was dimmed and the sounds were low. A couple of bedrooms were decked out in black satin with a stack of porn videos for entertainment, plus the obligatory sauna and jacuzzi,' recalls Christer.

'Björn would lose himself here for days on end, never knowing what time of the day or night it was. It could be the middle of the afternoon or midnight; as long as nobody could find him, he was happy. The owner would supply him with ten or more grammes of cocaine and he was happy as a pig. He would grab the drugs and greedily chop out a bunch of lines with his Gold American Express card on one of the glass-topped coffee tables. He'd snort several lines at once through a rolled-up note and soon he'd take off his clothes.

'He loved to sit around naked, and he'd get high watching the porn movies, snorting coke, chain-smoking and drinking tumblers of whisky or beer. Björn would have to finish every last grain of cocaine before he was prepared to see the daylight again.

'The more he snorted, the more he drank and smoked. And the more he did all three, the more he wanted sex.'

The owner of the flat would lay on some women from the local sex clubs for him – maybe four or five at a time. Christer remembers how Björn liked to fool around with them all at once before he made his selection and took just one girl into the bedroom. At first he would be polite and charming to the girls, but he would soon forget their names, referring to them instead as Number One or Number Five!

As his drug habit increased, so did his sexual depravity. He longed for the ultimate sexual high.

'One day when he was high, he told me he would like to fuck the moon if he could,' Christer told me.

All the time he was playing a sick game of Russian roulette, refusing to wear a condom despite the advice of his closest male pals.

Christer went on to tell me: 'Björn didn't want a

condom to ruin his pleasure. His ego was so swollen, he was convinced – in a God-like manner – that AIDS would never get him. I thought he was crazy, playing around with all kinds of women whose business it was to have sex with anyone who paid them.'

Despite the risks, Björn told Christer he had never once caught a sexually-transmitted disease in all his years, and he said he reckoned it was down to his punishing fitness routine and regular exercise.

Björn continued to confuse us. When he first met Jannike, he appeared to be a changed man. We thought he was so in love that he would never look at another woman again. He was obsessed with her in a way that we had never seen in a man before. But within a couple of months he was back to his old ways, staying up all night with the whores laid on for his delight. During Jannike's pregnancy he tried to go back on the straight and narrow, but hardly a month went by without him returning to his favourite haunt.

However, as any man who has ever taken drugs will tell you, cocaine can have a diminishing effect on a man's libido. Excessive use of cocaine produces the same results as too much alcohol.

But Björn had found a way round this. He discovered that if he was tied up and whipped, it quickly restored his manhood so that he was able to perform again. Christer told him he thought he was sick, but Björn assured his friend it was the best high in the world.

Christer recalls how as the livid red marks scored Björn's body his sexy tormentor warmed to her task: 'Admit you're guilty, and I may release you,' she said, taunting him with her tongue, the leather belt slipping between her fingers. The tennis star screamed in submission and the woman slowly removed the rope and mounted him, still holding him down by the throat.

Afterwards Björn went down on his hands and knees and licked her. When the woman left the room, Björn flicked on another porn movie and called up one of the sex lines in the United States. He would often run up bills of hundreds of dollars talking dirty across the Atlantic for hours on end.

'I felt embarrassed for him,' Christer told me. 'This guy had met the President of the United States and was Sweden's official ambassador to the world. He had mixed with all the movers and shakers and the most beautiful women were his for the asking.

'Björn had played football with Rod Stewart, sang with Elton John and Linda Ronstadt and was a close friend of Liza Minnelli. In the States, Bob Guccione and Hugh Hefner would lay girls on for him, while in Japan he would be invited to the most exotic geisha clubs. He was a member of an exclusive race of celebrities, travelling on private jets and gaining entrance to places we ordinary mortals could only dream about. Björn lived in a glittering and glamorous world and had everything going for him.

'And yet he had become a sick pervert who could only get his kicks from drugs and bondage,' Christer told me sadly.

'His old tennis friend Vitas Gerulaitis would visit "The Cave" whenever he was in town, but I think the novelty wore off for him too. He wanted to be where the action was rather than locked in some squalid basement.'

Björn wanted partners in crime, and he would try to persuade people to visit 'The Cave' with him. Once visited, few people were anxious to return. The police had got wind of the place and were keeping an eye on it. No public person in his right mind wanted to be seen visiting 'The Cave', but Björn has always considered himself above the law.

Björn didn't live in the real world any more. He had grown bored with having to act a certain way in public because of his high profile. And he was tired of women who wanted him only because of his famous name. He tried to explain to Christer one day that this was his problem, that since the age of 15 women had been at his beck and call, and he had pretty well lost respect for them.

Christer believes that the only woman he really adored was his mother, Margaretha.

'Björn wouldn't move without his mother's approval, and she seemed to believe that no woman was good enough for her son,' said Christer.

Today he's a 37-year-old man, and he's still living with his mother.

As Björn's dependency on drugs increased, Christer recalls how, when in Sweden, Björn often stayed with his parents, from where he would frequently call the owner of the basement flat and ask him to send a porn video over to their home. Inside the sleeve of the video there would always be a couple of grammes of cocaine neatly wrapped in little packets for him to snort while he was watching the movie.

'I watched Björn while he became so dependent on drugs that real life and all its associated problems were too much for him to handle. Cocaine made him paranoid and edgy and I could never really relax with him because it was difficult to predict his moods.'

One day Christer would be his best friend, and the next day he would be accused of sleeping with Björn's wife, or something else equally ludicrous. Björn would grow jealous and domineering, forever cross-examining Christer, wanting to know where he had been at certain times of the day.

'In Björn's sick mixed-up world, he saw everyone as his enemy,' Christer told me.

But there were some pleasant occasions that summer, too. At Björn's invitation, IMG's head tennis manager, Bob Kain, visited Stockholm on his way to Wimbledon. Björn's intention was to inform Kain about the plans we had for our new company. We rented a helicopter and flew Kain out to Sandhamn in the Stockholm archipelago to have lunch. On the way back Björn proudly showed him the archipelago from the air and pointed out Alstaholm and Viking's Hill. Kain was impressed and Björn was in one of his very best moods. I hadn't seen him as happy as he was that day since the time he'd come home from Hawaii with Jannike after their 'honeymoon' almost three years earlier.

About the same time Aje Philipson, whose mother was Sweden's richest woman, organised a private speedboat competition. Some twenty speedboats took part in the race, which ran from Philipson's country home on Ingarö to Sandhamn. Björn was among the competitors, and the King and Queen of Sweden were among the spectators. The King, who is an admiral in the navy and collects boats, was watching the race from a torpedo boat he had found in the navy's surplus stock that spring.

Björn's boat, *Dunderburken*, had been custom-made. It was 36 feet long, a bit over 10 feet wide, weighed almost 4 tons and was powered by two sets of Mercruiser motors with about 500 horsepower. The boat's cruising speed was between 35 and 40 knots, and its top speed was about 80. It was not surprising that Björn was the hands down favourite to win the race.

Björn approached the race as if it were the Wimbledon final. Two mechanics worked for weeks so that *Dunderburken* would be in top condition and there were two mechanics on hand for the race itself. The crew of three – Björn, Ingmar and I – were dressed in identical outfits for the occasion. Björn had hired a helicopter so that Rune, Margaretha, Jannike and Mia could follow us along the course from the air. In short, it was a very big and very expensive affair.

The starting shot was fired. We were a bit back in the field at the outset, but immediately caught up with the leading boats. Our boat sped forward like a cannonball, but I suddenly smelled something burning and saw smoke billowing out of the motors! We were scared to death, but fortunately all that happened was that the motors died and wouldn't start again. We were towed back to Philipson's pier, Björn swearing a blue streak the whole way. 'I'm going to sink this damn thing,' he hissed. 'Hell! This is worse than losing a Wimbledon final!' The mechanics quickly found the problem. Alverdal had set the carburetor incorrectly.

We eventually proceeded to Sandhamn by helicopter.

When we arrived everyone was seated in the restaurant. Jannike and Mia were waiting for us and had bought flowers to cheer us up. After the meal, Björn, who had recovered from the embarrassment with the help of a few drinks, gave an excellent speech and presented our flowers to Queen Silvia and to our host, Aje's wife. His final comment was greeted enthusiastically: 'I'll be back next year,' he promised solemnly, just as he used to do in his victory speeches when he won Wimbledon or the French Open.

The winner had driven a Flying Flipper, which was the same brand as my boat. 'We should have taken my boat,' I said to Björn. 'Then we'd have won like a shot.' Björn was very sulky, but then we took the helicopter to Alstaholm and did what Björn told me he used to do after important losses in tennis: we drowned our sorrow.

My large income allowed me to buy not only Stavsborg, but also a flat in Stockholm. I eventually found a maisonette at Grev Turegatan 70 and figured that both purchases would be good investments. The prices of cooperative flats were still shooting skyward and there didn't seem to be any change in sight. Therefore, when I found a fantastic penthouse flat in the centre of Stockholm, I bought it, too. After a short time I realised that I'd taken on a bit too much, so I put the flat on Grev Turegatan up for sale. The estate agent soon had a prospective buyer, a member of the Bonnier family, well-known for their publishing ventures. The price was a good one, and I was going to make a fair amount on the sale, so we reached an agreement and scheduled a meeting to sign the necessary documents.

Before we had a chance to sign the papers, however, I got a call from Björn. He wanted to find a flat for Jannike right away, and he had decided on my flat in Grev Turegatan.

'But I've already sold it,' I said, 'or at least I've promised it to someone.'

'You'll be able to change that somehow. She's got to leave the house now and I have to arrange something fast.'

'That's a bit difficult,' I said. 'A member of the Bonnier family is going to buy it, and it's not a good idea to get on their bad side. They own a number of magazines, Björn, and you might well end up in one or more of them if you're not careful.'

'Oh, that doesn't matter. Come on, now. I just have to have that flat.'

'In that case you're going to have to come along and explain it to the Bonniers. I have absolutely no interest in taking the heat for this.'

Björn ordered a helicopter and we flew to Smådalerö Island in the southern part of the Stockholm archipelago, where the Bonniers had a summer home. As we began our descent we could see an elderly man come out of the fine wooden house that stood closest to the landing site. By the time we jumped out he had almost reached us. He was obviously furious and shook his fist at us.

'Turn off the engines and don't scare my deer!'

It was Albert Bonnier, the patriarch of the family. I apologised and quickly explained our errand. He seemed to become more friendly and asked us up to the house, where the young couple to whom I'd promised to sell the flat were sunbathing. I suddenly felt very embarrassed.

After saying hello, I began, 'You see, Björn and I are best friends. He and Jannike are having some problems and I'd like to help him out.' I paused a moment and then began again. 'The truth of the matter is that Björn needs a flat right away and would very much like to buy mine, but I've already promised it to you. Well, you understand . . .'

No one said anything and I could see that they had really looked forward to moving into the flat. Maybe they'd even planned how they were going to decorate it. This wasn't at all easy, and I looked at Björn.

'You have to understand that it's not Lasse's fault,' he said. 'I hope you won't be too angry.'

They accepted our apologies without complaint, but I doubt they would have done so had there been a legally binding contract. Björn bought the flat for the same amount I'd paid for it two months earlier, which was less than the Bonnier couple had agreed to pay. Jannike moved in, as she would do frequently over the course of the next year before moving in for good.

The end of their great love affair was no different to all the previous temporary finales. The row ended as usual, with Jannike packing her bags at Viking's Hill and moving to the flat. Only this time she didn't come back. She took off for a week with my girlfriend Mia, and the pair of them did a lot of damage to Björn's credit cards – living it up and staying out all night. Jannike liked to take it out on Björn financially – where it hurt.

But when you have so many pairs of shoes, and so many dresses, the thrill of spending wears thin. Jannike simply wanted a more peaceful life, away from the uncertainty and away from the endless fights.

CHAPTER ELEVEN

Up at the White House, Down in Los Angeles

Early in the summer of 1987 the chairman of the Swedish Tourist Council, Gert Karlsson, phoned me at Project House. After chatting for a few minutes, Gert explained why he was calling. For the first time in twenty-six years a Swedish prime minister had been invited to the White House, the ultimate proof that the previously strained relations between Sweden and the United States were finally back to normal.

'I spoke with Prime Minister Carlsson's state secretary, Kjell Larsson, yesterday. Kjell is preparing Carlsson's official visit to the United States, and the Prime Minister evidently wants to organise the trip somewhat differently than is usually done. One of his ideas is to show off what Sweden has in the way of culture and science.' He paused a moment before continuing.

'And now Ingvar Carlsson has said that he'd very much like to have Björn Borg along as a member of the delegation to represent the Swedish tourist trade. Kjell emphasised that this was the Prime Minister's own idea, and that he'd be very pleased if Björn would agree to go.'

I noted that Gert's voice had a certain edge to it.

'We are very happy with Björn's work with us,' he said, 'although we hadn't thought he'd be as busy as he seems to be with other projects. In any case, I think this is a great way for both Björn and the Tourist Council to show why their contract was drawn up.'

I squeezed in a couple of questions.

'When will the visit take place? Do you have the exact dates?'

'During the first part of September, between the sixth and the thirteenth.'

'I'll do what I can, Gert.'

'Good! And when you talk with Björn perhaps you can stress to him that the government would really appreciate his help with this. I'm convinced that it would be very beneficial for Björn, too.'

Gert pointed out that it would be very good if I were to go along on the trip as Björn's 'assistant'. He gave me the Prime Minister's private phone number and told me to call Ingvar Carlsson as soon as I had spoken with Björn.

After that conversation I sat and thought for a long time. The government's invitation was like a gift from the gods. I had already contacted the advertising expert I had had in mind when discussing my business concept with Björn. He had been very enthusiastic about the idea and had assembled an excellent team to develop the concept for the Björn Borg Design Group, and Björn and I had spent a good deal of time discussing how we should announce the formation of our company and the fact that Björn was investing in his own name as a trademark. We would surely have the opportunity to make such an announcement at one or more of the many press conferences that would be held in the US in connection with the visit. But what would Björn say? For a number of reasons, he'd not been in the best of moods recently.

When I told him about the trip, he smiled a bit slyly and said: 'So, Carlsson needs help over there.'

I tried to explain the benefits he himself would gain from the visit and that the government felt that he should agree, not least of all in order to fulfil his contract with the Tourist Council.

'Oh, I only got that contract because the Social Democrats needed help in the elections.'

Björn wasn't really serious. He just felt the need to be stubborn.

'Think what it will mean if we're able to announce the formation of the Björn Borg Design Group in a setting like this,' I continued my sales pitch. 'The whole world will hear about it.'

'Don't be silly, Lasse, you can't fool me. You're the one who wants to go on the trip. This doesn't have anything to do with business.'

Later I had to put up with a lot of joking about my being so anxious to meet President Reagan, but it was worth it.

A couple of days later Björn came out to Stavsborg to visit. We sat on the veranda and talked about the trip. When we were done I phoned the Prime Minister, who answered after a few rings. After exchanging the usual pleasantries, I handed the phone to Björn, who greeted Carlsson politely and then said: 'I'll be glad to go along on your trip to the States! It'll be fun!'

I heard that the Prime Minister sounded relieved and that he expressed his thanks.

And then Björn added something entirely unexpected: 'But I want Jannike to go along on the trip, and Lasse will surely want to bring his girl along, too.'

The Prime Minister didn't reject the idea, but just replied that Hans Dahlgren, his foreign affairs adviser, would be contacting us about the practical details.

Dahlgren sounded troubled when he phoned me a few days later.

'I'm not very happy about the idea of your fiancées going along on the trip,' he said. 'It would be hard to do. We're not the ones who dictate the conditions for such a visit. We can have only fourteen people in the delegation, and the only wives will be those of the Prime Minister and of our ambassador in Washington, Wilhelm Wachtmeister. And you know that the government can hardly pay the airline tickets. Well, just as long as you understand . . .'

I told him that I understood. I had thought there might well be a problem with the idea and hadn't said anything about the trip to Mia.

'I'll speak with Björn,' I told Dahlgren. 'I'm sure he'll understand.'

But Björn *didn't* understand! When I told him what Dahlgren had said he just dismissed it.

'Oh, that's no problem. Jannike is going along and she'll be going to the White House dinner with me, too. They'll just have to make it happen or else I won't go.'

There was a lot of discussion about this matter, but it finally turned out the way the government wanted, for Björn and Jannike ended their relationship before the trip.

At the beginning of September I joined the Swedish delegation to the United States as it began its tour in Boston. Although Björn was very upset following the end of his relationship with Jannike, he didn't show it for a minute. He played his role perfectly: polite, pleasant and carefree, an exemplary ambassador for tourism. At press conferences he was careful not to compete with the Prime Minister, but seized every opportunity to mention the Björn Borg Design Group, which we had been working on throughout the spring and summer.

Three days later we flew to Washington, and the official welcoming ceremony in the White House. Aside from Raoul Wallenberg, the Swedish diplomat who had saved thousands of people from the Nazis during the Second World War, and Dag Hammarskjöld, the Secretary-General of the United Nations whose plane had been shot down over Africa in 1961, Björn was the only Swede President Reagan mentioned in his speech.

That evening Björn was one of the guests at the state dinner at the White House. I arrived with other members of the delegation who had been invited to the dance afterwards. I was thrilled to be asked by an official if I would like to meet the President; of course I would! When I was introduced to him, I explained that I was travelling with Björn Borg and asked whether he was going to watch Björn's tennis match with Vice-President Bush the following day.

President Reagan shook his head and said, 'No, unfortunately I can't. I have a meeting at that time.' As an afterthought he added, 'With the Pope.'

I found Björn as quickly as I could. Apparently, he had been a big hit at dinner. He was master at attracting people's attention, and he did it in a quiet, almost discreet way. It was usually very difficult to get him to participate in public events if he didn't think he'd be the centre of attention, and on the rare occasions when he felt he had been ignored he would become quite irritable. However, this night had been a success and now he wanted to leave.

The next morning we got up very early, for Björn's big event – a doubles match – was scheduled for seven o'clock. Björn and George Bush were to play Ambassador Wachtmeister, and Björn's old friend Vitas Gerulaitis on Bush's private court.

The match had been George Bush's idea, and TV camera crews and masses of journalists were on hand to report it. The mood was jovial, thanks largely to the playful Vitas. 'Björn, you're not to argue with our Vice-President,' he called out when Björn and Bush couldn't decide which of them was to return a ball that had landed between them.

At 6–5 and tie-break in the first set, and with Bush serving, Björn wished him luck with the words 'God bless you!' They won the point. On another occasion, the Vice-President missed an easy ball close to the net and told Björn, 'If I were John McEnroe, you'd have heard a very nasty word just then!'

Vitas and Wachtmeister won the second set, with the set ball having been played just as Ingvar Carlsson arrived.

'Make sure you win if you want to come along on the next official visit,' the Prime Minister called over to Björn when he saw how things stood. Björn took his words to heart, for he and Bush won the decisive set 6–2.

They had, Björn told me later, played serious tennis out there on the court. Bush and Wachtmeister often played against each other, and with the media present neither of them wanted to lose. Bush had played with great concentration, particularly during the last set. When we returned to Sweden, Bush sent Björn a photo from the match and a brief note, which read, 'Thanks for helping me win.'

The official visit continued with innumerable official lunches and dinners, press conferences, TV interviews, meetings with important dignitaries and visits to cultural and academic institutions, ending after a one-day trip to Chicago.

On Sunday afternoon Björn and I said goodbye to the Swedes who were flying home and flew to Los Angeles to participate in a marketing seminar on the Björn Borg Design Group. We had asked Marc Sussman, the head of a successful American marketing research firm that specialised in introducing Scandinavian firms to the United States, to arrange the seminar, and he had invited a number of potential business partners and licensees, including Jack Rothschild, the Swedish businessman who sold Björn's line of perfumes. I wanted us to prepare ourselves for the seminar on the plane, but Björn had worked a whole week, with excellent results, and now he had other plans. He looked at me with that teasing look in his eyes that I had come to know so well by that time.

'You'll have to take care of all that. You take care of the business, 'cause I've already done my part.' He continued with a happy grin, 'Now we're going to have fun! I'm going to show you Los Angeles and all the discothèques, just as I promised. I'm going to introduce you to my contacts and to some really special girls – top models! Lasse, we've done a great job, both of us. Now we deserve a few lines.'

I shook my head slightly. Of course I was looking forward to experiencing Los Angeles' night-life, and some sun, swimming and partying might be just the thing to cheer Björn up after the summer's turbulent events. After a few days I would be going back home to Sweden, while Björn stayed behind to play a charity match with Vitas. I had never been in Los Angeles, but with Björn showing the way I knew it would be a lively time . . . and that's what worried me now.

Vitas was waiting for us at the hotel in Beverly Hills. He and Björn exchanged a few remarks about the tennis match in Washington, then moved on to plan the evening's events together. I felt left out as they dropped me off at my room.

After I unpacked I went to Björn's suite. I had been there only a moment when Vitas came in, tennis bag in one hand. He went over to the coffee table, opened his canvas bag and took out a plastic sack. I knew it was cocaine and that the party was about to begin.

I was uneasy when I saw how much cocaine there was. Björn didn't have any self-restraint and usually kept snorting as long as there was any coke left. Jannike said that he was called 'the vacuum cleaner' by people who knew him in the States.

'Lovely,' he said. 'Is it good stuff?'

'Of course,' answered Vitas, handing him the bag. 'It's the best you can find.'

Björn poured out a small pile on the table and eagerly began hacking the cocaine with a credit card. Then he used the card to convert the pile into a few lines. I was uneasy about the amount, but I said nothing.

Björn leaned over the table and quickly snorted two lines, inhaling strongly. He snorted a third, got up with his eyes closed and gave me the rolled-up tube he had used.

'You're right,' he said to Vitas as he began walking around the room. 'These are really good lines.'

'You can't forget her, eh?' I asked.

He shrugged his shoulders. 'It's just something to get used to.'

I went next, then Vitas.

We sat there talking about women and about life in general. The cocaine had given me a false sense of clarity and analytical ability. I thought I could see right into Björn and his life.

When I looked at the clock I saw to my surprise that three hours had passed. My concept of time had been warped, minutes flying by as if they were seconds. In the meantime one of Vitas's friends had come in and snorted a few lines. I began to feel very restless.

'Why don't we go out? We can't spend the whole evening here,' I said.

'I can't go out like this,' said Björn. 'If you're thinking about broads, I've already taken care of it. They'll be coming soon. Trust me, I think of everything.'

As if on cue, a call from the front desk announced that we had company. A few minutes later three girls came up to the suite, but I had no interest in sex. I wanted to go out and see some of the night-life Björn had talked about so much. Vitas's friend also wanted to leave, so he and I bid the others goodbye and hailed a taxi outside the hotel. We went to a popular discothèque and although

I was having a good time, I couldn't really relax. I was worried about the amount of cocaine in Björn's suite. After a few hours I went back to the hotel.

Björn and Vitas were still entertaining the girls and seemed to be all right. I went to my room and tried to sleep, but it was impossible. The cocaine in my system wouldn't let me relax. My head felt entirely empty, my nose burned and my throat was completely dry. It was almost four in the morning. I walked around the room for at least half an hour before I was calm enough to sit down. I was still wide awake. I watched television for a while, then went to bed again. I lay there twisting and turning, and finally got up and gulped down a beer. The second one helped me to relax and at last I dozed off.

The telephone rang, waking me with a start. I looked at the clock and saw that it was just after five. I couldn't have slept more than a few minutes. I picked up the phone. It was Björn. His voice was thick and I was sure he was about to cry.

'I'm tired of living. There's just nothing to live for.'

I ran down the hall and knocked on his door. I could hear him moving about inside, unfastening the safety chains.

'Who is it?' he asked.

'It's Lasse.'

Björn opened the door. He was alone and looked absolutely terrible. After letting me in, he walked around the room and began talking about his unsuccessful life. He said that he had called and talked with Jannike.

'How the devil could you call her when you're in this state?' I asked.

'I want everything to be fine again,' he said in a tired and unhappy voice.

'But, Björn, you have lots of things to live for,' I said. 'You've got a wonderful son to devote yourself to and there are other girls, as many as you want.'

We continued talking and finally he drifted off to sleep. I stayed there for a long time looking at him. Fame and wealth he certainly had, but they couldn't protect him, or anyone else, against the feelings of anxiety and loss that accompany a shipwrecked relationship. He must have worked very hard to keep his misery to himself during the official visit, but he had years of experience in hiding his feelings in public. I didn't know if I could help him, but I was very conscious that I was going to have to keep my knowledge of Björn's problems to myself.

The September sun felt wonderful as I dozed at the side of the pool. We had slept until we woke up by ourselves, but I still felt exhausted. The presentation of BBDG was to take place the next day, and I had to get myself back in shape. I closed my eyes and tried to ignore the small talk around the pool. I thought about how guilty Vitas had looked a few minutes ago when I had bawled him out in his room. I had almost never been as angry as I was then, and told him that he had almost killed my best friend.

Björn was sitting a short distance from me, hiding behind a large pair of sunglasses. Jack Rothschild, who had checked into the hotel that day, was sitting in a deck-chair close to him and talking nonstop. The topic was how he and Björn could earn more money from their

collaboration, based on Björn's old promise that Rothschild could launch a Borg perfume for women, too. I
considered Rothschild more of a problem than an asset,
and I wanted Björn to get himself out of that obligation
at any price. There was no doubt that Rothschild's
company, Romella, was well run and profitable, and his
ideas well conceived. His Björn Borg perfume had become
a market leader in Scandinavia in a single season. However,
I was opposed to what I saw as his short-term sales success
based on using Björn for publicity rather than building
long-term respect for the product itself. His strategy was
just the opposite of the one we had developed for BBDG
and I had told Björn that he should try to get Rothschild
to adjust his tactics to our long-term goals or try to get
out of the licensing agreement with Romella. Björn understood exactly what I meant. 'Don't worry about Jack,' he
had said. 'I'll take care of him and make sure nothing
goes wrong.'

My thoughts were interrupted by Björn calling me over
to where he and Rothschild were sitting. He still had his
sunglasses on and looked a bit pale under his suntan. The
night's activities had clearly left their mark. When I sat
down, Rothschild excused himself and left.

'I've been thinking this over,' Björn said. 'I think we
should go ahead and make the deal with Jack. We
promised him and I think things will go well.'

I groaned inwardly, for it wasn't difficult to see that
our consultants would criticise us harshly for making such
a decision.

'It's the wrong thing to do,' I said.

'I've made up my mind,' replied Björn.

In that case, of course, there was no use protesting further. When Jack Rothschild came back, I had no choice but to shake his hand and wish him luck. He smiled like the California sun and I sighed silently to myself. Sometimes business decisions were completely irrational. In his present condition Björn could hardly think about the issues, much less discuss them in a sensible way. I dived into the pool to cool off.

We made our presentation to Marc Sussman the next day. It was a real success. Björn made an excellent impression when he gave his talk and most of the potential licensees for our trademark wanted to do business with us.

CHAPTER TWELVE

Business Matters

BBDG's business concept was ready for Björn's and my signatures on 7 December 1987. At a gathering at Stavsborg that day, we and eleven others signed a 28-page document bearing the title 'Björn Borg Design Group – Comprehensive Strategy'. The other signatories of the document were Jannike, Rune Borg, Bo Alexandersson, Christer Björklund, Björn Gullström, Bengt Hanser, Staffan Holm, Lars Modin, Stig Sjöblom, Rolf Skjölde-brand and Olle Söderberg, all of whom had been involved in the creation of Björn Borg Design Group (BBDG).

I have to say at once that the Björn Borg Design Group was the best thing I have ever been engaged in developing. Thus I have every reason in the world to explain the difference between my view of BBDG and its develop-ment, and the picture that was painted by the media in 1989 and by Björn and his lawyers. This chapter deals with BBDG's business concept and how we developed it.

To my way of thinking, the successful development of a business requires a sufficient amount of working capital, visionary leadership, tough-mindedness and creative people. It is not essential that one be able to summarise the business concept in a few catchy phrases, but one must be able to formulate it in a simple and comprehensible way so that it can be understood and shared by all the interested parties. The company's leadership must not only understand the meaning of the business concept, but must also be able to agree on and carry out a series of measures to realise the business concept in what is, in my opinion, the only measurable way: namely, the bottom line or profit.

The name Björn Borg naturally had commercial value during his tennis career. Various manufacturers would pay Björn's company a one-time fee and royalties often amounting to 5 or 10 per cent of the sales or profits, for the privilege of using his name. The most common way to make money on Björn Borg's name, however, was to have Björn endorse a product and the trademark under which it was sold. A company would simply use Björn Borg the man in its advertising for the product and pay for his services. During his tennis career Björn signed many such endorsement contracts with a number of firms, including the 'big three': Donnay, Diadora and Fila. In order for such a contract to function, it was necessary for consumers to see the connection between Björn Borg and the product as a credible one. Credibility might be quite natural, as in the three cases mentioned above in which Björn endorsed certain types of tennis equipment, or it could be created by clever advertising executives, as in the cases of the Stiga lawnmower which was linked to Björn by the slogan 'a master on grass'. Companies purchased Björn's ability to attract people's attention. The effectiveness of the advertising depended upon simple messages, such as success, honesty, gentlemanly behaviour, a healthy and sound lifestyle, and so on. Björn's endorsement contracts were always based on the idea of minimising his personal commitments and maximising the payments he received.

When contracts included the right to make television commercials, it was even more expensive to purchase Björn's services.

Endorsement contracts, then, are one way for a celebrity to earn money. They are based on the idea that the individual in question will attract attention only for a limited period of time. In Björn's case this was the most natural way of doing business at the beginning of his career, for who could have predicted that his time at the top would last all of eight years? During this time his matches were broadcast all over the world. No one who watched television could avoid knowing who Björn was. Thanks to that and to his special charisma, he became one of the world's best known names and faces.

I was surprised that so few people attempted to take advantage of the enormous possibilities that his *image* presented. Björn was swiftly transformed from being simply a tennis star to being an image. Remember Björn during a finals match at Wimbledon: he hits the winning ball, falls to his knees and lifts his hands to the heavens in his well-known victory pose. After he has left the court, the image of the victor remains: the unbeatable Borg kneeling humbly. All of this came to be a burden for Björn. He forced himself to live according to rules that were made for Borg the superman, and he always had to think of his image. It was impossible for him to live a normal life, to smoke or have a few drinks at a pub. No matter what he did, he had to think of what people would say. Nor did he have the spiritual strength to stop playing the superman or show his vulnerability as a normal person with feelings, and strengths and weaknesses.

One company understood the value of using Björn Borg's image early on. In 1981, at the peak of Björn's career, a licensing contract was concluded between the Japanese store chain Seibu and IMG Tokyo. Seibu's designer created a collection of fashions and a marketing concept under the name BORG. This contract with Seibu was the only one in which IMG sold the Björn Borg image. I am not entirely sure that the IMG people really understood its business potential. When I later introduced them to the BBDG business concept, they said they had not taken better advantage of these possibilities because Björn always preferred short-term contracts with high cash payments and had rejected the licensing contracts they had proposed to him.

When I marketed Björn in Scandinavia, I discovered that IMG only passed along offers that involved limited-time contracts with fixed remuneration. The companies making proposals, for their part, were interested in developing new products to be marketed under the Björn Borg *trademark*. They wanted long-term licensing contracts that would give them the chance to earn back the money they were investing in product development and marketing, and thought it better for all parties involved if they instead shared the profits generously when their efforts began to be successful. IMG's and Björn's lack of interest meant that nothing came of the many excellent offers they received.

The three main contracts I negotiated on Björn's behalf prior to the founding of BBDG turned out to be compromises for this very reason. These included the Eiser contract for the Björn Borg Menswear Collection, the

Kullenberg contract for the Björn Borg Sports Club, and the Romella contract for Björn Borg fragrancy lines. It was difficult to find a solution that would reconcile the companies' desire for long-term contracts and Björn's financial demands. For example, the discussions with Eiser created such uncertainty that they took upon themselves the extra expense of developing a logo, 'The Diamond'. If the contract with Björn were not renewed, then at least they would have 'The Diamond'.

I noticed early on that Björn believed that everyone wanted something from him and that they really only wanted to *exploit* him. It was an attitude that he never changed as long as I knew him. As far as I could see, his attitude was partly a result of the way IMG indoctrinated its clients, who learned early on not to discuss their business dealings or form close contacts with anyone else without IMG's participation. In this way, IMG retained control over its clients' affairs. Moreover, IMG's clients thereby learned to view other companies, not as business partners, but rather as outfits that were trying to exploit them. IMG thus functioned *in loco parentis* for its many young clients, assuming responsibility for their business training. This attitude occasioned many long discussions with Björn. I could understand it during his active career, but definitely not thereafter.

There were, of course, other reasons, too, for Björn's attitude. His abuse of drugs and fear of being exposed as an addict became deeply-rooted; his sudden wealth was another reason. Moreover, his isolation and loneliness during his professional tennis career had made it difficult for him to open himself up to others and to develop mutual trust. All of this was seriously to hamper his development as a businessman in the long-run, while the other side of his personality – his charm and magnetism, and the fact that he seemed to prefer listening to talking was a tremendous resource. I thought it would be possible in the long-run to train him as a businessman, not least because he seemed to be so interested.

I realised that I was correct in seeing business possibilities for the Björn Borg image when I read a study, made during his heyday, that showed that he was the world's most well-known individual after the Pope and Mohammad Ali. The image Björn had succeeded in creating during his tennis career titillated many people, and an air of mystery surrounded him. With his sportsmanship on the courts, his charm and quiet manners, moreover, he had for the most part succeeded in hiding the fact that he was really rather superficial, shy, even a bit boring, and that he had no deep or well-developed interests. Nor did he disappear from people's consciousness after he quit tennis. Most people retained a very sharp picture of Björn years after his great matches, just as if they wanted to preserve those moments and that time. Björn was a symbol of invincibility or perhaps, in a more philosophical vein, of everyone's hope for immortality.

The question was whether I had the same confidence in my partner and friend Björn as I had in the Björn Borg image. As with love, friendship sometimes makes us see things less clearly than we should. On the one hand, Björn Borg exposed his image to tremendous risks by living the way he did. On the other hand, I viewed him as someone who was more gifted than most people. I thought that he

Björn Borg. An early Design Group advertisment.

Above: Masquerade time on Itaparica. Björn and I as Julius
Caesar and Robin Hood.

Opposite: The party goes on. Björn tucks in while Jannike and a
friend show off their Brazilian tans.

Top: Björn and I relaxing with our hoofed friend.

Above: My girlfriend Maria Bohlin and I spent a lot of time with Björn and Jannike.

Top: Happier times when Björn and Jannike travelled everywhere together.

Above: Björn with Jannike, Maria Bohlin on the right and Christer Gustafsson in a neck-lock.

Top: Björn, his mother and a friend enjoy a drink or two!

Above: The key people in the Björn Borg Design Group until its closure in July 1989. Left to right - Stig Sjoblom, myself, Björn Borg and Staffan Holm.

Top: Björn with Ingrid Carlsson, the wife of Swedish Prime Minister, Ingvar Carlsson.

Above : Fun and games during our trip to America in 1987.

would finally put his life in order in the light of our new plans. Then, too, I was naturally influenced by Björn Gullström, who had taken it upon himself to steer Björn in the right direction following his career in tennis. Gullström considered me an appropriate partner for Björn, not least because I was economically independent, which meant that he did not have to worry about me trying to enrich myself at Björn's expense.

When I thought about all these things I understood that the business concept had to be based on an entirely new commercial use of the Björn Borg name that would lead to preserving and strengthening the image. It could not be based on Björn continuing to participate personally in the way he had done thus far. On the contrary, his personal participation should be reduced.

Somehow the rumours about Björn's use of drugs and his jet set lifestyle never really penetrated the mass media in Sweden in the way they did elsewhere in Europe and in the US. One reason, of course, was the fact that Björn no longer lived in Sweden and had no strong ties with his native land during his tennis career. Then, too, most people had a great deal of respect for him. As a consequence, it was his own version of reality that got out, which was naturally a good thing for us in our public relations efforts around Björn as the founder of BBDG.

The Björn Borg trademark as it 'looked' in the spring of 1987 enjoyed quite a good position, despite the previous use of his name and his dissolute lifestyle and difficult private life. In March of that year, Björn offered me an opportunity to buy 40 per cent of the shares in Björn Borg Enterprises Ltd, his Jersey-registered company, and thus in the Björn Borg trademark. Regardless of why Björn stopped playing professional tennis, it was very important that he did so while he was still at the peak of his career. In that way the Björn Borg image retained its association with success.

There was no unifying theme or trait to characterise the various products Björn had endorsed over the years, and this was a hindrance in the development of the trademark. It took a lot of work to make the business concept clear and sharp. But I had some things to go by.

The interesting thing was the Björn Borg image, not Björn Borg the man. In the short-term, however, it was obvious that even Björn Borg the man continued to have commercial potential which could still be exploited as a source of income for Björn Borg Enterprises and for the marketing of the Björn Borg trademark. To put it simply, he could endorse his own trademark. Björn's own role was therefore extremely important and very sensitive, but neither of us knew in the beginning just what his new role should be. I *did* know that it was essential to remove the taint of the negative aspects of Björn's private life and, in order to be credible, it was necessary for him to behave according to his image as much as possible – at least in the beginning. In short, he had to be on his best behaviour. Once the trademark was well-established, he would be able to achieve his goal of being a successful businessman with few demands and little stress. He wanted to have unlimited freedom and to avoid having to work hard.

For my part, I wanted to build up BBDG into something really worthwhile, and to earn money from it.

There were other principles, too: the effort was to be

a long-term one; it would require perseverance and patience; the trademark was to be launched globally; and we had to create a concept which had no links to the old business connections. Finally, I also understood that the way we organised ourselves would be important for the business concept.

To get help with the concept I contacted Bo Alexandersson, a man with a long past in advertising and marketing who had impressive contacts in the advertising world. It came very naturally to me to sit down with Bosse and discuss my idea. His sharp eyes followed me from under his heavy eyelids as I wandered all over the place and tried to explain the situation.

'Bosse,' I said, 'we have to develop this concept quickly so that Björn and I can decide how to proceed.'

He leaned back in the sofa. 'What's the big hurry? This can turn out to be something really big, and in that case there's no reason to throw together a plan too fast.'

I hesitated a minute under Alexandersson's quizzical gaze. What could I say? How open could I be about my fears and doubts without running the risk of frightening people away from the project?

'No, we shouldn't be careless with the design,' I said. 'It has to be the best we've done. But remember that time is ticking by. We have to launch the whole thing before the market loses interest in Björn. And, who knows, he may lose interest himself.'

Bosse nodded silently and thought for a long time about what I had said.

'I'm going to need help,' he finally said. 'I have to collect all the relevant information. Then you will probably want to have a good-looking package so that it will be possible to sell the trademark.'

'Naturally, and you'll be responsible,' I replied, pleased that he seemed to believe in the idea. 'Hire whoever you need, but keep the budget in mind. Why not organise a competition?'

'Of course, with a signed racket as first prize,' smiled Bosse as he stood up. 'You know what it costs to hire good people, but I'll see to it that you get an estimate of the costs.'

During the following weeks I met frequently with Alexandersson to find out how his work was proceeding. Björn and I met almost every day, and I reported to him as soon as I had anything to report. It was a very happy time for Björn Gullström.

'Have you noticed?' he chuckled. 'The kid gets in his car and drives to work almost every day! Do you think you can get him to study something in preparation for working with the trademark? Should we hire some sort of tutor?'

Bosse Alexandersson worked intensively with the development of the trademark, bringing in Bengt Hanser, Lars Modin and Rolf Skjöldebrand, all of whom clearly belonged to the Swedish advertising élite. They produced a series of drafts, and Bosse kept me informed of their progress.

At a meeting in the conference room of the Deltagram advertising agency, which Modin owned, I was presented with a sheet of paper on which was a green rectangle containing the words: Björn Borg Design Group.

I looked up at Modin. A graphics designer, he was unobtrusive and pedantic in nature, a bit awkward and surly, a recluse, and a pronounced aesthete. Before I discovered that Lars had great talent in his special area, I thought he was rather strange and found it difficult to have confidence in him. Next, I looked at Alexandersson with some irritation. 'Here I give you the chance to work with what is perhaps the best-known name in the world and ask you to develop a good-looking logo that cleverly describes the fact that Björn Borg is now an image and not a tired ex-tennis star, and you give me a bright green rectangle on a sheet of white paper!'

Bosse raised his eyebrows. 'But you yourself just said that you need something that states that Björn is an image!'

I looked helplessly at Bengt Hanser who was sitting across the table from me. Bengt was considered the dean of Swedish advertising and had been the founder of the Swedish Advertising Association. He smiled.

'You see, Lasse, it's very hard to make a trademark out of Björn Borg. He's such an unbelievably well-known person.'

Bengt's quiet provincial dialect and his air of authority made people sit up and listen to him. I could see that he was right. The group had not had an easy assignment. Nonetheless, I was still uneasy about the symbol.

'But why make Björn a green rectangle?' I asked again.

'To show in the trademark itself that BBDG is something other than Björn Borg the tennis player – namely, a business organisation,' answered Bengt. 'First of all we have to create confidence in Björn's business idea among prospective licensees. None of us has doubted for a moment Björn Borg's ability to attract consumers. Most people know his name and know about his tennis career, even if it's been five years since he quit. For that very reason the consumers, his new audience, will have high expectations when Björn goes out and accepts public responsibility for his own name in a business context. Since you're not happy with what Eiser and Romella have done, then it's right to create your own trademark. But remember one thing – the new trademark will be influenced to a very large degree by how Björn Borg lives and functions today. Borg can't live a life that gets him into the boulevard press more frequently than into the business press.'

'But he doesn't want to, either,' I protested. 'Björn is known for good things like careful preparation, good health, politeness, respect for others, willingness to fight, and persistency. No one is jealous of him; everyone thinks it just that he got to be the best. Now he wants to lead a normal life, just like everyone else. Family, friends, work. Don't forget that he is a celebrity and that he's followed everywhere by the press. He sells papers . . .'

I could hear how what I was saying sounded like a speech in Björn's defence, and sensed the others staring at me.

'We're not saying that Björn's lifestyle jeopardises business,' said Bosse. 'But when you start up, Björn will find himself in the limelight again. You're going to have to spin the information so that the papers write what you want them to and so that you avoid a lot of gossip.'

Bengt Hanser nodded. 'What Bo is saying is very important,' he said. 'When you talk about the new business, people have to be clear about the fact that Björn has all his good qualities in his baggage, as well as all the good contacts he has made over the years and all his experiences. He has to be seen as a man who is still curious about life, but who has a special interest in sports and a healthy lifestyle.'

'Exactly!' I had unconsciously used Björn's favourite expression; now I felt the creativity in the air. 'I'll suggest to Björn that we set up a programme for his public appearances and other assignments that we can send out to the press on a regular basis. In that way we can detract attention from his private life so that he can have some more privacy.'

Hanser nodded approvingly. 'That's an important part of the public relations work for the trademark, of course, but don't forget that this is the real message,' he said, tapping his pen on the green rectangle.

'Now you've got to explain the rest, Bosse,' I said.

Alexandersson rose. 'This is the Björn Borg trademark,' he said, 'and it's rectangular to distinguish it from the private individual. This rectangle still represents all of the positive images people have of Björn Borg the individual. Thus, the trademark will contain his name. Now, you and Björn Borg want to do a number of things. For example, you want him to become a businessman despite the fact he never graduated from elementary school.'

'That's not true,' I protested. 'Of course Björn graduated from elementary school. He had average grades of 4.4. He always says so himself.'

Alexandersson shrugged his shoulders to indicate that that was hardly something to boast of if you wanted to make a career in international business. 'And then you want to sell a whole lot of products with Björn's name on them despite the fact that you don't know much about how they're made. How can Borg put his name on things with any credibility if he doesn't know anything about them? He's going to guarantee that the customer is buying a product of quality, and how can a tennis player do that unless the product is a racket or a tennis ball?'

I sat quietly and listened.

'You can't *start* a trademark,' Bosse continued. 'Therefore we think that it's better to start a design group because a group of designers and product developers can create products that Björn can stand behind.'

'But we're not going to produce everything ourselves,' I objected. 'Above all we're going to sell licences for the trademark to companies that are competent to produce quality products.'

'Yes, but someone has to choose the right companies for you, and those companies must for their part cooperate with an ex-tennis star. By working with the right companies and distancing the trademark from Björn Borg the individual, we think you'll be able to find the right consumers. The ones who spend a lot of money on fashions and new things.'

It was clear that I was going to have to work full-time and that we would need a functioning organisation to blow new life into the name Björn Borg. Still, I had to give Björn credit where credit was due. When he played tennis, he had viewed his business activities as a nice source of extra income. I had now succeeded in getting him to believe that there was a business value in his name without his having to play tennis, and I myself had seen how enthusiastic Björn was when it came to BBDG at this point. Now I had to convince my partner that we needed to be very consistent when we did business under our new trademark.

I got up from the sofa and began pacing back and forth. I told Alexandersson and the others in the room: 'Björn has never had anyone who thought only about him and his affairs. He has always been just one client among many, even if he was perhaps the most important one. It's not so easy for him to judge his own commercial shelf-life or how to prolong it, but it won't be a problem to get him to see how important his own lifestyle is in this context.'

I felt my comments were drifting in the direction of a new defence of Björn, and it didn't sound very convincing. But I suddenly felt I had reached a new sort of clarity.

'The business concept is identical with the following message: Björn Borg has founded the company in order to take responsibility for the future business-like use of his name. In this way he will guarantee that both he himself and the licensees will make more money and continue to do so for a longer period of time. This should make the licensees feel more secure about doing long-term business with a firm that owns the Björn Borg trademark and that has employees or consultants who are experts in matters of design, production, marketing and sales. An organisation that is, in short, an adviser to the licensees.'

My speech was interrupted by the entrance of Rolf Skjöldebrand. Rolf and I had known each other for several years and had come to the increasingly hot media business from different directions. His magazine *Ake Skidor* (Skiing) had been a serious competitor of my 'SkiAlp' project. Now Rolf had returned to working exclusively in advertising. He was a partner in the Skjöldebrand & Sjögren advertising agency, which would later be bought by the multinational corporation Saatchi & Saatchi.

Skjöldebrand's strength as an advertising man clearly lay in his stragegic thinking. He was unsurpassed in his ability to see the connection between a company and its activities, on the one hand, and how the consumer viewed its trademark and the trademark's positioning, on the other. Sköldebrand presented his strategy, which clarified the points we had been discussing, and ended with a six-point programme.

'This is what I think we have to develop,' he said.

1. A credible marketing concept.
2. An organisation suited to the goals.
3. A programme for Björn Borg's personal appearances.
4. A decision on the name, symbol and identity of Björn Borg Design Group.
5. A decision about a product programme for the trademark.
6. A decision about how to get the current licensees to use the new business concept.

I reported the consulting group's proposal to Björn, and we discussed it thoroughly on several occasions. Björn liked the business concept and the name BBDG, but we were both a bit hesitant about the logo. Even though Björn thought it was a clever idea and well suited to its purpose, he always wavered and was indecisive when we talked about it.

'Are they really serious about me being a green

rectangle for the rest of my life?' he would say and snigger a little.

After our return from the US we worked hard on polishing the business concept. Björn had seemed to be totally dedicated to working and being productive when he came home from Los Angeles, and I think that he was a bit ashamed about having been so depressed that one night in the hotel there. Things had once again been patched up between Björn and Jannike, and they seemed to be living a normal life.

Björn put a lot of time into the company that autumn, and I was very hopeful. The escapades of the summer and Los Angeles were over, and I hoped they were behind us for good. Björn attended all the meetings and especially involved himself in the question of how his name should be used in the future and how the trademark would look. When the vote was taken, he favoured Lars Modin's rectangle, which we decided to keep and to test in the marketplace.

The strategy that we all signed on 7 December 1987 was built above all on the quality approach. We described it in the following way: 'Björn Borg Design Group aims first and foremost to develop and sharpen – with the greatest professionalism, judgement, and taste – the name Björn Borg to be an image in a number of business areas on the world market where it has decisive commercial prospects.'

The idea was to grant licences for the use of the Björn Borg trademark to various markets all over the world under the name Björn Borg Design Group. This did not preclude the possibility that BBDG might itself produce certain types of goods. We would also be able to design products for companies. The logo in the form of the rectangle with the name Björn Borg Design Group was to be on every product manufactured and sold. We aimed to use good materials, thoughtful design, style and taste. Our message to future business partners was hardly a modest one. We wrote in our strategy that BBDG should 'choose licensees, rather than itself being chosen at general presentations'.

The target group for BBDG products was also defined in our strategy. Björn Borg as an image was primarily directed at active, fashion-conscious young men between twenty and thirty-plus and at people who felt they belonged to that group. They would be offered quality products, including everything from men's clothing to accessories, shoes and cologne. BBDG would also design products exclusively for certain companies. We divided the products into three categories. The first included products produced by BBDG and marketed under the Björn Borg trademark, such as clothes, cosmetics, sports clubs, tennis equipment and travel products. The second category was made up of products designed by BBDG, but not marketed under the Björn Borg trademark, including watches, eyeglasses, fashion accessories, hi-fi products, videos, furniture and communications equipment such as mobile telephones. The third category consisted of endorsement contracts, and included such things as the Tourist Council, mineral water, cars, events and the bedding for tennis courts.

Clothes would serve as the foundation of our activities. Initially we had hoped to develop a cooperative arrangement with Eiser International, which had the world rights for marketing Björn Borg Menswear everywhere except in Japan, where the licence was held by Seibu. But Eiser still hadn't succeeded by 1987, and was unable to bring about the changes we demanded. We finally negotiated with Eiser's owners and used Stronghold Invest AB as a vehicle to buy Eiser International on 23 December 1987. Following that purchase, we rechristened Stronghold as Björn Borg Invest AB.

Björn and I had agreed to finance the development of BBDG by selling some of the real estate owned by Björn Borg Investment AB and using the rest as collateral to borrow money. I was to assume ultimate responsibility for developing the company, while Björn would, in his own words, 'personally oversee the entire enterprise as chairman of the board, and play an active role as ambassador and scout for my companies'.

We agreed that an international fashion organisation should have its headquarters in central Europe. Björn decided that the location should be Monte Carlo, which had the advantage of low corporate tax rates, and he applied for permission to establish two companies there – Björn Borg Design Group SAM and Björn Borg Management Services SAM to assist our licensees. Staffan Holm became managing director of the former company; Stig Sjöblom of the latter.

Björn and I and our secretary Mary Ahl constituted the staff in Stockholm, and we decided to hire consultants for any other services we needed. Having a small number of employees and low overhead costs were goals of ours at BBDG. With these things in place, the play could finally begin. Was the world interested in BBDG and in the Björn Borg trademark/image?

CHAPTER THIRTEEN

Audit by the Poolside

It was time to market the BBDG concept, and Björn and I prepared an international sales trip. He chose the countries we were to visit and participated in approving the materials we would take with us. He was very painstaking and it was clear that he was pleased at being able to make a contribution based on his experience. He decided we would begin in the Far East. The area's consumption of fashion products was rising steadily, there were excellent opportunities for high-quality production at competitive prices and Björn was very popular in that part of the world.

IMG helped us organise the trip. During our trip to the United States the preceding September we had negotiated a new contract between IMG and Björn Borg Enterprises Ltd, according to which IMG would receive a commission on any licensing agreements BBDG concluded with clients referred by IMG. IMG was to be an active partner not only in marketing the BBDG concept but also in helping with its administration. BBDG and IMG sent out invitations to clients in every city Björn and I were to visit.

At the end of January 1988 we flew to Singapore. In each hotel where we stayed we booked a conference room, unpacked our BBDG display and made presentations almost nonstop from morning until early evening. We signed up interested companies one after another, sometimes several at once. In two weeks we had covered Singapore, Jakarta and Hong Kong.

After a four-day diversion to Abu Dhabi to attend the Scandanavian Festival, where Bjorn appeared on behalf of the Swedish Tourist Council and I began negotiations for a licensing contract for the whole Middle East, we went to Tokyo. By that time we had learned the routine but were beginning to feel the effects of so much travelling. Changing time zones, the heat, constant packing and unpacking, and all the meetings were sapping our strength. I sometimes felt as if I had a tape recorder in my mouth that was always ready to play our presentation for strangers. From Tokyo we went to Sydney, and returned to Sweden at the end of February.

We were off again on 16 March, this time heading for Toronto and New York, then back to Japan and Singapore. At the same time Staffan Holm, the newly appointed managing director of BBDG in Monte Carlo, was conducting a series of presentations throughout Europe.

It quickly became clear to all of us that the BBDG concept was a success, but that it would be very difficult to coordinate the licensing to produce an image of uniform quality and price throughout the world. Therefore we agreed that our long-term strategy must concentrate on design and production of our own products and that licensing would have to take a back seat. In the meantime we had to maintain the momentum and proceed with the official launch of BBDG, which was held at the Monte Carlo Country Club during the tennis tournament, the same tournament that had served as Björn's swan song five years earlier.

While the sun shone in Monte Carlo, storm clouds were gathering over relations with IMG. Our cooperation during the sales trip had been successful, but Björn, who had been generally displeased with the company for several years, thought that its reporting, administration and management of the finances of Björn Borg Enterprises Ltd was unsatisfactory. He informed IMG that he wanted to end the relationship and recruit a new head of finances.

I was not entirely in agreement. Surely, I thought, it would be better to work out our differences and maintain a good relationship with IMG, particularly in view of its worldwide network. It was simply the best in the business, and we could use its knowledge and connections. But Björn was adamant. He felt that the company had earned enough from its relationship with him, and now that it was no longer performing in the manner he demanded it was time to cut his ties. He didn't need IMG any more. We would have to reorganise the company ourselves.

As joint owners of Björn Borg Enterprises Ltd, Björn and I were naturally interested in maintaining close control over the business, which now began to expand in terms of investments and employees. Björn was used to short contracts; long-term planning with high investment of capital was new to him and his exaggerated caution with money, encouraged by Margaretha and Rune, made him unsure of himself. I knew that Björn and his parents were suspicious that the employees were enriching themselves at Björn's expense. The extent of Björn's concern on this matter was revealed one day when he phoned me at the office in Monte Carlo from his parents' house in Cap Ferrat.

225

'I want to go through all the invoices,' he said. 'You'll have to bring them out here right away so that we can do it.'

We were in the midst of some difficult planning, and I had no desire to sacrifice a day's work to sit and watch Björn review the invoices, but he would not listen to any arguments and refused to come to the office. Cursing to myself, I filled the back seat of my car with the relevant files, put the pedal to the floorboards in the little Alfa, and left Monte Carlo behind me.

The house that Björn had bought for Rune and Margaretha in 1975 is a lovely two-storey villa in lush grounds surrounded by a stone fence. On the other side of the wall, just about thirty feet away, is the Cap Ferrat Zoo, enclosed by a high fence. I used to joke with Björn about which side of the fence we really belonged on. Björn would laugh, and Rune would usually join in.

As I was getting out of the car and beginning to take the files out, Björn approached with that special, annoying smile on his face.

'Come,' he said, 'we'll sit by the pool. It's just as well that we get started right away.'

It was an awkward situation. Björn knew that I knew that the meeting was just a display of power, a tweak of the nose. It revealed how insecure he was and perhaps also how easily he could be influenced by other people who were close to him, especially by his parents. We each sat in a chair in front of the pool. I nursed a cold drink and tried to relax in the hot sun. I watched out of the corner of one eye as Björn eagerly leafed through the invoices. Sometimes his gaze fixed on something and he would stop to consider it before leafing further through the papers. Throughout the visit I felt Rune's presence in the background. Dressed in shorts, he seemed to be working in a flower-bed, but I noticed how he watched us intently. Rune had become a self-absorbed and serious man who always seemed to be brooding and was increasingly isolated from his surroundings.

Rune had managed Björn's tennis shop in Monte Carlo and thought he knew the city and its business climate. He was always prepared to share his knowledge with us and considered us rather ignorant, but the fact was that after nearly fifteen years of living in Monte Carlo, he still knew hardly a word of French and had difficulty with such simple tasks as going to the bank. Rune Borg had not had any real job in life for years other than his self-assumed one of continually watching over his son's life.

While he and Margaretha worried that other people might exploit Björn, they had, of course, lived entirely off their son since he was a teenager. They had absolutely no friends and acquaintances except for Margaretha's parents and, of course, Björn. For the most part they were alone and isolated at Cap Ferrat or, in the summer, at Alstaholm. The classic relationship that can develop in a family consisting of a weak father, a dominant mother and an only son had become increasingly evident. The ties between Margaretha and Björn were strengthened, while Rune became more and more 'invisible'.

A bit more than three files and an hour and a half later, I awoke from my drowsiness.

'What's this?'

Björn stared at me with the look that millions of TV-viewers had come to recognise from the great tennis championships, a look that revealed no feelings. I peered at the invoice he held in his hand. It was for the purchase of an Alfa Romeo 33, which had been bought for 40,000 francs.

'Björn,' I said, 'that's the company car, the one in the driveway. Don't tell me you think it's too expensive!'

The irritating smile returned.

'You know I've got damned good connections when it comes to cars. I could have got it for 30,000. Don't do that again without asking me first. I've got fantastic contacts when it comes to cars.'

I sighed to myself, knowing that it was pointless to discuss the matter. I had been appointed to run the company, and the only thing I wanted to do was return to town and pick up where I had left off a few hours ago. I looked over to where Rune stood fiddling with his flowers, and he quickly averted his eyes. I forced myself to wear what I hoped would be a happy smile.

'Of course, Björn, you're the boss. Perhaps I'd better drive back to the office and get to work now.'

'Exactly,' he said, delivering the word, as always, like a whiplash. On the way back to Monte Carlo in the car I decided that what had just happened would never happen again.

A short time later in Stockholm Björn and I discussed how we were to settle the matter of BBDG's organisation once he severed his relationship with IMG. I proposed we engage a firm of well-known and vigilant auditors, such as Price Waterhouse. With a certain note of triumph in his

228

voice, he said: 'I have two top men who will help us. They know finance and administration inside and out, and they have great contacts.'

'Who are they?'

'John and Julian.'

John Webber and Julian Jakobi were the finely-tuned pair of financial advisers at IMG's London office who administered Björn's fortune. John Webber was around 50 years old, intelligent and dignified. He had been with IMG for many years and was head of the financial division. One of his responsibilities had been the management of Björn's growing fortune during his tennis career and Björn had come to trust him. I liked him too in the beginning and appreciated his straightforward and apparently genuine manner.

Julian Jakobi was Webber's closest assistant. He was 35 and considered by many to be arrogant and ambitious. He had been sent to IMG's Monte Carlo office, where much of his work involved helping the Borg family in every way. He made himself more or less indispensable to Rune and Margaretha, who, in turn, told Björn how invaluable Julian was.

It was obvious to me that IMG wanted to get in on Björn's business again, and planned to do so through Jakobi and Webber. But Björn refused to accept that. He believed the two Englishmen were more loyal to him than they were to IMG.

'But they work for IMG, and you said you don't want to have anything to do with them,' I replied. 'Are you sure that they don't want to have control over you again now that they see you can be something great with BBDG?'

'No, no,' said Björn. 'There's no danger of that. It's not official, but they have their own company. It's called Godfrey Allen and they're going to leave IMG to work full-time on it. This has *nothing* to do with IMG, trust me.'

In some ways I thought it was a good idea that John and Julian engaged themselves more and more in Björn's interests. That would calm him down and make him feel secure, and if they added as much to the company as Björn thought they would, that would be fine with me. But that they should also serve as the company's auditors – how would that work?

Not long afterwards a fax landed on my desk. It was an internal IMG letter written by Mark McCormack that revealed that Godfrey Allen was in fact fully owned by IMG and that its profits went back to IMG. I took the letter and drove immediately out to Viking's Hill to show it to Björn.

'What's going on, Björn? You said that Godfrey Allen didn't have anything to do with IMG!'

He read the fax carefully and seemed genuinely surprised by the contents. He said that he would speak with them. I didn't want to embarrass him any more, so I dropped it at that for the moment.

A few days later John Webber phoned me and said that he had talked with Björn. They had agreed that Price Waterhouse was to be our auditing firm, and he added that he thought it was a good choice. On the other hand, Björn wanted him and Julian to become members of the board of directors of the parent company, Björn Borg Enterprises Ltd. I had no choice but to accept this plan, but I was unsure of them and how their involvement would influence the work with BBDG.

CHAPTER FOURTEEN

Family Problems

Although Jannike and Björn had been reconciled after his return from the United States, the relationship soon began to deteriorate again. It was clear that Jannike was frequently very unhappy. On one occasion, when Vitas Gerulaitis had been visiting Stockholm, he and Björn had spent most of their time at 'The Cave'. Returning to Viking's Hill, they found Jannike unconscious on the floor, apparently having taken a large number of sleeping pills. They took her to the hospital to have her stomach pumped, and Björn had succeeded in keeping the incident secret.

Björn dealt with the episode in an ice-cold manner, reminiscent of his performance on the tennis court. I found his coolness almost frightening. He wasn't at all shocked or upset by Jannike's apparent suicide attempt. It didn't seem to matter to him at all that his girlfriend – the mother of his son – had attempted to take her life. All he appeared to care about was that nobody found out.

This wasn't just a cry for help on Jannike's behalf. It was serious. She had taken enough sleeping tablets to end it all for good. Her life with Björn had grown so unhappy that she couldn't see any other way out of it. To my knowledge, Björn made no attempt at finding counselling or help for her after the incident.

Cocaine had made Björn's personality extremely

erratic and he was prone to unfounded jealousy and wild imaginings. Björn was such a disloyal person himself – always cheating and picking up girls – that he judged everybody by his own standards. At that time, he was convinced that Vitas was having a fling with Jannike. And, even though Björn no longer cared for her, he was damned if any other man was going to have his woman.

I joined them at Viking's Hill after Jannike was released from hospital. I remember she was standing in the kitchen in complete shock. Only then was it dawning on her how close she had been to death. She was shaking and couldn't talk properly. It was clearly the end to all her dreams.

The end came in June, and when it was really over, Björn did what he usually did in these circumstances – he broke with her completely. 'She's got to leave!' he spluttered. 'I don't want to see her again.' And he didn't.

I had seen it happen before, like the time he broke with Christer Gustafsson. The two of them had been friends for well over ten years, but during the autumn of 1987 Björn pulled down an iron curtain on a very confused and upset Christer. Christer suddenly became invisible for Björn and he didn't understand why. Björn never explained to Christer or to me why he ended their long friendship so abruptly, but he forbade me to have anything more to do with Gustafsson.

My theory is that Björn's long abuse of drugs was responsible for his becoming increasingly suspicious and imagining that people in his immediate circle were betraying him in any number of ways. He even thought that Christer had had a relationship with Jannike. Moreover, it had become more and more difficult, if not impossible, to discuss Björn's problems with him, although he would sometimes come to my flat in the evening to visit. Whenever the topic of drugs came up, however, he would simply dismiss it. No matter how I weighed my words, drugs were banned from our conversations. The difference between us was that I banned them from my life.

Mia would often go to bed early, and sometimes, when I said that I was also tired, Björn would ask if he could stay in our living room for a while. He wanted to be alone. The next morning we would find thirty or forty cigarette butts in the ashtray. He had sat there the whole night. It wasn't hard to conclude that he weaved fantasies in his brain during those lonely hours, fantasies that he began confusing with truths.

Björn's career-long tennis coach, Lennart Bergelin, had also ceased to exist for Björn one day without either a farewell or an explanation. Although Bergelin never said anything about it, he suffered terribly from Björn's sudden silence and iciness. In the years following that break Lennart Bergelin had two heart attacks without Björn ever so much as expressing his concern. Lennart's son, Niklas, told me that his father couldn't understand what had happened and that the whole family wondered how Björn could act in such a way after everything the two of them had been through together. Several years after Björn had dumped Bergelin, Lennart's wife, Munda, phoned Margaretha Borg and asked her directly why Björn had acted like he had.

Margaretha's answer was: 'It's not so strange. Lennart

never supported Björn when things were at their worst for him.'

'But, Margaretha,' exclaimed Munda, 'we've never known that Björn was having problems! Why hasn't anybody said anything?'

The explanation was very simple. Lennart wasn't needed any more. Björn uses people as long as he has a need for them and after that they cease to exist for him. Without a word, brutally but very effectively. It was impossible to talk with Björn about these matters; he would simply refuse to say anything. He saw it as being his business and no one else's.

During the summer of 1988 Björn met the Italian singer Loredana Berté through mutual friends in Milan and spent some time with her on the Mediterranean island of Ibiza. When Björn came back to Stockholm, he told me that he had never had so much fun in his life. He and Loredana became engaged almost immediately, and spent much of the rest of the summer together in the Stockholm archipelago. When Loredana was home in Milan, Björn frequently chartered a private plane at company expense to visit her.

Loredana had seemed a bizarre choice of girlfriend for Björn: not particularly pretty, and older than him with something of a reputation. I said to him, 'Björn, why is it you cannot date some normal Scandinavian girl?', and he said to me, 'Lasse, they would never understand me.'

And I suppose he was right. Loredana had certainly been around, she wasn't shocked by drugs and she knew the ways of the world.

Björn had met Loredana in Italy almost ten years earlier, when she was living with another tennis star. He had found their lifestyle enviable, and wanted to recreate it for himself. Loredana knew lots of interesting people and was always great fun to be with.

Says Björn's former close friend and associate Ingmar Alverdal, 'The Swedish people didn't warm to Loredana Berté, with her extreme ways and affectations, but in private she provided him with the mother figure which he craved. She cooked for him and nurtured him like a mother would. He felt safe with her.'

From the beginning, Björn was anxious for Loredana to enjoy being in Sweden. He arranged Swedish lessons for her and encouraged her in every possible way to continue her career in Stockholm. There was a great deal of interest in her as Björn's new fiancée, and she was invited to appear on a television show. Loredana was very, very nervous and apparently made herself totally impossible during the taping of the programme. The host of the programme later said that Loredana was the worst diva with whom he had ever dealt.

Björn didn't give up. He was determined to help his fiancée win the hearts of the Swedish people, sometimes in unusual ways. One autumn day Ingmar Alverdal asked if he could borrow my car, which was large and roomy, to run some errands for Björn. When I saw the car again two days later it was fully loaded with hundreds of records, every one a copy of Loredana's latest single. I asked what was going on and Ingmar blushed. He told me that Björn had told him to go to as many record shops as possible in the Stockholm area and buy all the copies he could find.

Armed with a thick wad of Swedish banknotes, Alverdal had driven around for two days in order to buy Loredana's way to the top of the Swedish pop chart and thus make her feel better about her fiancé's native land. Unfortunately, this brave attempt did not succeed.

One of the reasons Björn was so anxious for Loredana to feel at home in Sweden was the approaching custody battle over Robin. Everything suggested that the decision would be made in the courts, and it was to Björn's advantage to show that he had a wife, a home and a stable existence, particularly in light of what Jannike might have to say about his suitability as a carer for his son.

Björn hardly had a stable life with Loredana. He told me that he had stopped using drugs, but I also found out that he had given instructions that I was not to be informed about anything to do with his private affairs.

Björn wanted Loredana to play a major role in the custody fight for Robin and even persuaded her to meet with Jannike. Loredana rose to her new task admirably, chatting to Jannike on the phone and arranging cosy shopping trips and lunches, but the pair never saw eye to eye.

On one occasion they had supper together and the evening ended in catastrophe, with both of them swearing never to speak to one another again. They were two highly volatile women fighting over one man – incapable of having a friendship without it ending in bitching. Nevertheless, Robin had become of great importance in Björn's life. When he was sober, Björn was the model father, caring, attentive and lots of fun to be around. If Robin cried in the middle of the night, then Björn was at his side, cuddling him and reading stories. As a baby he nursed him, changed nappies and did all the things any loving parent would do.

But when he was on a bender, that was an entirely different matter. Then Björn didn't think twice about dumping Robin with his parents while he went out and had a good time, failing even to tell them when he would return.

One late autumn evening, I was working in my flat when the phone rang. It was Ingmar Alverdal.

'Do you know where Björn is?' he asked.

'No,' I said. 'I have no idea. Why?'

'Loredana is hysterical. Björn was to pick up Robin at the day-care centre, but he never showed up. Rune and Margaretha had to fetch Robin instead. Björn has disappeared and Margaretha wants to report the case to the police.'

'You know damn well what he's doing! He'll come home at dawn. Don't set something in motion that we'll all come to regret.'

I hung up and sighed deeply. An hour or so later the phone rang again. It was Margaretha Borg and she was very upset.

'Where is he?' she shouted. 'We've called the police and they're looking for him everywhere. They'll just have to find him, no matter what. This can't go on any longer. We've got to save him. I don't care what the papers write or what happens to the business . . . Björn can afford to abandon it!' Then she added with a bite to her voice, 'But of course you can't!'

'Oh yes, Margaretha,' I said as calmly as I could. 'I can afford to abandon it, too. It's clear that Björn has to have help, but he told me he had quit. Calm down. I'll try to get hold of him.'

I slammed down the phone and made a face. Then I picked it up again and dialled the number for 'The Cave'. After a while a tired voice answered. I said who I was and asked if Björn was there.

'No.'

'OK,' I said. 'You have about ten seconds to tell me whether Björn is there and if everything is normal. Otherwise the police are going to pay a visit. Björn's mother has reported him missing.'

'Well . . . OK, he's here,' came the answer after half an eternity.

'Then everything is as usual?'

'Yes.'

I hung up and immediately dialled the number for Viking's Hill. Margaretha answered.

'It's OK,' I said. 'I know where he is. He'll come home in a few hours, so call off the police.'

She mumbled something and I hung up quickly to avoid a long and heated conversation.

Through Ingmar I learned that Björn returned home around five in the morning, completely exhausted. Loredana had been beside herself and had destroyed a large part of the furnishings.

The next day Björn called to tell me off.

'What the hell are you doing? You're not to talk with

my mother about things like this. Talk with Rune instead! I'm closing down. There's a 50 per cent chance that I'll close down the company now.'

'I think you should thank me instead,' I said tiredly. 'She and Ingmar called the police – they were only half an hour away from your hideout. I fixed things so that the police were called off. It would have been great if they had waded in.'

He looked for a way to get the upper hand.

'I think you should keep your employees in check,' he finally said. 'Alverdal shouldn't call the police.'

A day or so later I met Stig Sjöblom, who was uneasy and almost indignant.

'What the hell is going on?' he asked. 'I knew that Björn used a little cocaine at parties sometimes, but this seems much worse. It sounds like real abuse.'

'What do you mean? What have you heard?'

'According to Ingmar, eighteen trash bags full of furniture, porcelain and other things Loredana had broken were carried away from Viking's Hill the other day. Björn had apparently been lying low in some sort of hangout. What's going on?'

'It's a family problem,' I said evasively.

'Sure, but listen. Ingmar had notified the police, and some sort of raid was organised. You know what the police said when he called?'

'No . . .'

'They hardly reacted at all. They just said, "He's probably just hiding out with one of his whores some-place". And you know what else? This morning Ingmar called and told me there's been a big meeting with the family and Loredana. Our doctor was there, too, from what I understand. He promised to help. Björn apparently opened up and talked about his problems, and Loredana said that she hadn't known it was so serious. Tell me now, Lasse, what the hell is going on?'

I didn't answer right away. There was no need to burden Stig with everything I knew, so I formulated what I said very carefully.

'First of all, I don't think it's so very serious. And I think they have to be given a chance to solve their problems within the family. Look at it this way: it's a good thing that they're dealing with it.'

That's what I said, but privately I cursed my fate. Stig, I and many others were involved in a very promising business and there was only one uncertain factor: Björn Borg.

Stig tapped his watch. 'The clock is ticking, Lasse. We've not much time left, and we have to make it all the way before it's too late.'

There were many dangers in this situation: that we would be in *too* much of a hurry, would build up our organisation too fast and incur too many costs before we started generating revenues. Although Webber and Jakobi kept close track of all our expenditures and pounced on anything they thought too expensive, they created other problems by feeding Björn's existing suspicions and anxieties about costs.

My private life had also changed. After two years together, Mia and I broke up that summer. I decided to do something I had never done before – to live alone. I was in no hurry to throw myself into a new relationship.

CHAPTER FIFTEEN

High Appraisal

We had all worked hard building BBDG throughout 1988. Our preliminary budgetary work that spring showed that we would need to increase our share capital by $8 million and our bank credits by $4 million. Björn and I had agreed to contribute the necessary capital, and Björn Gullström had helped us negotiate the loan with Gotabanken. Impressed with our development up to that point, the bank had provided the $4 million on three conditions: that we were prepared to increase the share capital to $8 million, as we had foreseen; that we appointed a professional with experience in international industrial activity to chair the board of directors; and that Björn and I signed sureties for $2.4 million and $1.6 million respectively. This surely would be removed when we paid in our money.

While we looked for a suitable chairperson we continued to develop our organisation. We hired top people in their professions to staff the headquarters in Monte Carlo and the office in Stockholm, and later did the same in the United States and Singapore. We bought Eiser, and with it a useful network of agents and licensees in Finland, Greece, Italy, Norway, Switzerland and Spain, thereby laying the foundation for our main clothing business. We began negotiations with another of our licensees to create a shoe company, and started to develop two new business areas: BBDG Retail Operations and BBDG Accessories and Travel Articles. In every case we hired the best people in their field to run the new businesses. In November Björn and I had gone to Japan to renew a licensing agreement with Seibu, and had agreed terms to coordinate the development of Björn's new collection of tennis fashions. At the same time we had forged deals with new companies for a line of spectacles and the development of sports clubs bearing Björn's name. All three contracts were due to be signed in February.

In December Gotabanken introduced us to Håkan Frisinger, who had recently retired as the managing director of Volvo. He was precisely the sort of person we needed: a professional industrialist, calm and confident, with considerable knowledge, contacts and experience. I presented him with all the information about BBDG and waited eagerly to hear whether he would agree to chair our board. About a week later Frisinger phoned to accept our offer. Björn and I were elated.

On 2 February 1989 I went to the very impressive London offices of Price Waterhouse to hear the results of its first appraisal of BBDG. The opportunity of investing in the firm was one of the carrots Björn and I had used to recruit certain key figures, and the results of the appraisal would guide us on setting the price of the shares we would offer them. We did not need to be reminded that we had promised the bank to increase the share capital to $8 million. Above all, Price Waterhouse would now tell us whether we had done our work well and had a sound business.

Björn Gullström and Stig Sjöblom were already there, having spent the morning with two of Price Waterhouse's experts discussing various aspects of our tax position. After a working lunch in the conference room David Foley, head of the corporate finance division that had carried out the audit, presented the judgement.

Reading from a copy of the printed document he had handed us, Foley confirmed that on 31 December 1988 100 per cent of the shares in Björn Borg Design Group had a value of $40 million. Price Waterhouse had concluded that BBDG had

> developed very positively through the seed and start phases, and ... is now entering its growth period ... the company's strength lies in its professional and capable leadership, a well thought-out and executed strategy, a strong name that is known in the market-place, a unique Scandinavian image, a clear market potential in the United States, strong and developed business ties in Japan, and further potential for sports clubs and sales in Asia and Australia.

We had succeeded! I stared hard at the table and savoured the moment. I had no doubt that Björn and Stig were sharing my thoughts: imagination, hard work and clever and dedicated colleagues had helped us to lay a solid foundation. Our dreams were coming true ... so far.

There were a number of sensitive areas. Foley pointed in particular to the fact that our products had been market-tested to only a limited extent and that our designs needed to be made more international. We could certainly do something about that. And then:

> Especially in this initial development stage there is continued dependence on Björn Borg as an individual ... A key ingredient in the business concept that has been developed for the Björn Borg Design Group is the integration of personal qualities and characteristics associated with Björn Borg's name, image and accomplishments. Fundamental to this is the fact that, especially at an early stage, there is a close connection between how things go for the company and for Björn Borg the individual.

I ignored the wave of unease that washed over me.

In addition to the bank loan, which provided the ongoing business financing, we had to find venture capital for special investments. It seemed sensible to me to use traditional, solid and recognised partners, and I had made a preliminary presentation to a major finance house in London. Björn had other ideas. 'You don't have to worry about that,' he said. 'Financing is no problem. John and Julian will take care of it; they have all the contacts in the world.'

And so it was that following our meeting with Price Waterhouse we were going to see Keith Harris. Harris headed the European operation of Drexel Burnham Lambert (DBL), an American brokerage firm in which Julian Jakobi had placed part of Björn's assets and which he now recommended. DBL had made itself famous through its so-called junk bonds, a very controversial but popular method of raising venture capital at the time, and Harris questioned us about our needs, our budgets, our share plans and a multitude of other details. He was fascinated by our idea and didn't take long to reach his conclusion.

'Gentlemen, I congratulate you,' he said. 'You're bankable.' This meant that any commercial bank would be prepared to give us terms for our future financing. 'I don't believe you need DBL's services at this point. That which is valuable in Björn Borg Design Group is the shares, and I recommend that you keep them internal. Broaden your bank contacts to get the best conditions. I would be glad to introduce you to some international bankers here in London.'

We were impressed by Harris when we left his office. He was a professional. We understood from what he had said that we would not suffer from a lack of financing, something that is always a risk for new firms. Our London visit, in other words, had turned out to be a great success.

Our last meeting was with Mervyn Parry, a lawyer who was to examine an option agreement for our employees. He seemed to me an excruciatingly pedantic person who thrived on details and apparently loved showing us how thorough he was. What I thought should have taken half an hour took an eternity, or, more precisely, an hour and forty-five minutes, but when Parry eventually got to the point, I woke up. He proposed that our employees should not be allowed to buy shares in BBDG until the company began producing profits. I thought that was an excellent idea, for in that way they would be even more motivated to do their absolute best so that the company would succeed.

*   *   *

That evening Björn Gullström came to my room at around seven o'clock. We had not had a chance to exchange many words as we raced from one meeting to another, and had both been fully occupied with our own thoughts. 'Gullis' had become something of a spiritual father for Björn and me. Not only did he try to guide us personally, always concerned that things be done justly and that neither of us be treated badly by the other, but he also provided the company with expert advice on legal and tax matters. Both Björn and I had total confidence in him and always listened to what he had to say.

Today Gullis had heard the Björn Borg Design Group given a high appraisal by one of the world's most respected auditing firms. He sat on the very edge of the bed and tears began to stream down his cheeks, moving evidence of the relief he felt after all the tension of recent months.

'I know that you understand what this means to me,' he said, wiping away the tears with his hand. 'Now maybe we can finally straighten the boy out. He actually became a respected businessman today.'

Everyone in the company knew how much Gullström had worried over what would happen to Björn after his tennis career. Now he could breath easier, at least for the moment. We hugged each other, and Gullis went to his room. The next day he would return to Sweden and tell Björn about our meetings in London, while Stig and I would fly to Singapore to see Paul Naruse before going to Japan to sign three important new contracts. I sat staring out of the window for a long time that night, thinking about the future.

CHAPTER SIXTEEN

Loss of Face and Empty Hands

Stig and I took the lift down to the lobby of Shin Takanawa Prince Hotel at 8.15 on the morning of 8 February. Our eyes were bloodshot, we were tired after the night's work and the seriousness of the situation weighed heavily on our shoulders. We both hoped desperately that the news of Björn's suicide attempt in Milan had not been played up in the media. I stopped short when I saw the advertisement next to the newspaper stand. The picture of Björn seemed to dominate the whole wall, and above it were large and boldly printed Japanese characters. It was the first and only time I have ever understood Japanese, for the headline screamed out the news that Björn Borg had tried to take his own life. Stig and I looked at each other and groaned. We bought a few Japanese papers and went out into the street to catch a taxi.

Björn Borg was a great idol in Japan. A study made a few years earlier had shown that over 80 per cent of the adult Japanese population knew who he was despite the fact that his active career had ended. The drama of the last twenty-four hours was thus hot stuff and the papers made the most of it. We sat in silence in the back seat of the taxi and looked at the headlines and the pictures. There was one picture in particular that was used in several of the papers. It showed Björn leaving the hospital wrapped in a blanket. He looked tired, his smile more like a twisted grimace.

I wondered what he was thinking at the moment the picture was taken, exposed as he was to the eyes of the world and left to the public's damnation or pity for the first time in his life. For once he was in no position to control the situation and it must have been bewildering and painful for him. He must have been very angry at having put himself in this situation without being able to blame anyone else. I fought those thoughts and concentrated on my immediate problems. Was there any way we could turn the situation around, lessen the shock, and take the edge off the scandal? Finding the answers to those questions would take a very creative and functioning brain. I looked at Stig; he seemed quite clear and alert given the circumstances. How did I feel? Surprisingly alert, I decided. Adrenaline was coursing through my body. There was so very much at stake, perhaps the whole business concept we had been working on for almost two years. Our survival instinct was guiding us both as we sat in that taxi in Tokyo's tortuous morning traffic.

Our first meeting was with Seibu Menswear, with whom Björn had a long-standing licensing agreement that required him to visit Japan regularly to make public relations appearances. Björn, of course, was tired to death of such visits. Therefore, although our primary purpose in visiting Seibu in November had been to induce Seibu to extend the existing clothing contract for another five years, which would give us an average of about $800,000 a year, our secondary aim had been to sell them on our overall strategy, in which the image of the product was more important than the image of the person.

Allied to this was our desire to create a uniform international design for BBDG's fashion collection. Often, clothes designed for one cultural or domestic market are difficult or impossible to sell in another. Björn and I had worked hard at trying to get Seibu to accept our design for its domestic market. The Japanese executives had listened with interest, and had agreed to travel to Europe to assess our clothing line on the spot to see what parts of it they could use in their domestic market. In the new five-year contract there was a clause saying that Seibu could abandon its own designs and use ours at any time during the contract period, although at additional cost. It was this contract that Stig and I were on our way to sign.

At Seibu's impressive office complex we were directed to a visitors' corner to wait for our hosts. Japanese business people have a well-earned reputation for punctuality, so it was not a good sign that we were still waiting twenty minutes after our meeting was scheduled to begin. At last a delegation, led by the head of Seibu Menswear and including his chief negotiator, the manager of the sports division, two of his closest colleagues, the chief designer for the special collection of Borg clothes, and an interpreter, approached us. Later we would hear that when the head of Seibu Menswear had gone to the managing director's office shortly before we were to meet to get the signed contract, he found the managing director waiting with a worried look on his face and a morning paper in his hand. The head of menswear, who had not read the papers that morning, was thoroughly shaken when he saw the headline about Björn. He was thus very subdued when he joined the others a few minutes later to discuss the situation. Now everyone was extremely polite and we were shown into a conference room.

The chief negotiator picked up the newspaper and, speaking in staccato sentences, went right to the heart of the matter. The interpreter was clearly upset as she explained what he had said.

'He says that the top leadership of the company is very disturbed over everything they have read in the papers about Mr Borg's suicide attempt. The Japanese are super- stitious, and many are religious. Suicide attempts are very much frowned upon in our country. He says that Seibu has the right to an explanation of what has happened and to know what measures Mr Borg intends to take.'

It was crystal clear to me that Seibu's managing director had already made his decision and that it made absolutely no difference what we had to say. There was no way we were going to be returning home with the signed contract, but it was important for us to create an opening for the future. I decided to hold the flag high and began a mild counterattack.

'But surely, my friends, we are not talking about a funeral, are we? I have spoken with Mr Borg and he feels fine now,' I lied. 'He is so famous and so much is written about him that these things easily happen. But the only thing that has happened is that he has suffered an ordinary case of food poisoning. He is now resting at his parents' home.'

The Japanese conferred with each other for a few minutes. Then the chief negotiator, speaking through the interpreter, said: 'We wish to see Mr Borg here. We wish to confirm with our own eyes that he is healthy and in the best of shape.'

'Of course,' I answered. 'I will talk with him as soon as possible and inform you when we will be able to return. We understand, of course, that this publicity is not at all good either for you or for us. But Björn will be playing a number of exhibition matches here in Asia against John McEnroe in April. At that time he will also be granting a number of television interviews. We can also arrange public relations activities at your department stores. He has been training for several months and is in top condition.

'And one more thing. What has just happened is, in fact, linked to what we have discussed previously, namely, that we must promote the trademark rather than Björn Borg the man. This shows us how an insignificant event can have disastrous consequences. Björn's name is so well-known that we always run the risk of misunderstandings in the media. That is one of the reasons we have developed the BBDG concept.'

The Japanese group sat silently and contemplated what I had said. Then the chief negotiator said: 'Seibu's position remains that signing the contract should be postponed for a while. The company wishes to wait and see the effects of what has happened and of the measures you intend to take.'

We left the Seibu building after the forty-five-minute meeting. We were not as unhappy as we might have been. Despite the fact that the contract had not been signed, it seemed the situation was not entirely hopeless and that, with a healthy Björn to put on display, we might still succeed.

It was clearer than ever before that the weeks ahead of us would be extremely important ones. It was absolutely necessary to repair our reputation and restore Björn's good name. But what did Björn himself want? I had begun to wonder whether he was really prepared to de-emphasise himself in favour of the product. Was he afraid of ending up in the background? Was he concerned about being cast aside? I tried to convince myself that the answer to both these questions was no. After all, Björn was the majority shareholder and had said repeatedly that he wanted to avoid being in the public eye, that he longed for peace and quiet, and a normal family life. But, of course, there was plenty of evidence to suggest that he couldn't manage such a life and didn't want it.

Stig and I took a taxi back to the hotel and went up by my room. We took off our jackets, ordered coffee and sandwiches, and prepared for our next meeting, which was to be with a representative of Toyomenka, Japan's third largest trading company, and a local businessman who had introduced us to the firm. Toyomenka invested in various promising projects and had become interested in Björn Borg Sports Clubs.

The trademarked clubs constituted a relatively new business concept within BBDG. They would offer golf, tennis, squash and healthcare facilities as well as hotel rooms, shops and restaurants, all of which would be available only to people who had taken out expensive memberships. In Canada I had already negotiated with a company that wanted to build a Björn Borg Sports Club at Whistler Mountain near Vancouver. We were to receive a one-time payment of $1 million, 10 per cent of the stock, an exclusive sports cabin and $100,000 a year for Björn's personal appearances at the club. Now Toyomenka wanted to invest in one or possibly two clubs on the outskirts of Tokyo, and was willing to pay $200,000 a year for five years merely for the right to continue working on the business concept. If they did in fact subsequently decide to build such clubs and use the Björn Borg trademark, we would receive a one-time fee of several million dollars, a percentage of the membership fees and other revenues. In the long-run, this part of our business had the potential of generating very large revenues.

We had been in my room for about fifteen minutes when the reception desk relayed a message from our Japanese business contact: he was abroad and would be unable to attend the meeting since 'he had not made his scheduled flight back to Tokyo'.

'Talk about lame excuses,' sniffed Stig. 'He doesn't dare look Toyomenka's representative in the eye. He must be afraid of losing his damned face.'

About half an hour later Toyomenka's representative arrived. He was a very polite man, who really believed in the sports clubs idea and had put a lot of time into developing it further and selling it to his bosses. We saw immediately that he was crestfallen. He hesitated before looking us in the eye.

'I have spoken with my managing director, who is in the United States,' he said solemnly. 'He signed this contract last week, but now he says that I am not to give it to you under any circumstances. He says he is shocked over Mr Borg's suicide attempt and that it is now unsuitable to open a sports club bearing his name.'

He looked at us as if to say that he had done all he possibly could on our behalf, but it had come to nothing. No one dared to invest millions in a sports club emphasising health and fitness that was based on a name connected with suicide and drugs. That was the simple truth we now faced.

I suddenly felt physically ill. Sweat glued my shirt to my body. It was an absurd situation. Think what would have happened had we come just one day earlier! The contract would have been ours! We would certainly have been forced to do some damage control, but the contract, which could have been worth enormous amounts of money, would have been ours . . .

I sang the same song now that I had sung at Seibu a couple of hours earlier, but this time without any result.

'I'm sorry, really sorry,' said our friend from Toyo-menka, backing out of my hotel room.

We sat there and considered our fate. We knew we had to try to overcome the depression that was threatening to overwhelm us or BBDG would have two new candidates for suicide on the payroll. On the way to lunch we picked up a fax from the reception desk. It was from Keith Harris at DBL in London, wishing us luck. It seemed years ago that we had sat in Harris's office and he had congratulated us and told us that BBDG was bankable. In fact, the meeting had taken place just five days earlier. We appreciated Keith's gesture.

During lunch Stig and I planned our next moves.

'OK,' I said, 'it's best that you return to Singapore and help Paul with the Reunion Tour as much as you can. Stay

254

as long as you must and save whatever can be saved. The tour is vitally important now.'

Stig nodded. I would return to Monte Carlo that night.

The third and last business meeting was with Hoya, one of the world's largest manufacturers of eyeglasses and frames. We had negotiated a five-year contract for frames carrying the BBDG logo that would give us at least $100,000 a year, but now we had a replay of our meetings with Seibu and Toyomenka. Unfortunately, it was not possible for the company to sign any contract at the moment. They wanted to wait and see what happened with Mr Borg, and they wanted to meet him in person before they could think of going any further. Like Seibu, Hoya had left the door a bit ajar, so there was a small hope for the future.

The end result of these meetings was that only Björn could save the situation, only he could put all the speculation to rest. We were back to square one, where everything depended on Björn Borg the man, not on the image of the products. It seemed that the work and money we had invested in developing ideas, designs and marketing strategies had been wasted. Equally depressing was the fact that I had no idea what my partner was thinking or how he viewed the future. Björn was still refusing to speak to anyone.

A few hours later, on the plane to Paris, I opened an American magazine and read a long article about Jannike, based on a television interview in which she had completely belittled Björn. He was a broken man without a future, she said, and she felt sorry for him.

Jannike must have been pleased to get the upper hand over Björn. Her strategy was simple: everyone would see what a bad father Björn was and that he certainly should not have custody of Robin. What would her next move be? Would she reveal to the papers everything she had experienced with Björn? About his abuse of drugs? I closed my eyes and thought of the television series *Dallas*. I fell asleep wondering which role each of us was playing.

At about ten o'clock the next morning, the taxi pulled up in front of our office in Monte Carlo. I took out my bags, paid the driver and went into the building. I was anxious to meet the others to hear what they had to say, to know what they were thinking and feeling.

The office was like a funeral parlour. Where there had always been the constant buzz of discussions, exclamations, comments and laughter associated with creative activity, I found silence and depression. The welcome I received was muted and in many cases amounted to nothing more than a nod of recognition. I felt as if people blamed me for what had happened. Well, why not? I was the one who had initiated the enterprise and convinced a collection of creative people to leave their excellent jobs and their pleasant and promising lives in Sweden. All for a business concept based on an ex-tennis player who had now let us down terribly. Thus, I too had let people down. I could feel the looks aimed at me as I dragged my bags through the office towards my little corner.

Had everything gone as we had planned, we would soon have been discussing the convertibles, the appraisal of the company and the price of buying shares. There would have been optimism and great motivation. Now we all wondered if there was any future.

I picked up the phone and dialled. As usual it rang several times and as usual it was Margaretha who answered.

'Hi, Margaretha, it's Lasse. How's Björn? Can I speak with him? I've just arrived in Monte Carlo.'

'He's feeling better now, but he's not up to talking to anyone yet.'

'But Margaretha, it's necessary! I *must* speak to him!'

'I'm sorry, but he can't.'

I sank down in my chair. The fighting spirit that Stig and I had developed during that night in Tokyo just evaporated. Common sense screamed at me: 'Get yourself out of this, for God's sake! It isn't going to work! You have a partner who has abandoned everything and who doesn't give a damn about the company. He won't even talk to you.' But still, I had to talk to him before deciding to do anything drastic. In spite of everything, there might just be a natural explanation for his behaviour. There was only one thing to do for the moment, and that was to get the employees together to discuss what had happened.

'Have you talked to him?'

Rolf Skjöldebrand opened the quickly summoned meeting with the question on everyone's mind. I could feel at least eight pairs of eyes looking at me searchingly.

'No,' I said. 'I just phoned Cap Ferrat, but Margaretha said that he still doesn't want to talk to anyone.'

There was a furious outcry. They had spent the whole time right in the middle of the hornets' nest, plagued

257

by the media, inquiring creditors, customers, banks, subsidiaries and other interested parties, without being able either to confirm any news or pass along any reassurances. Now their frustration and anger overflowed.

'Damn!' exclaimed Staffan Holm. 'Let's drive over to his place. It's just half an hour away. This is crazy! He hasn't even called. We have to find out what's going on!'

'Bring him here instead so that he can explain himself here at the office,' said someone else. 'The journalists are hanging around in droves out here. What are we supposed to tell them? He has to make himself available to the press. He's got to go out and explain himself.'

Rolf had apparently been thinking along other lines. 'There's nothing wrong with the business concept. That remains. Why not just continue without him? We can still call the company BBDG and just use the initials. We can make it without him!'

No one else seemed convinced and the angry discussions went on for a long time. Local and foreign newspapers that had been collected in the office were thrown on the table one after another to underline what people had to say. I could see their confidence disappearing. Our employees had seen Björn and me as a strong and closely-knit ownership team, but now the ties between us didn't appear as resilient or as credible. Everyone in the room was conscious of that fact that Björn wouldn't even talk to me!

The only positive aspect of the meeting was that everyone had a chance to express himself and get his frustration out in the open. We broke up after about an hour, having decided that I would continue trying to get in touch with Björn. There was nothing more important than that at the moment.

Following the meeting I phoned Håkan Frisinger at his home. Frisinger sounded uneasy and had trouble trying to keep calm.

'What happened? How is Björn, anyway? Was it really a suicide attempt?'

I told him the truth: that I had not succeeded in getting in touch with Björn and that I was going to try again. Then I told him what we had experienced in Japan.

Frisinger was, understandably, worried not only about BBDG, but also about himself. He had never been involved in anything questionable and had accepted his post with us only after giving the matter considerable thought. Now I could feel his anxiety at being involved in a potential scandal.

I decided to take a break to shower and change the clothes I'd been wearing for nearly thirty hours. Just as I was leaving the office my secretary stopped me.

'There's a call for you, Lasse!'

'No, not now. Tell them I'll call back later.'

There was a pause.

'He insists that it's very important!'

'Who is it, then?'

There was another pause.

'He says his name is Ulf Nilson and that he's calling from *Expressen* in Stockholm.'

I immediately froze in my tracks. I knew Ulf Nilson very well. He was the paper's celebrated international reporter. Although based in Paris, he was seldom there: wherever something of great interest was happening, Ulf would turn up. His articles were given great play in his paper, often serving as the headline story of the day, as most people who came into contact with him knew very well. That went for Björn, too. Björn had a pretty good idea of his standing with most journalists and had developed a seemingly unfailing ability to use them for his own purposes. He had made a promise to Ulf when we'd met earlier during the Swedish Prime Minister's official visit to the United States. Like me, Nilson had been invited to the White House after the dinner. He had found me and Björn and made his approach immediately. There had never been a real interview with Björn since he left tennis, Ulf said, and he would very much like to do one emphasising Borg the businessman.

Björn had thought for a moment.

'OK,' he had said. 'You'll get the first interview I give as a businessman, but I'll choose the time. We're not yet done with our planning.'

Nilson had accepted these conditions and had been trying to get the interview ever since, but Björn had repeatedly put it off until finally last December he had agreed a date.

Now I took the phone.

'Hi, Lasse,' came the voice on the other end of the line. 'Björn and I agreed a couple of months ago that I would interview him this Saturday, but I can't for the life of me get hold of him. I only get that Alverdal guy and he doesn't seem to know anything. Have you talked with Björn since what happened in Milan?'

'I just arrived from Tokyo and haven't talked with Björn yet. I'll try to reach him, but I'm not exactly sure when . . .'

'It doesn't matter. I'm in Stockholm for the moment, but I'll be in Monte Carlo as soon as I can. I'll take along a photographer and be down there tonight or tomorrow morning. I'll contact you then.'

'Sure. We'll get the interview worked out for sure,' I said putting down the receiver. Now what was I to do? What would Nilsen write if Björn refused to be interviewed at the last minute?

That evening I tried again to get hold of Björn, but without success. Margaretha repeated yet again that Björn still wasn't up to talking to anyone. I made a number of other calls, including one to Gullis. I told him about the possibility of the Nilson interview, and he told me that he had been summoned to Gotabanken in Stockholm earlier that day. In view of the headlines the bank was uneasy and wondered what was going to happen to our company. Between the lines, the bank had threatened to break off its commitment to us. That certainly didn't make me feel any better.

Ulf Nilson showed up at the office the next day with his photographer, Torbjörn Andersson. Nilson was dumb with surprise when he learned that I still hadn't talked with Björn. Given the situation, I had found it necessary to tell him the truth about that.

'That's just great,' he exclaimed. 'He hasn't even sent any word? Well, it would be best for Björn to let me interview him, because otherwise I can guarantee that there will be some pretty unpleasant things in the paper about him.'

I asked Staffan Holm to tell the two journalists about

BBDG and the concept behind it while I made another attempt to get in touch with Björn. It was a wasted effort. I felt terrible. I was about to lose face in front of two representatives of Sweden's largest newspaper. What would Nilson think – and write – about our company if Björn wouldn't even talk to me, his partner? And what chain of reactions would such an article set in motion?

My thoughts turned again to abandoning the whole project. My sense of impotence was digging deep holes in my soul and I was convinced I was headed for a nervous breakdown.

Ulf Nilson came over to where I was standing and staring despairingly at the silent phone.

'You know,' he said, 'this business concept seems to be very thoroughly put together. If I understand it correctly, it could be a great success.'

He appeared to be genuinely impressed and I thanked him for his praise with a tired shrug of my shoulders. But he wasn't finished, and as he continued, his tone of voice moved from puzzled to indignant.

'Why doesn't Björn come here? You say it was just a small case of food poisoning. Hasn't he recovered yet? He won't even speak to you. What's the problem? He's sitting out there at Cap Ferrat and leaving all the employees to fend for themselves!'

By this time he was in full swing.

'Is he hiding? I have to tell you that if Björn hasn't let me know by tonight that the interview is on, I'm going back to Stockholm and writing a damning article about him. I'll write that he is trying to destroy a good business idea out of pure spite – or maybe out of stupidity. Just so you know.'

I shrugged my shoulders again. What could I say? Nilson seemed to have made up his mind and I wasn't sure that I cared one way or the other any more. Perhaps it would be best this way, to have everything fall apart fast. I could begin doing something else, something more down to earth and less high-flying.

My new girlfriend, Eva, whom I had been seeing for a few months, had flown in from Stockholm the same day, and that evening we went out to dinner with Christer Björkman, a colleague from the office. Understandably, none of us was especially cheerful. My mind was plagued by unanswered questions. Should I really jump ship? What should I get involved in if I did? What would happen to the other people in the company? We had just ordered when I was summoned to the phone.

'Hi, Lasse!' It was Ingmar calling from Stockholm. 'Björn wants to talk with you immediately. You're to phone him as soon as you can. And you're to get hold of Ulf Nilson as soon as possible, too. Björn wants to do that interview first thing in the morning.'

'That sounds great,' I said tiredly. 'But why the sudden urge to talk?'

'Well, I think Björn Gullström has talked with Björn, or perhaps with Margaretha. Gullström seems to have said that unless Björn agrees to the interview everything will be ruined. Nilson will return to Stockholm and destroy Björn once and for all, and *Expressen*, of course, will push the whole thing as aggressively as it can. That would probably mean the end of the company.'

I sighed, finished the conversation and hung up.

Gullis would later tell me that he had talked with Margaretha for hours. He had pleaded and begged in call after call. He had explained to her what would happen if Ulf Nilson carried out his plans to write a very negative article about Björn: that all of BBDG's employees might leave the company, which would mean that the business would collapse; that the company might be forced into bankruptcy, which would involve expenses of at least $10 million for Björn personally; that, in turn, might lead to Björn having to file for bankruptcy, since he didn't have the liquid assets to meet such expenses; and if *that* were to happen, then Björn's trust fund would have to step forward, which might lead the Swedish tax authorities to confiscate most of his fortune. In short, there was a real threat of a major catastrophe.

Gullis had finished by saying, 'Margaretha, you must understand that this is deadly serious and that there's no time to think about it or to give vague answers. If you and Rune want to help prevent the catastrophe that threatens to destroy Björn's life, then do it now!'

Margaretha had been unresponsive during most of the conversation but had finally come to her senses and agreed to try to convince Björn.

When I called their hotel, the receptionist told me that Ulf Nilson and Torbjörn Andersson were out and were expected back in about an hour. At least they hadn't returned to Stockholm yet, to my great relief. I then phoned Cap Ferrat. Björn answered.

'Hi, Lasse,' he exclaimed. 'How are you?'

He sounded as if nothing at all had happened! Or as if

I had been the one who'd had his stomach pumped.

'Oh, I'm OK, but how about *you*? Why haven't you called?'

'Fine, just fine. It's been a little rough, but things are fine now. We'll have to talk about it later. Regarding the interview with Ulf Nilson, we'll do it tomorrow morning at nine.'

'Nilson has been at the office all day,' I said. 'He talked about returning to Stockholm, but he's still at his hotel as far as I know. I'll get hold of him.'

'Perfect,' said Björn. 'Loredana and I and Mum and Dad are flying to Stockholm tomorrow afternoon. We've borrowed a private plane. Come along with us so we can talk on the plane.'

I thought of Eva and hesitated.

'I don't know. Eva is here and we had planned to fly home together.'

'Oh, that's no problem. She can come along, too. There's plenty of room.'

'I'll discuss it with her and we'll see. But, OK, I'll fly with you in any case. We really do need to talk.'

'Exactly. I'll see you at nine in the morning. Take care of yourself!'

I staggered back to the table. I was happy that I'd finally spoken with Björn, but I was also rather shocked that he acted as if nothing at all had happened.

'I've talked with Björn,' I said and sat down. 'He's going to do the interview tomorrow.'

'Great! How is he? What did he say?' Christer Björkman wanted to know.

I looked around the crowded restaurant.

'Oh, he was just fine, no problems. By the way, you can call the others and tell them that Björn's doing the interview.'

I had no desire to say what I was really thinking, so I changed the subject and we finished our meal feeling more hopeful.

During our walk back to the flat I told Eva that Björn wanted us to fly back to Stockholm with his family in a private plane. She looked at me.

'No, I can't sit with them for three hours after what's just happened. I simply can't do it. But you go ahead. It's just as well that you and Björn talk alone.'

I reached Ulf Nilson about an hour later.

'Everything's set for the interview. Nine o'clock tomorrow morning. I'll be at your hotel at half-past eight!'

'It was about time Björn said something nice,' came the laconic answer.

CHAPTER SEVENTEEN

A Polished Interviewee

The next morning Andersson drove us to Cap Ferrat. Nilson sat next to him in the front seat telling jokes and I sat in the back feeling nervous. How would Björn behave? What would he say? I assumed that the mood would be somewhat depressed and wondered what Björn would do about it.

We pulled up in front of the Borgs' villa a few minutes before nine. Björn, Loredana, Margaretha and Rune were all standing there, waving and smiling, when we got out of the car. It seemed almost as if the two journalists and I belonged to the family, except that I was very well aware that the Borgs couldn't stand reporters, no matter how good they were.

Björn looked pretty good, but I knew him so well that I could see he wasn't in the best of shape. He wasn't exactly shaky, but he had to make a great effort to appear relaxed and untroubled. He had a day's growth of stubble and was wearing a light blue sweater with diagonal stripes. When I saw the brand name on his sweater I raised my eyebrows. Björn noticed and said happily, 'Yes, I have to advertise for the company, so Mum sewed on the logo.'

I groaned silently. He had had the Eiser logo, which we had abandoned long ago, sewn on his sweater! Good Lord, he really must have been confused if he couldn't even remember what the BBDG logo looked like. Oh well, we couldn't worry about that now. Nilson stood joking with Margaretha and Rune, but Björn had arranged everything. Loredana quickly excused herself and disappeared, and Björn's parents soon followed her example.

Björn took over.

'Come on,' he said. 'Let's go into the living-room.' He looked at Nilson and laughed.

'Uffe, you're the first journalist I've ever let in this house. You should feel honoured!'

Nilson *looked* as if he felt honoured.

We followed Björn into the house, through the hallway with the bedrooms on either side and up a staircase to the first floor. The kitchen was to our left and the large and lovely living-room to our right. Through the picture window we could look out over the Mediterranean and see Nice far away to the right. Nilson and Andersson were impressed, but Björn took their compliments lightly and invited us to sit down on the sofas that dominated one part of the room. Margaretha came in with coffee and we made polite conversation for a few minutes. Then Nilson took off his jacket, got out his tape recorder and placed it on the table in front of Björn. The interview was under way.

I sat next to Nilson and listened, but I said hardly a word during the interview. Björn and I had not been alone for one second and therefore hadn't had a chance to discuss how he would answer whatever questions Nilson might ask about the company. But Björn had never asked for any advice before and certainly didn't need any now. He knew precisely how to handle journalists. He had been around them almost daily for nearly twenty years. He had been asked every conceivable question. Björn could frequently tell after an interview what the reporter would use as a headline, how much play the article would be given and what angle it would present. And he was a master at choosing the right moment for publicity. Sometimes he would remain silent for a month or two and then, when he wanted to have something written about him for a given purpose, he would make a statement. The journalists would crowd around him and the articles they wrote would be almost precisely what Björn had planned.

Björn was the conductor and the journalists were his orchestra. He almost always got them to play as he wanted them to, but if it didn't sound just right he could become very angry indeed. Björn knew precisely what was going on at this particular moment: Nilson had a world-class scoop and would swallow just about anything he was given.

Nilson tried his best, but he fell into the same trap as all the others by underestimating Björn's cool and his impudence. For my part, I was alternately impressed and astonished by Björn's performance. The impudence! Time after time Björn smiled somewhat gloomily and wound his way out of the occasionally difficult questions with total ease. He seemed to be perfectly calm no matter what he said. I thought about what he had told me so often in the past: 'There's no one who can catch me, Lasse, no one!'

The article was published on 13 February, occupied four pages of the paper, was prominently mentioned on the front page and took up the whole placard advertising the paper that day. The headline read 'A lot is at stake for me', and below, 'Björn Borg talks with Ulf Nilson . . . About the future, the pills and Loredana.' The article began:

269

Björn is in Sweden at the moment. To escape from
the press, which has been after him and Loredana
like animals during the past week, he borrowed the
soccer club Milan AC's jet and arrived in Sweden
unnoticed. When you read this, he has probably
just left the court at the SALK hall in Alvik after a
tough workout. He is in good condition – he weighs
the same as he did when he won at Wimbledon –
and in a great mood. At the same time he doesn't
deny that he is unhappy, shaken and raging mad
over what happened in Milan on Tuesday – and on
the after-effects of the scandal: 'I feel that I have
been treated in a clearly unjust way in the media. I
didn't try to commit suicide. I've never taken drugs
– *not a single time in my whole life.*'

Then came Nilson's first direct question.

'Do you dare look me straight in the eye and swear
that you've never experimented with cocaine, or
heroin or any other drug.'

He looked me straight in the eye – that well-
known, hard look from the tennis court, where
honour and money were in the balance. 'Never.'

'Are you dependent on pills?'

'No!'

Further on, Nilson wrote about the background to the
interview.

There is a story behind the interview that says a
great deal about Björn Borg the man: that's why I'm
going to tell it. We hadn't seen each other for many
years when we met at the White House in connection with Ingvar Carlsson's visit. As Sweden's

ambassador for tourism, Björn had been invited to dinner with Reagan; I was among those who were allowed to come for coffee afterwards.

'There's never been any real interview with you as an adult,' I said. 'I'd like to do one.'

'I'll go along with that,' said Björn.

'No one else can do it first and we'll sit down seriously.'

'OK.'

That was in September 1987. We agreed on times and places for the interview three or four times, but something always came up: a tour for Björn, a world championship boxing match for me and so on. It was not until Christmas that we were able to agree on an absolutely certain date: Saturday, 11 February. Lars Skarke, Staffan Holm and Bengt Hanser of the Björn Borg Design Group put together a programme that we followed. I flew from New York to Stockholm and then went on to Monte Carlo, where the company has its headquarters, but then it happened: Tuesday, 7 February, Björn Borg to the hospital early in the morning, stomach pumped, possible suicide attempt.

'There goes your interview,' said my friends.

'I don't think so,' I said and did my best to seem credible. 'Björn is a Swedish athlete. If he's made a promise, then he's made a promise. If he can stand on his legs at all, he'll keep his promise.'

I perhaps only half believed what I was saying, but I kept it to myself, flew to Monte Carlo and waited. Photographers were hanging in the trees around Björn's parents' house and a large number waited near the door. The *Daily Mail* in London offered 150,000 kronor for the first interview. An American paper offered 120,000 and another dozen offers arrived, all in six figures. By selling himself in a number of different distribution areas, Björn could have earned several hundred thousand kronor, but he kept his promise.

We met on Saturday for the longest interview he had ever given. We sat in the wonderfully beautiful living-room, with its view out over the Mediterranean, and some time in the middle of our talk Björn chuckled and said, 'Uffe, no journalist has been in here in twenty years. No journalist has *ever been* in here.'

We talked a long while, chuckled a good deal, teased each other and babbled on, but the basic tone was very serious. Björn was very conscious of the fact that having had his stomach pumped had hurt him and his company, and hurt them badly.

'It's unjust,' he said time and time again, and added that unjust headlines and rumours can do just as much harm as ones that are true. His mother, Margaretha, and father, Rune, said hello, but then sat in the kitchen; Loredana greeted us and disappeared in the large house. It was clear that Björn wanted to speak for Björn and Björn alone, that he wanted to concentrate and get to the bottom of things. Neither Loredana nor his parents were to be in the picture – arguing with Björn is as meaningless as spitting against the wind. He had things to explain and he wanted to do it *himself*.

After that long passage, Nilson began to put questions again.

'You were of course conscious of the fact that there is some drug use among tennis players. Your friend Vitas Gerulaitis admitted his abuse of cocaine.'

'I was conscious of that, but I've never participated. Never. I hate drugs. All drugs. I hate what drugs do to young people and I could never think of touching the stuff.'

'OK, let's talk about what happened in Milan.'

'We hadn't been there in five or six weeks. Then we came home to Loredana's flat and I ate something that made me sick.'

'It has been said that you had gone out alone after a serious argument and that you came home at half-past six in the morning.'

'Entirely false.'

'You never went out?'

'No.'

'How do you explain the fact that Loredana didn't get sick?'

'Perhaps she ate less.'

'Why did she call the ambulance? It was obvious that that would lead to unfavourable publicity. Having your stomach pumped early in the morning is something you should try to avoid if you want to be a model for youth and be considered a serious business leader. . .'

'I know, I know. But she was worried. I wasn't unconscious, as someone has said, but I was foggy and sleepy.'

'How many sleeping pills did you take?'

'Two or three.'

'Not sixty? To take your own life?'

Björn looked very angry for a moment. Then he said, 'If someone takes sixty sleeping pills he doesn't leave the hospital a couple of hours later. That is impossible.'

'Did you try to commit suicide?'

'No.'

Later in the article, Nilson wrote:

When Björn is done working out he drives to Björn Borg Design Group's office in Alvik. He works there every day during the two-week periods when he cares for Robin.

'I'm *always* in Sweden then. I schedule all the trips I have to make for negotiations with suppliers and distributors and others out in the world during the fourteen-day periods when Jannike has Robin.'

After work he picks Robin up at the day-care centre and drives home, where Loredana is waiting.

'First I play with Robin and talk with him. Then we eat. Loredana is fantastic with food, and I have always liked Italian food best. I can't fix anything myself, but she's great at it . . . Afterwards I put Robin to bed – that's something I always do myself – and then we have a couple of hours to ourselves. We might watch TV or a video or just talk. I think the most important thing is to talk with one another, to tell each other what's happened during the day, to discuss things . . . We don't have an au pair. We don't have any help or any servants.

I'm *never* going to have any.'
A few questions further on:

'But you were never married to Robin's mother.'

'No. But we are friends, and we're doing the best for our son. He's the one who counts. He's the one we're raising. He's got to grow up, and that's not so easy in today's society. Society is becoming tougher and tougher, with drugs and all sorts of things. Parents have to give their children as much support as possible.'

'So Borg the playboy is actually quite old-fashioned?'

'Yes. I'm oldfashioned. I pay my debts, show up on time, stand behind what I've promised. I feel great.'

'You've had your disappointments, of course, but have you yourself done anything that you're ashamed of.'

'No. I'm quite happy with what I've done. And the future looks bright . . .'

The interview lasted almost two hours. When it was over I was completely exhausted just from watching such a powerful demonstration. In those two hours Björn had done more than a large company's public relations department could possibly accomplish in several years. He had made Nilson believe his version of events and do just what he wanted him to. It is almost absurd in this context that when Björn met Ulf Nilson in New York somewhat later he was furious with him, not because *Expressen* had sold the article to foreign newspapers – that was just fine – but because they had received *money* for it. Björn thought that it was reward enough for the paper to earn money on the increased sales his interview had produced. To his way of thinking it was a matter of exchanging services: he got his message out and the paper sold more copies.

Long afterwards I would often think: dear, wonderful, damned Björn Gullström, godfather to my only son, why did you have to convince Björn, via Margaretha, to give that interview? And I would curse myself: why you idiot, didn't you let Ulf Nilson fly back to Stockholm and write everything he had threatened to write? That would have been a suitable end to our dream.

After that long Saturday morning our business concept rested entirely on a series of public lies. Everything had been transformed into a game, and at this point I had no idea what role Björn had given me. I would find out later and it wasn't very pleasant.

Nilson and Andersson left about half-past eleven, very pleased with their day's work. Björn waved goodbye to them as they drove off and I couldn't help raising my arm a little too. A private plane was to fly us from Nice to Stockholm several hours later, so I sat down by the pool to wait while the Borgs packed their bags.

There were a good number of people at the airport and, as always, there was quite a commotion when Björn strode through the building. Most people had presumably read the headlines during the week, and they turned their heads and whispered to one another as Björn and Loredana walked past. Rune and Margaretha followed a few steps behind, and I came last with my head full of thoughts. Since we were taking a private flight, we didn't need to check our bags. The passport control officers took care of us first and we were in the plane within minutes.

It was a small plane, designed to hold ten passengers in comfort, and Björn had instructed Rune and Margaretha to sit all the way in front, with Loredana immediately behind them.

'Come,' he said. 'We'll sit where we can be alone.'

We went to the back of the plane and sat down. The others were sitting about thirteen feet away and would hardly be able to hear our conversation. Initially, Björn and I avoided the burning questions, but we soon got around to talking business. I reported the results of my trip to Japan and told him about the reactions at our office in Monte Carlo. I also told him what people were saying at our other offices. Björn didn't seem to be very concerned by what I had to say, and I was not sure whether he was treating the situation lightly or was ashamed of himself.

Everything I had been through for the past few days flooded my memory. I was sick and tired of his problems with women and drugs. I was tired of dancing to his tune. I looked at him and thought: you're too egotistical and immature, a spoiled brat. Can't you grow up, pick yourself up and think of someone other than yourself? You've let me and the other people in BBDG down. At first you wouldn't talk to me and now you don't even say you're sorry, but just sit there nonchalantly and unperturbed. I've had it with you.

'Björn, I don't want to be part of this any more.'

That was all there was to it, I'd said it.

He gave me a questioning look. 'Quit? You don't mean what you're saying, do you?'

I swallowed and took a deep breath, but I didn't say anything. None of the others seemed to hear what we were talking about. All three of them had sunk down in their seats and were motionless, as if they were sleeping or reading, although I could easily imagine that all six ears were straining to hear everything we were saying.

'No, now we're going to work and earn money,' Björn continued in a serious tone of voice. 'We can't give up now, we just can't. Now's the time we have to fight. Together! What happened in Milan is no problem, I can promise you that. You know, if Loredana didn't have the contacts she has it would have been ten times worse. Now everything is fine, I guarantee it.'

I looked at him.

'What do you *mean*? Have you had the hospital records altered? Those are pretty good contacts – is that why you have hidden out and kept silent for five days?'

Björn looked out the window and was quiet for a long while.

'Don't think about it any more. I'm just saying that nothing more is going to come out from that direction. Things are going to calm down, count on me.'

Suddenly he looked very small and defenceless, and close to tears. He was far from the unbeatable Borg who could sometimes be arrogant and sarcastic, even spiteful. He actually seemed vulnerable. His gaze shifted from one thing to the other, but wouldn't meet mine.

'We must, Lasse,' he urged. 'We just can't give up now! There's no problem. I promise.'

I thought hard and knew the whole time that I was very close to saying yes. I couldn't help feeling sorry for him, remembering all the fun we had had together, all the trips we had taken, the tennis match when he had hopped around on one leg. I thought about our joint plans, about our intense discussions and conversations, how we were going to show the world, about everything I had experienced and everything we might have ahead of us. If only. . . .

'Come on, Lasse,' said Björn again. 'I promise everything will be perfect from now on. No more trouble or nonsense. This will never happen again. And I'm going to work very hard!'

Sure, Björn, that's the way things can be, I thought to myself. But you're trouble and so is the life you lead, the only life you seem able to lead. I was torn by conflicting feelings. Björn was a great risk to the company but I didn't want to give up now. I thought about my idea and about all the colleagues who had put their hearts into BBDG. Was I going to let them down, just like Björn had? You don't lie down ten yards before the finish line just because you're tired. You pull yourself together and fight on. I thought so hard I could hear the gears grinding in my head.

'OK, Björn. But then it's just going to be business between us. From now on we're going to keep our private lives separate. I'll live my life and you can live yours. I don't care what you do, just as long as you behave.'

He tried to smile and shrugged his shoulders a little.

'Sure, that OK. The main thing is that we fight for the company together. That's the most important thing, that we don't give up because of this.'

For the rest of the trip we discussed the company's problems and thought about a public relations campaign.

We decided we would go out as soon as possible to try to salvage whatever contracts we could.

Ingmar Alverdal, with his permanent fixture, the mobile telephone, was waiting for us at the airport. He had arranged for limousines to take us to our homes, so I quickly said goodbye to Björn and his family and went to Stavsborg. Eva was already there. I hugged her hard and kissed her.

'How was the trip?'

'Fine,' she said. 'Ulf Nilson was on the same plane and we talked quite a bit. You know what he told me? He said that he had already written most of the article, that it will be in Monday's paper and that it's going to be a good one, although he's not sure Björn is telling the truth. How was it on the plane with Björn, by the way?'

'I told him how disappointed I was in him. But we're going to go on with the company anyway. We've got a tough job ahead of us, that much is clear. We'll just have to start all over again. But at least he has now promised to behave and to do as much as he can.'

Eva looked at me inquiringly. 'Lasse, are you sure you know what you're doing?'

I assured her that I did.

CHAPTER EIGHTEEN

The 'Predators' Ball'

The interview in *Expressen* had at least mitigated some aspects of the chaotic situation that had developed after the events in Milan, and Ulf Nilson followed it with a second article the next day. That article had covered two full pages and dealt with Björn Borg the businessman and BBDG – in other words, the story that Nilson had originally been promised. We immediately arranged for a content analysis of the articles by specialists in media coverage. The report contained no surprises, confirming that although not all of Björn's statements in the interview were believable, the articles had 'a positive value'. It was true that Björn's image had suffered a serious blow, but the damage would be repaired if 'suitable measures were taken'. Thus, 'it is of decisive importance that Björn's contacts with the ... media concentrate on his business activities ... and that he preferably avoids the tabloids.'

This was more evidence, if it were needed, of Björn's skill in using the mass media to shape his image the way he wanted. Some reporters, however, couldn't care less about what picture Björn wanted to convey. Following his presumed suicide attempt, for example, the French magazine *Paris-Match* published an article that portrayed Björn as a human wreck who had failed at everything he had undertaken following his tennis career, a punch-drunk ex-athlete. Stig had immediately contacted a French lawyer, who had concluded that Björn could sue the magazine for a lot of money and probably win the case. Stig had informed Björn of this at a meeting at the office and asked how he should proceed.

'No, forget all about suing them,' Björn said.

'Why? We have a good chance of winning the case according to the lawyer. You can get at least half a million francs.'

'Because what happened in Milan is *never* going to happen again.'

'Oh, sure,' said Stig. 'Of course it can happen again.'

Björn gave him a strange look. 'What? What do you mean?'

'But Björn,' Stig replied, 'you can never tell when you'll suffer from food poisoning again, no one can tell.'

Björn couldn't help smiling.

Instead of suing *Paris-Match*, Björn, master of the media, invited a reporter and photographer from its competitor, *Le Figaro*, to Viking's Hill, the only journalists ever given this honour. The result was a big 'at home with' article in which Björn was presented as virtue and conscientiousness personified, and was given the opportunity to deny everything *Paris-Match* had written.

Following our conversation on the plane, and at my insistence, Björn and I had agreed to formalise our partnership. Our relationship had become almost strictly limited to business matters and it was appropriate that it be regulated by a written partnership contract. I was to draw up a list of my claims on the company, since I hadn't accepted any salary during the nearly eighteen months that we had been working with BBDG and I had had a number of expenses for which I now wanted compensation. I would now pay Björn $100,000, as per the option agreement from the spring of 1987, in return for which I would receive 40 per cent of the shares in Björn Borg Enterprises Ltd. Last but not least, I was to pay $2 million to the Jersey company, which was to constitute my part of the increased capitalisation that we had agreed to with Gotabanken. The incident in Milan had given the bank cold feet and it had asked several times whether the $8 million had been invested in the company.

In addition to these contractual arrangements, we planned a number of public relations moves to restore the company's image. Björn agreed to undertake an extensive trip to give everyone who wanted it a chance to see him. He was to show that he was bright and healthy and in the best of shape, a fresh-looking business leader.

After my divorce, I was religious about spending a winter holiday with my daughters, Anna and Cissi. We had become accustomed to going off somewhere far from offices, conference rooms, telephones and schools to ski or to sunbathe and swim. I had been travelling almost constantly over the past year and we had seen each other all too seldom. I naturally longed for them and I had a bad conscience. Moreover, I felt completely exhausted after the events of the past few weeks, so I had decided to really splurge and to take Eva and the girls to Bermuda, a paradise completely devoid of stress or pressure.

On 25 February we checked in to the Marriott Hotel on the south-east side of the island. The beach and the sea were just a stone's throw from the hotel, and there were two first-class golf courses right next to it. The most longed-for holiday of my life could now begin.

It lasted two days. Then the telephone rang. It was Julian Jakobi. He was calling on behalf of Björn, with whom he had been meeting in Stockholm over the past few days, and he had the following message:

'Björn has been thinking about your option. He has reconsidered and feels that it should be for 25 per cent and not 40.'

I was speechless. At no time had anything been said to suggest that we would alter our existing agreement.

'But I don't understand. Björn hasn't said anything about any change to me.'

'Sorry, but that's the way he wants it now.'

After the conversation I sat and thought things over. I remembered what I had said on the plane from Nice: that now our relationship was going to be limited to business, that I wanted to live my own life, and he could live his. Hadn't Björn been able to take my reaction? Was this my 'punishment'?

I could also imagine another possible reason. Björn had now had time to think about Price Waterhouse's appraisal of the company. When he realised that my share of 40 per cent was suddenly worth millions on paper, he reacted as he always did in similar situations: he felt he had been exploited, that someone was trying to make money out of him. That the appraisal demonstrated that the business concept was sound and that his own share was judged to be worth $24 million apparently did not matter to Björn. Nor did he seem to care that his behaviour had nearly sabotaged the entire project. Björn felt that his interviews with the press represented his part in putting everything right again. After just one week he was big and strong again: 'No one can catch me, Lasse, no one!'

I felt terribly tired and disappointed, and thought that he could at least have left me alone during my holiday. With a sigh, I dialled the number at Viking's Hill.

Björn confirmed what Jakobi had said. Since he was going to contribute $6 million in additional capital and I was going to contribute only $2 million, he and Jakobi had figured out that I was entitled to no more than 25 per cent of the shares.

I reminded him of our agreement. He wouldn't discuss it with me, but simply referred me to Julian.

I understood the logic in their figures, of course, but we had agreed on the distribution of the share capital long before, and it had never been changed in the option agreement. Only now that the appraisal had been made did Björn think that my 'carrot' – the reward I had been promised for making BBDG a success – was too large. Such tactics did not, in my opinion, reflect a high standard of business ethics.

'But, Björn,' I said, 'we talked about this last week, and there wasn't any problem then. Why have you come up with this now? I can't accept any new conditions.'

'Then I'm going to close the company down.'

'Well, you're the one who decides that.'

Then Björn changed his tone of voice. 'Or we can

do the following. Put up more money and you can buy more shares.'

I understood that he was testing my level of interest, so I answered without hesitation, 'Sure, I'm ready to buy as soon as I can get my hands on the necessary money.'

But I would never actually be given the chance to buy more shares.

The negotiations went back and forth. I talked with Stig, Gullis, Jakobi, Webber and time after time with Björn himself without making any progress. I received a mass of fax messages with various calculations and proposals. One minute my share was to be 25 per cent, the next minute 20, then 25 again.

I decided not to accept any of the offers. If Björn wanted to close down the operation, that was his business and I told Jakobi precisely that. When I told Gullis, he said, 'You know how Björn can be. He never changes his mind once he has something like this in his head. Think about the employees, if about nothing else. If you leave now, he'll close down. That's just the way it is. For them there will no longer be any driving force in the company. Think about it.'

I didn't have any intention of giving way, despite what Gullström said. I insisted that I should receive the proportion of the shares that we had initially agreed. Deep down, I didn't think that Björn would make good his threat to close the company, since he had too much to lose by doing so. But what was he really after? I decided to ignore the phone, which had already destroyed three days of my holiday, and spend my time with Eva and my daughters, which had been the point of the trip.

But at the reception desk there was a new message. 'Urgent, urgent – call Björn Gullström.'

Gullis didn't have any good news for me.

'Lasse, Björn has asked me to call you and give you the following message: if you don't accept his terms you know what will happen.'

'What the hell does he mean? Is he mad?'

'I don't know. He just said that you know very well what he means.'

I tried to think, but my thoughts were interrupted by Gullström's voice, 'What's really going on? This is creepy. Hell, he's threatening you!'

Yes, it certainly sounded like a threat, but to this day I have no idea what Björn really meant. I could only agree with Gullis – it was unpleasant and even absurd.

'Go along with what he says, for God's sake!' Gullström's voice sounded even more strained. 'It's the only solution. This has gone too far. We can't close down now, when we're so close!'

I paced back and forth in my room thinking all night long. Sometimes I would go out on the balcony and listen to the waves breaking in the dark on the beach below. The next day I phoned Björn.

'What are you doing? I can't understand why you're threatening me. It's damned unpleasant, I can tell you.'

'You're the one who's going to decide what you want to do. And I want to know now,' he replied icily.

It was hopeless. Completely dejected, I said, 'OK, you win. I'll accept the 25 per cent. I haven't the stomach to argue about it any longer. But this is wrong, and you know it.'

'Good,' he said immediately. 'Then it's a deal. Now let's get on with it.'

A day later we said goodbye to Bermuda. I had hardly had a chance to be together with my daughters. Business had dominated my holiday and now occupied my thoughts on the plane home.

'What is Björn like, anyhow?' almost everyone had asked during the job interviews.

'He's a great guy. Honest and first-class in every possible way,' I had replied. I had been the perfect sales-man, keeping up appearances despite the fact that I was familiar with the other side of Björn's personality. In doing so I had risked my credibility. I looked out through the window. I knew that I was strong in times of adversity and that I would somehow get out of this dreadful situation. But I didn't feel especially well.

On the last day of March Håkan Frisinger opened his first board meeting with Björn Borg Design Group with a brief talk in which he drew parallels between BBDG and Volvo, where he had been involved in making its trademark internationally known and respected, just as we hoped to do with BBDG.

'At Volvo we worked according to a few key words, namely, creativity, credibility and continuity,' he said. 'I think that we should strive to live up to these concepts within Björn Borg Design Group, too. And I would like to add two more to the list: discipline and concentration. My first proposal is that the head of the company draw up an internal company policy in accordance with these important words.'

We had met a few times over the course of the last few months. Frisinger was a man of considerable dignity, friendly and modest, but also firm and decisive. He listened more than he talked, and when he finally did say something he always chose his words carefully and used them sparingly. He had long ago learned to delegate small matters to others, and he expected that they would be handled with the same thoroughness that characterised his own actions. I had already learned a number of things from him, like the time I had become too enthusiastic and talked about how 'fantastically BBDG had developed'.

'Lasse,' he said and smiled just a bit, 'as head of the company you should never use such expressions. They'll just be tossed back in your face if things are not quite as "fantastic" as you've said they'd be. Say instead that BBDG "is developing according to plan". Moderation is always best.'

I had taken up the question of his salary with him, but he had cut me off.

'Salary? No, we can discuss that when the company begins to turn a profit. Until then it will be just fine if you cover my expenses in connection with our meetings.'

The meeting of the board had taken place at our office in Monte Carlo. Sitting around the table were Björn and I, Julian Jakobi, John Webber, Björn Gullström, Håkan Frisinger and Stig Sjöblom, who acted as the board's secretary without having a vote. In addition, Johan Denekamp and Rolf Skjöldebrand had been asked to attend.

Rolf had been nurturing the idea of creating a new

logo for the company. He had taken me aside some days prior to the board meeting and showed me his finished proposal. It was identical to the logo we were already using, except that the words Björn Borg Design Group had been replaced by the initials BBDG. Neither Skjölde-brand nor anyone else in the Monte Carlo office had forgotten Björn's silence right after the events in Milan, and they had said many times that they didn't trust him. The widely recognised business strategist Skjöldebrand believed so strongly in the business concept that he felt it was entirely possible to carry it out even without the person on whom it had originally been based. He had asked me to discuss the new logo with Björn and to take it up with the board of directors.

That was no modest request. I could hardly tell Björn that the personnel wanted to remove his name from the logo because they didn't trust his ability to behave himself and because he set a bad example for the company. He'd have gone through the roof! At the same time, as the head of the company I had to listen to what the staff had to say and to present their thoughts. I promised to raise the matter with Björn. I did it very carefully and almost as an aside.

'Björn, the lads in the office aren't fully happy with the logo. They think it's a bit too chatty and that it would be better if it only said BBDG.'

Björn looked at me with ice in his eyes and said just one word. 'Never!'

I told Skjöldebrand what Björn had said and we decided not to raise the issue with the board. I myself thought Rolf was wrong. The trademark was called Björn

Borg and it was appropriate that the logo should carry his name.

At the meeting Rolf took up an entirely different matter instead. Rohdi Heintz's contributions as a designer had been discussed a great deal inside the company. He was a clever professional with a great deal of experience, but his clothes were not compatible with the image we were trying to create for BBDG, and so Rolf proposed that Rohdi should be replaced as our chief designer.

It was no easy decision. Rohdi had been in the picture since the beginning, when Eiser had started Björn Borg Menswear in 1983, and he had worked loyally and with great enthusiasm. We discussed the matter thoroughly and voted to approve the proposal.

Next, Johan Denekamp presented our financial situation to the board. Among other things, he reported on the projected results of the company's activities for the 1989 fiscal year. For this start-up year we had budgeted for losses of about $3.8 million, but, Denekamp explained, there was now some uncertainty in that forecast since we didn't know exactly what economic consequences the events in Milan were going to have.

Julian Jakobi soon asked for the floor. His first statement was characteristic of his and Webber's contributions during the remainder of the time the company existed.

'I've found a number of different costs that I would like to comment on,' he began. 'I think that BBDG could easily save a good deal of money,' he looked quickly at Björn before continuing, 'among other things, by booking airline tickets and hotel rooms in a more systematic way.

I've heard that someone paid $1,000 for an airline ticket
that we could actually have got for $200 less.'

I looked at Björn, who was watching Jakobi approvingly.

'I am offering myself as an adviser in such matters,'
continued Jakobi. 'As I have said, I think BBDG can save
a lot of money here.'

'Good, Julian,' said Björn. 'Make an appointment with
Lasse and see what you can do.'

Håkan Frisinger didn't bat an eyelash. I wondered if he
was thinking the same thing I was. Jakobi's tactic was
crystal clear: he wanted to impress Björn and score a few
points with him. For a member of the board to offer to act
as some sort of a consultant on how to save money was
more than a little silly. If Jakobi thought that money could
be saved on our trips, as a member of the board he should
simply demand that it be done. *That* was his job, not to
do it himself.

Björn did not understand that, nor would he over the
course of the next few months. It became increasingly
clear that Jakobi and Webber, although members of the
board, did not have the best interests of the company as
their primary goal. All of their contributions were directed
at protecting Björn's 'interests' against those of the
company. This was certainly evident when the question of
financing was raised at the meeting.

It had been decided that we would turn to Drexel
Burnham Lambert to attract external capital into the
company. A few days after the board meeting Björn and
I were to undertake a public relations trip to Japan to
promote a Reunion Tour of exhibition matches against
John McEnroe, prior to which I was to visit Los Angeles

and attend the so-called 'Predators' Ball', DBL's annual conference. Within the world of international finance, attending the 'Predators' Ball' was an obvious thing to do. The conference brought companies in need of financing together with banks, funds and other institutional investors who were willing to make capital available to promising businesses in almost any field, in return for suitable interest rates. Björn and I had each received an invitation, and Björn had been positive about going with me. Our task would be to make as many financial contacts as possible. I had spoken a number of times with Keith Harris, and he too thought it would be a good idea if Björn went to Los Angeles. I now raised that issue again. Björn nodded, but Jakobi raised objections.

'I don't really like the idea,' he said. 'Drexel may take advantage of the fact that Björn is coming to do some public relations for themselves. If Björn goes, he should have some sort of assurance that Drexel will really help with BBDG's financing and that it isn't simply a matter of some public relations trick around Björn.'

I looked at Frisinger again. He didn't bat an eyelash this time, either, but he did look at Jakobi circumspectly.

'You're right, Julian,' interjected Björn quickly. 'It's clear that we have to have some sort of assurances from them. Otherwise you never know what will happen. It's happened before.' He leaned back and wrinkled his forehead. 'Yes, that's what we'll do. Drexel will have to fax something to me at home. I'm returning to Stockholm this evening. If I receive an assurance from them, then I'll go to Los Angeles. Otherwise I'll forget about it and fly directly to Japan.'

There were a number of objections I felt like making at that point, not least of which was that it was Jakobi who was putting obstacles in the way of Björn's cooperation. It was Jakobi, after all, who had referred us to DBL in the first place. He should have been talking Björn into going, but now he claimed to be worried that the American firm would exploit Björn. Once again he was putting on a show for Björn, of course, and it was not in the best interests of the company. BBDG was no longer considered bankable. Our own bank had threatened to withdraw its support of BBDG after the fateful night in Milan. If it were to make good its threat, we would have to arrange for financing in some other way. Nonetheless, here was Björn playing the diva again just a month later, cheered on by Julian.

The last item discussed at the meeting was the public relations trip to Asia. Many sponsors, including the main one, an Italian jewellery firm, had abandoned the Reunion Tour following Björn's 'illness' in Milan, but we were still hopeful that Paul Naruse could rescue the situation, although I knew that it did not look very good at the moment.

Three days later I was sitting in the bar at the New York Hilton with Keith Harris, who was visiting his firm's head office on his way to the conference in Los Angeles. Earlier that day I had met Saul Schoenberg, the head of BBDG-USA, to go through the budget. Saul was thorough, efficient and cost-conscious. He had stuck to the plan we had developed and had organised the US market in a very detailed fashion. We could be calm, for Saul had the situation under control.

'Well,' said Keith, sipping his beer, 'what's going to happen? Is Björn coming?'

Harris had maintained contact with us after our meeting in London in February, and I knew that he had taken soundings on our behalf and even tried to 'turn around' people and companies who were hesitant about us because of the rumours about Björn.

I was prepared for the question, but it was an embarrassing situation. I could hardly tell him that Björn feared that DBL would pull off a public relations coup if he visited the conference. That would be an insult; even more important, it would not seem very intelligent.

'Well, you know what a fix Björn is in,' I began rather uncertainly. 'He's always very busy and now he's in the process of preparing for the trip to Asia and the matches against John McEnroe. Björn really wants to show up in top form, and he'd prefer to fly directly from Stockholm to Japan.'

Keith listened with raised eyebrows. 'But you need help with your financing. That must certainly be more important than anything else!'

'Oh, well, I'll tell you the truth,' I said, deciding to stop beating around the bush. 'Björn would like to have some sort of written confirmation that DBL really intends to help us with our financing. If he gets it, he'll come immediately!'

Keith burst out laughing. 'What are you guys doing, anyway?' he exclaimed almost merrily. 'Sure, Björn Borg Design Group is an exciting business concept, but we can get along very nicely without your company. You have financing problems, right? We are prepared to try to help to the best of our ability, but a written confirmation from Drexel as a condition of coming to the "Predators' Ball"? You must be joking!'

I could feel myself blushing. 'You have to understand how often Björn has been exploited over the years. It's hardly surprising that he's oversensitive at times, is it? Please, Keith, write a few lines on a piece of paper and I'll fax it to Björn.'

'Jesus,' said Harris, rolling his eyes. 'Tennis players, who do they think they are, anyway?'

He took out a pen, asked the bartender for a piece of paper, and jotted down a few lines.

'Will this do?' he asked. He had written that Drexel Burnham Lambert intended to do its best to help Björn Borg Design Group find suitable investors, that Björn's participation in the 'Predators' Ball' was important to that effort and that Harris personally looked forward to meeting Björn and discussing the issue of financing.

'That looks fine,' I said, thanking him at the same time.

A few minutes later the message had been faxed to Viking's Hill and half an hour later Björn phoned me in my room. He said he was happy with the message and that he would take the first available flight to Los Angeles.

Our hotel was not far from the newly constructed and gigantic Beverly Hills Hilton, where the 'Predators' Ball' was to take place. Keith Harris and I had flown to California together and made plans to have dinner with Björn, who was to land about the same time we did.

Björn was in a good mood when I rang his room, and I could hear Loredana's voice in the background. That she had come along on this important trip could have been a problem. As a celebrated star, Loredana was concerned about being the centre of attention and was capable of creating a scene if she felt she was being ignored or slighted. Moreover, she loved to dress in provocatively short and tight-fitting skirts, which were on the border of what was considered acceptable, at least in business circles. For these reasons I was uneasy about Björn's taking Loredana to the conference and to the many meetings that were held in connection with it. I needn't have worried. Loredana had no desire to attend boring business meetings while she was in Los Angeles and she had arranged her own programme.

That first evening Keith Harris, Björn, and I had dinner at an Italian restaurant. Keith joked, did all the talking and soon had Björn and me in the best of moods. The restaurant was frequented by business people, many of whom Keith knew. Every once in a while he invited potential investors to our table and introduced Björn and me.

'Björn Borg Design Group is an exciting company,' he told them, presenting the basic concept. 'It's a good opportunity for investors and can produce good profits.'

Björn and I listened intently. It was interesting to hear the powerful investors' reactions to what Keith and we had to say. Everyone seemed positive. One Swiss businessman who joined us indicated that he had $10 million that he wanted to invest in a company like ours. That evening continued in this fashion until Björn got up and said, 'I'm afraid I have to go now. My fiancée is waiting for me at my hotel.'

* * *

Just after nine the next morning, Björn and I arrived at the
Beverly Hills Hilton, where the conference was already in
full swing. Three thousand people had been invited and it
seemed as if they had all come. Men streamed through the
lobby and the adjacent areas, greeting business acquaintances and old friends. They stood around in small groups,
their conversations peppered by laughing and shouting. It
was like the beginning of a new school year – everyone
wanted to know what everyone else had been doing since
the last time they had met. There was an atmosphere
of anticipation, curiosity and excitement everywhere you
turned.

The major topic of discussion was DBL's legendary
broker Michael Milken, who was not present. The week
before the conference he had been accused of insider
trading. The papers had been full of articles about it and
opinions were divided. Milken, who in 1987 had earned
the unbelievable sum of $550 million in salary and com-
missions, protested that the only thing he was guilty of was
having revolutionised the financial markets, and he was
now busy preparing his defence.

DBL had suffered from the publicity, of course, but
the company was considered sufficiently solid to survive
the situation. Business continued as usual and during this
conference DBL's handling of the transfer of ownership of
the giant Nabisco company – a transaction involving $5
billion – was to be discussed at a seminar.

Björn and I walked into this whirlwind of powerful and
influential investors and businessmen, and absolutely no
one took any notice of us. In this setting we were outsiders,
cats among ermine. We stood there a bit lost until Keith

Harris took us in tow and showed us around. This was no conference in the normal sense of the word. Instead, it was a large number of conferences, seminars and meetings that continued nonstop from morning until evening in many different rooms. Keith introduced us to various people, and we found ourselves busy talking about BBDG with one person after another and handing out brochures. One of our listeners, a huge American, slapped Björn on the back in friendly fashion.

'So, you don't want to invest any more of your own money in the company,' he laughed. 'You're after other people's money, are you? Yes, yes, I understand. Well, I can only tell you that Drexel's the right company for you!'

Eventually Frederick Joseph, DBL's chief executive officer, learned that Björn was at the conference and came over to say hello. After exchanging the usual pleasantries, he began to talk about tennis. Björn had previously been asked if he'd like to play a little tennis that evening with some of the company's customers and he had agreed. Now it turned out that a suddenly convened meeting had got in the way.

'We'll have to do tennis some other time,' Joseph told Björn. 'I hope you won't be offended.'

'No, no,' said Björn. 'That's OK.'

The day flew by. When we finally left the conference hotel we were both satisfied. We had made valuable contacts and were agreed that we would not lack for financing in the future. On the way back to our hotel, Björn said, 'We were right to come here. This shows you what sorts of contacts John and Julian have!'

CHAPTER NINETEEN

'Is this a PR trip for John McEnroe Design Group?'

Björn, Loredana and I landed in Tokyo on the evening of Thursday, 6 April. We were to be in Japan for five days, during which time Björn and I were to meet with Seibu and Hoya in an attempt to win back the five-year contracts that Stig and I had been unable to take home in February. Björn was also to do some public relations work for Tretorn, be interviewed on a number of television chat shows and take part in a major press conference in order to re-establish his 'lost honour'.

Paul Naruse had worked out a detailed plan with IMG's Tokyo office and a Japanese public relations firm, and even before we began a Japanese IMG executive had asked me to arrange things so that Loredana did not come to the meetings. I forwarded that request to Björn, who had a ready answer, one he had used before, when Jannike had been in the picture.

'Sure,' he said, 'it's no problem.' Then he paused dramatically before adding, 'But then I won't come either.'

Björn did pretty well on the whole. He was in one of his working-mode periods and was determined to regain the faith of those who had doubts about him. He even tried to charm me. One of our appointments was a visit to a Seibu department store in one of Tokyo's suburbs. Björn was to participate in a tennis demonstration on the

301

roof of the department store, where a temporary tennis court had been prepared for the occasion. There were masses of spectators around the court, and Björn demonstrated his special techniques and gave advice and tips to a number of promising young Japanese players. During the demonstration he summoned me and, after introducing me as his business partner, gave me a lesson in how to serve, to the amusement of the audience.

The managements of Seibu and Hoya were very pleased to see Björn healthy and fresh, and they signed the contracts we had been denied two months earlier. Toyomenka's 'no' to the Björn Borg Sports Club project, however, had been a final one.

The big press conference was held at a hotel in downtown Tokyo. Paul and his colleagues had succeeded in getting the most important Japanese newspapers, magazines, and radio and television networks to attend. Over a hundred journalists showed up to see and hear Björn Borg. Björn, Paul and I took seats on the raised podium along the narrow end of the large conference room, and Björn opened the press conference by welcoming the journalists.

'Nice to be here,' he said, as he always did in similar situations. Björn never prepared himself for such public appearances. He just said what was suitable for the occasion, and therefore he usually said pretty much the same thing. He had a number of favourite expressions, which he used until he tired of them, replacing them with a new set. An analysis of the content of his public statements would show that he usually didn't say anything at all. Sometimes, however, he could surprise his listeners.

After his words of greeting, Björn gave me the floor. I was tense and nervous, but I managed to get through my ten-minute presentation of Björn Borg Design Group fairly well. Then Paul gave a talk about BBDG Asia, following which the journalists were given the chance to ask questions. The idea of embarrassing someone is alien to the Japanese, so although everyone was naturally curious about what had actually happened in Milan, no one dared ask. The result was that, aside from one or two negligible questions, it was very quiet in the room. The journalists sat there thinking about the burning question, but none of them could get it out. You could almost hear how they suffered. Then Björn took a surprising initiative.

'I understand that you are curious about how I feel,' he said with a smile. 'Well, as you can see, I feel just fine. I really appreciate your concern for my health. I have received an unbelievable number of letters from my fans here in Japan and I want to take this opportunity to thank them.'

I looked at him and he was still smiling. As far as I knew, he had not received a single letter from Japan – he had never told me about any – but it certainly sounded good!

'What happened in Milan was entirely innocent,' he continued. 'I simply ate some bad fish and suffered a case of food poisoning. It can happen to anyone. As I said, you can see yourself that I am healthy and in the best of shape!'

Then he smiled his best smile again.

The only difficult question came from an English journalist who wrote for an English-language paper in Japan.

'Björn, hasn't what happened in Milan nonetheless sabotaged part of your image?'

Björn had been asked similar questions before and he gave his standard answer: 'As everyone understands, you can't leave a hospital after just a couple of hours if it is as serious as a number of people have suggested.'

Oh yes, Björn, I thought to myself. Someone with your physical condition and stubbornness can.

Björn thus got through the press conference famously. His performance was humble but sure-footed and he was able to be just as charming as he needed to be. That evening a number of television channels broadcast and rebroadcast the clips in which he made his statements. That alone was worth the whole trip.

We flew to Singapore on 11 April. BBDG Asia was to celebrate its opening that evening with a reception at the hotel where we were staying. Björn and John McEnroe were to play the first match in their Reunion Tour the next day. Paul had pulled together a good turnout for the reception, as well as for the match, and the Swedish ambassador in Singapore was among those present. Björn began by saying it was 'nice to be here', and after a number of other speeches he and I each cut a piece from the large cake decorated with BBDG's logo, symbolically launching our activities in Asia.

John McEnroe and his manager, Sergio Palmeri, arrived at the hotel later that evening. Björn and Loredana had already retired to their suite, so the task of welcoming them was left to me.

Björn had phoned McEnroe at the end of 1988 and got

304

his agreement to participate in the Reunion Tour. They had made several similar tours over the years, filling stadium after stadium. Tennis fans never forgot their intensive battles at Wimbledon and the US Open and gladly took the chance to relive them. This time McEnroe agreed to participate for Björn's sake. Money was unimportant to him; it was strictly a question of doing an old tennis pal a favour. McEnroe had been worried after Björn had had his stomach pumped in Milan and Palmeri had phoned me.

'John wonders how things are with Björn. Will there be any matches in April?'

I had calmed his fears and now everyone was in Singapore, including Ilie Nastase and Manuel Orantes, who were to play doubles matches against the local players prior to each of the Borg and McEnroe matches during the tour.

The World Trade Center in Singapore was packed, which meant that six thousand people had come to see Borg play McEnroe. The two had met over lunch at the hotel. Now evening had come, and they were sitting in the locker-room preparing to go out on the court. I was surprised to see that Björn seemed quite stressed and was remarkably quiet. McEnroe, on the other hand, joked with Palmeri and seemed entirely at ease. As they were to go out to the court, I heard Björn say to John, 'Take it easy out there, now.'

McEnroe laughed. 'You should talk. Don't you remember the time you drove me off the court in Toronto?'

They had played an exhibition match there a few years earlier. McEnroe had showed up entirely out of shape after not having played for a long time. Björn had been in good shape and had been playing matches frequently, and he had no difficulty at all in making John look bad on the court. Such behaviour was not at all popular among the top players, who took exhibition matches as a relaxing way to earn money while playing some real tennis. Moreover, their professional pride demanded of them that the fans be given a good show. The players often agreed that one of them would win the first set and the other the second set, so as to give the crowd the chance to see them play a tie-breaking set. It was an unstated rule that no player was to embarrass another by winning by too large a margin.

The two players arrived on court in cars provided by Volvo, one of the sponsors. Björn was the first to open his car door and step out into the spotlight, and then came John. Their appearance was accompanied by an enthusiastic announcer and thunderous applause from the crowd.

One can hardly claim that McEnroe was especially merciless towards Björn during the match, but Björn was not easy on himself. He ran like a madman and tried to kill the balls as soon as he could. Sometimes he hit them far outside the lines, and when there was a real volley, McEnroe was calmly able to direct the play from the middle of the court. I got the impression that he tried to engage Björn in volleys, but that Björn was trying to make points as fast as he could, only to miss. During the second set Björn was noticeably tired and just hit the balls around a bit here and there. Nonetheless, McEnroe let him win a few games, with a final score of 6–3, 6–3. It was not a good match.

Afterward, Björn was as angry as a bee. He put on a

sour smile during the press conference and said only a few short sentences. In the car on the way back to the hotel he swore, 'What the hell was John doing? Why did he play like that? He could have taken it easy.'

I didn't think there was any reason to complain about McEnroe. Sure, he had toyed a bit with Björn during the match, but he would surely have given his opponent the second set if only Björn hadn't been so tired that he simply threw away so many balls. I hoped that Björn's tension and irritation would disappear before the next match and be replaced by a better mood, better tennis and better entertainment.

We had booked a table for the whole entourage in one of the hotel's dining-rooms for later the same evening. We arrived and sat down one by one: Ile Nastase, Manuel Orantes, Paul Naruse, John McEnroe, Sergio Palmieri and I. And then we waited. And waited. Björn and Loredana never showed up. They didn't send any message, but I understood that they had chosen to have dinner in their suite by themselves. McEnroe wondered what was going on – whether Björn had become ill – and both Paul and I found it an awkward situation. After a while, however, we just ignored the glaring absence, had a very good dinner, and went off to a discothèque. McEnroe, Nastase and Orantes told stories from their tennis careers and, on balance, it turned out to be a very pleasant evening.

Manila, the capital of the Philippines, was the venue for the second match. On the plane that morning I was seated next to John McEnroe. He took out a book and quickly became absorbed in his reading. After dozing for a while, I asked him what he was reading. He showed me the cover of the book: *How to Be a Better Parent*. It seemed a bit comical to me, and I laughed. Here was the greatest madcap and rebel in tennis, or perhaps in the whole world of sports, whose angry outbursts and the disciplinary sanctions against him were so frequently written about fully engrossed in a book on childrearing! He understood what I was thinking, smiled and shrugged his shoulders lightly. Then he told me about his sons, Kevin and Sean. He elaborated on the meaning of giving one's children a healthy sense of self-confidence. I told him about Anna and Cissi and the divorce, and McEnroe listened and asked a number of questions. On that flight he was as different as he could possibly be from the generally accepted picture of McEnroe the irascible loudmouth.

I did get a glimpse of the famous McEnroe temper when we landed in Manila. The Philippines is not a country that has many major sports events, and thus the match between Borg and McEnroe was an occasion of unimaginable magnitude. When we deplaned we were met by a horde of journalists and photographers who wouldn't leave the stars alone for even a fraction of a second. Borg and McEnroe had literally to fight their way through the passageway into the airport terminal. When one of the photographers got too familiar, McEnroe exploded.

'Fuckin' animals!' he screamed. 'You're animals, not people! Leave us alone, damn it!'

What John didn't think about was the fact that relations between the United States and the Philippines were terrible at the time. The US had given temporary asylum to the deposed dictator Marcos, and after that neither the Star-Spangled Banner nor American citizens were very popular in this nation of islands. The journalists and photographers turned on McEnroe, shouting, 'Fuckin' American, go home!'

Björn had become concerned at how things were developing. He looked at his tennis colleague and commented dryly, 'It wasn't such a good idea to say that, John. Now you're going to need bodyguards.'

McEnroe immediately screamed, 'Bodyguards! I want bodyguards!'

He never got any bodyguards, but we were quickly taken to a VIP room, where we were left in peace and quiet until transport to the hotel in Manila could be arranged.

Björn, Loredana and I stayed in the same suite, and I got to see a different side of Loredana. She took very good care of Björn and made sure that I felt at home, too. She was considerably softer and more down-to-earth than she liked to make herself appear in public.

The second match was played that evening. John was worried in light of what had happened at the airport, but when we arrived at the stadium his fears were put to rest. Fifteen thousand excited people had come to watch the two tennis legends play. I sat with Sergio Palmeri, and we looked at each other and smiled when we heard the tremendous cheers that greeted Björn and John. The excitement was so intense that it sent cold shivers down my spine.

Just as he had been the night before, Björn was in a great hurry out on the court. As soon as he had an opportunity he laced into the ball – and it went out.

'What's wrong with Björn?' asked Sergio. 'Why does he want to decide balls so quickly?'

I knew that Björn was in bad shape and therefore afraid that he wouldn't last the match if there were long volleys back and forth, but I just shook my head. This evening's match was not very good, either, but at least Björn did win one set. The final score was 6-1, 3-6, 6-3 to McEnroe. The crowd was enthusiastic. They had seen two remarkable superstars in action and, since their knowledge of tennis was not all that good, they had not been disappointed. Björn was more satisfied that evening and mumbled something along the lines of, 'John was pretty OK this evening.'

Back at the hotel the Philippine Tennis Association had arranged a reception in honour of Björn and John. The two stars did what was expected of them, greeting people, conversing, being pleasant and signing autographs. Afterwards Björn and I sat in the bar and had a beer. Björn said that he was going to go up to the suite to have dinner with Loredana. He wanted me to go with him.

'Why? You can't avoid the others all the time!' I didn't understand why he was always sneaking off. Was he embarrassed because he was out of shape? 'John is starting to wonder what harm he's caused you. Can't all of us eat together, instead?'

Björn agreed, and Loredana joined us. Björn and John sat next to one another and chatted. I sat across the table and joined in the conversation from time to time. It was clear that their friendship was a superficial one. For the most part they just exchanged pleasantries, put the right questions and talked a bit about sports. There were many silences, as if they were each trying to figure out what they would say next.

Early the next morning Sergio Palmeri had to leave the group and fly home to Italy. The rest of us flew on to Taipei for the third day's match. When we checked in at the airport, McEnroe tapped me on the shoulder and said, 'Now you'll have to be my coach.'

'But what about Björn,' I said.

John grinned. He seemed to be in a very good mood. 'Björn? Oh, he has Loredana.'

A few hours later John's mood and mine were considerably worse. We had checked into the hotel and then Björn and I had visited a shop where Seibu, which did a lot of business in Taiwan, sold Björn Borg clothes. By this time it was one o'clock in the afternoon and a press conference was scheduled to begin. There was only one problem: no Björn Borg. The minutes passed by, the twenty or so journalists began to get impatient and McEnroe paced back and forth. When a quarter of an hour had gone by, John came over to me and asked with a calm, but strained voice, 'What is Björn doing? Where is he? Is this the John McEnroe Design Group that's making a public relations trip? It's starting to seem like it.'

Björn arrived a few minutes later. He ignored the fact that he was late and simply took his seat on the podium. I noticed that he was beginning to look worn out. Matches every day, public relations appearances in between and the constant travel were rather exhausting, but I could see that he was slowly beginning to slide back into the role of Björn Borg superstar, the man who was always worshipped and sought after. He was beginning to forget that this was a public relations trip and that its purpose was to restore his reputation and good name.

That evening it got to be unbearable. We had agreed from the beginning that I was to leave the trip the next morning and return to Stockholm, where a series of important meetings awaited me. Gunnar Ström was to show the autumn collection, and I was to give seminars and review sessions for our people and agents abroad in connection with the showing. Björn summoned me at the hotel.

'Come here!' he hissed. 'You knew it, but you go right ahead and fly home!'

'Knew what?'

'That we have to ride several hours on a bus to get to Hiroshima tomorrow. That, of course, is why you want to fly home.'

'I have no idea what you're talking about.'

'Don't give me that! I know very well.'

I contacted Paul and it turned out that there weren't any tickets available for flights from Taipei to Hiroshima, where the final match was to be played on Saturday evening. They were going to have to land at Osaka and take a bus to Hiroshima, a trip that would take a few hours. We decided to get new tickets so that Björn could fly directly to Hiroshima. I phoned everywhere I could think of, even Sweden, where I reached Ingmar Alverdal, who promised to look for tickets at his end. In the middle of this commotion we had to go out to the tennis arena. Björn was still in a terrible mood. He took Loredana with him and sat in one car, while McEnroe and I got into a different one.

'It's too bad it's turned out like this,' said John.

'Yes, he must be very tired,' I said.

We talked all the way to the tennis stadium. McEnroe, who had obviously thought things over quite a bit, did most of the talking.

'It's too bad,' he said. 'I thought that Björn and I would be real pals during this trip, but there's just no way. Why did he bring Loredana along? The idea was that we would have a chance to reminisce about the old days and have fun together. But he just isolates himself. Hell, he just runs away! I know that he has problems, but I still don't understand him. I've gone along with this tour to help him. It's for his sake, you know. He could at least go so far as to try to be decent to me.'

Then McEnroe began to speak of the false glamour that surrounds well-known people, of the superficiality and the lifelong deceptions. He told me about his wife, Tatum, growing up in a family of film stars, which was anything but a secure childhood. And he told me about a good friend of his who had a close relative with a drug problem and how it hurt the whole family. McEnroe shook his head.

'You have to keep your distance from all of this, to know who you are,' he said. 'That's why I am so concerned that my children will have the right upbringing.'

At the arena I continued calling around to find plane tickets. I finally reached Alverdal in Stockholm again, and to my great relief he told me that he had succeeded in getting tickets for a direct flight from Taipei to Hiroshima the next day. I told Björn the good news, but he didn't say a thing.

That evening the stands were only about half full and

313

Björn played as he had during the first match in Singapore, sloppily and carelessly. Once again he hit balls out unnecessarily. John won the first set, but was determined to give Björn the second one. He was even ready to give him the match so that Björn would have at least one victory. But towards the end of the second set Björn had had enough. He waved me over and gave me orders: 'See to it that a car is ready to leave in fifteen minutes.'

And I heard how he told McEnroe: 'It's just going to be this set.'

A few minutes later it was all over. Björn took his rackets, his bag and Loredana and snuck off. I found a few excuses to explain why he wouldn't be showing up at the press conference, and then I went out and got in the car with them.

'I'm really pretty disappointed, Björn,' I said. 'This is, after all, your public relations trip. Why are you going on like this? All the others are standing up for you – just look at John.'

'Go home,' he replied defiantly. 'Just let me do my job.'

'What the hell is wrong with you, anyway? You've got your tickets now. Straighten up! I'm not sneaking out on you, if that's what you think.'

'Don't give me that!'

For the first time during the whole trip Loredana raised her voice. 'Quit arguing! Remember that we're all exhausted.'

At the hotel I asked whether they would be having dinner with the rest of us. Björn shook his head.

'We'll see you in Stockholm next week,' he said.

I wished him luck for the last match and we said goodbye. Loredana gave me a surprisingly warm hug and then they went to their suite.

A bit later I found John and Paul in the hotel bar.

'Is Björn coming?' John asked.

'No,' I said.

He shrugged his shoulders. 'This is China and I like Chinese food. Is that OK?'

We took a taxi to a restaurant. It was late in the evening, but we still ordered a full meal. John started with spring rolls.

'I love this,' he said when the food came.

He took an eager mouthful and then another. Then he froze completely for a second.

'Ants!' he roared so that the servers crouched behind the serving table. 'There are ants in the food!'

We looked. McEnroe was right – ants were crawling all over his plate. He began to spit and blow his nose in his napkin.

'What the hell should I do?' he yelled. 'I'm going to be sick. I might die!'

'Order a large vodka,' I said. 'That cures almost anything.'

The whole thing was a real scream, and Paul and I tried to stifle our laughter. When John saw us a smile began to spread over his face.

'Right! In with the vodka!' he called out, and then he began laughing. He laughed so hard that he had to lean over the table to try to get his breath back.

'Oh, God,' he said. 'I've eaten Taiwanese ants!'

He was served his vodka and drank it so fast that he

coughed and got tears in his eyes. That was the opening shot for a very happy night in Taipei. We went on to a discothèque. John became giggly and talkative and paid for several rounds of drinks. We talked, laughed and had a great time.

The next day I flew back to Sweden while the others flew to Hiroshima. John McEnroe won the last match 6–2, 3–6, 6–2.

CHAPTER TWENTY

The BBDG Ship Sets Sail

Monday, 17 April 1989, was a big day for all of us. That was the day BBDG was transformed from a business concept into a productive company. It was nine o'clock, and Gunnar Ström, the head of BBDG's Clothes division, was about to introduce our first autumn collection. Gunnar was 39 years old, tall and broad, with wavy blond hair. He was an enthusiastic and cheerful man, and a complete professional, with fifteen years' experience in the business. Since joining us as head of BBDG Clothes six months earlier, he had worked intensively with his colleagues to develop the new collections. For a number of reasons, one of the collections Gunnar had concentrated on was underwear. First, he had once worked for Jockey, the market leader in underwear in Scandinavia, and he knew how it should be made. Second, underwear is one of the most profitable types of clothing. Third, Rohdi Heintz had already designed Björn Borg underwear during his years with Eiser, and it had sold well, so Gunnar 'only' had to improve and develop the product.

Gunnar gave the sign, the lights were dimmed and a pair of synchronised projectors began showing a series of pictures of the underwear, the equally important packaging and the specially designed display cases.

About forty people had come to the showing at

BBDG's new offices in Alvik, a suburb of Stockholm. These were our distributors, and they came from the United States, Canada, Italy, Greece, Switzerland, Spain and Singapore, as well as Sweden. We had finally achieved the goal of presenting *one* collection that would be sold in *all* markets, departing from the former practice of each market determining what its collection would look like. Now the distributors had come to assess the sales potential of our new products for their markets and to place their orders.

I sat at the back of the room and watched people's reactions. Since this was the very first presentation of BBDG-produced products, the mood was optimistic and enthusiastic, but also a bit strained. I was reminded of the première of a film or play. So far, the reviews seemed to be good. But, then, Gunnar and his colleagues were the best people in the business in Sweden.

It was nice to be back in the normal swing of things. I had arrived home from Taiwan the day before and gone directly to a Stavsborg that was full of visiting distributors. Optimism, involvement and faith in the future characterised BBDG during those days. We had finally begun! The memory of the Milan incident had faded and no one realised that a threatening shadow loomed over the enterprise. I myself had stopped thinking about Björn and the mood swings he had demonstrated on our trip to the Far East. Instead, I was caught up in the enthusiasm in Alvik. It was great to be with the gang again.

After lunch Rolf Skjöldebrand took the stage. He talked about the promotional campaign that was to come.

It was strategically planned and consisted of two parts: image advertising in trade journals and fashion magazines throughout the world and, when we had developed more products of our own, product advertising in various markets with the distributors.

An hour later it was time for the high point of the day. It was now Anders Arnborger's turn. He and fashion designer Thomas Hedenstedt had designed the collection of tennis clothes we had christened 'Active Wear'. For years I had dreamed of this: marketing tennis wear under Björn's name that had been designed and produced in cooperation with the former star himself. The world's best tennis clothes made by the world's best tennis player. In view of Björn's previous endorsement contract with Fila, we had not been able to do it until now.

Again the lights were dimmed and the projectors began to hum. The first pictures of BBDG's tennis wear collection were met by spontaneous and well-deserved applause. The clothes had been designed in accordance with Björn's own ideas. The material was very airy and the cut ensured that nothing was too tight. The jersey was longer in back than in front so that it stayed in place even when you served, and the BBDG logo, a green rectangle with the words Björn Borg Design Group stacked in four lines, appeared right in the middle of the chest. The pockets in the shorts were made of an elastic material so that they readily accommodated the second serve ball.

It took three more days to present the various collections Gunnar's division had designed. Everything was characterised by two things, quality and functionalism. At last we were on our way, moving away from Björn Borg the man to Björn Borg the trademark. The BBDG ship had cast off and the real cruise could now begin. I could feel that we had wind in our sails. Despite everything.

I had still not invested the $2 million that was to be my contribution to the increased share capital. Of course, I didn't have $2 million in cash and had no desire to sell any of my property. Following the events in Milan, it proved to be difficult to borrow money for the purpose, but John Webber and Julian Jakobi were very anxious to help me and I was grateful to them. They had initially suggested a bank in London called Aitken & Hume International, in which IMG owned a good deal of stock. That may have been one of the reasons Aitken & Hume denied my request for a loan. Then John and Julian quickly put me in touch with another London bank, the FennoScandia Bank, which granted the loan. I put up Stavsborg and my shares in Björn Borg Enterprises Ltd as collateral.

On 18 April 1989 the $2 million was transferred. I felt very good since it had taken such a long time to raise the money and Björn had put a lot of pressure on me. I was a bit surprised about John and Julian's unusual helpfulness when it came to getting the bank loan, but I was sure that Björn had told them to help me. Of Björn's share of the increased share capital, $4.2 million had been paid on 10 March, but only $1.2 million of that went to increase the share capital in BBDG, while the remaining $3 million went to paying off a loan BBDG had taken out with Aitken & Hume International, a loan for which Björn had already put up private collateral. It would have been better for the company if Björn had put the whole $4.2 million into

BBDG and BBDG had repaid the bank in the autumn after it had made deliveries to its customers and received their payments.

Despite urging and requests from a number of directions, Björn had refused to invest the remaining $1.8 million he was supposed to contribute until I had produced my share.

'But, Björn, you have to invest the money. You know that we need it very badly,' I had said.

'Oh no,' he said, 'I'm not going to pay until you get your money.'

'But the bank's the one that will determine when that happens, and it's going to be very soon. The most important thing is that the company has the capital as soon as possible.'

'Don't give me that. I'm not paying until you do.'

By 20 April Björn's payment still hadn't been made, so I phoned him again.

'Now I've put in my money. Why haven't you put yours in? You said it was available at any time.'

'Oh, that'll be taken care of.'

'Björn, this is really very important. You have to put the money in now!'

Nonetheless, we had to wait another week.

At about the same time Gullis phoned me. 'You have to pay Björn your option money. He has been after me about it a number of times.'

'Sure,' I said. 'But if the $100,000 was for 40 per cent of the shares and I am only getting 25 per cent, then I should be paying $62,400. Isn't that logical?'

He called me a day later. 'I'm sorry, Lasse. You have to pay the $100,000. Björn exploded when I mentioned the figure you gave me. And he wants the money immediately. He's off to the US and needs dollars.'

I sighed and did what I had been doing all spring, gave into Björn's demands. But it didn't feel right. Did he have to squeeze every dollar he could out of me? Couldn't he be fair? And why couldn't he phone me himself? Why did he always use a messenger? For the moment, however, I had to pay Björn only $60,000; by 1 June I had paid him exactly $100,062.

During this period Björn devoted himself to his private life. He was with Loredana most of the time, and they saw a good deal of Henning Sjöström, who had been a very successful lawyer in the 1960s and 1970s. They were preparing themselves for the custody battle over Robin.

The Milan incident had put a real brake on BBDG's forward movement and created a crisis of confidence in the minds of many of our business contacts, especially banks and suppliers. Moreover, it had brought significant additional costs in the form of extra public relations activities, difficulties in selling BBDG in new markets and cancelled orders. We had also lost valuable time – every day the company stood still cost us money.

The paralysis had now begun to disappear and the wheels to turn again. The board of directors was working to solve the company's future financing needs. Gotabanken had expressed the desire that we recruit another bank so that the risk could be shared. The bank made it clear that it would not broaden its trade credits in the manner it had earlier promised and therefore, on the advice of Jakobi and Webber, we went further with our discussions with DBL. That's where we were going to find the solution.

Our next board meeting was held in Stockholm on 19 May 1989. Håkan Frisinger had emphasised the importance of the board having good control over the situation and therefore wanted the meetings to be more frequent than before; the BBDG ship needed to be piloted expertly past all the reefs and rocks. Keith Harris and a colleague of his from DBL had been invited to attend and had prepared various alternatives for our financing.

Johan Denekamp made the first presentation, responding to the board's request for a worst-case study of the numbers for the 1989 fiscal year. This is always done when a company is seeking investors to ensure that the financing will be adequate. Denekamp's figures pointed to a worst-case loss of $7.4 million.

Webber asked me to comment on those figures. I confirmed that the company was developing according to plan, but that our development costs had increased. The loss would be greater than the $3.8 million Denekamp had estimated at the last board meeting, but in my judgement the loss would be no greater than $4.2 million. The loss was made up entirely of development costs, such as the purchase of companies, the registration of trademarks and the development of the organisation. These costs would be balanced in the normal way by being prorated over the next few years, when revenues would be produced.

The board instructed me to present these figures more

precisely at the next meeting and to present our cost savings in detail.

We then turned to the question of financing. Following its previous discussions, the board unanimously agreed that we needed total credits of between $14 million and $16 million to finance the business in the long-run. This amount included Gotabanken's credit for $4 million, which meant that we required an additional $10 million to $12 million. Again, this estimate was based on the worst-case scenario. These monies would secure BBDG's position until it began producing a profit and became self-supporting.

Keith Harris responded with a number of different financing suggestions. In return DBL demanded that it be given an option to buy 20 per cent of the shares in BBDG at a price reflecting the Price Waterhouse appraisal.

During the lunch-break Björn huddled with Webber and Jakobi to discuss DBL's proposal. I was not invited to participate despite the fact that I thought my views as one of the two shareholders might be of some interest. They weren't. Following his discussion with the two Englishmen, Björn left; he had other things to do.

When the meeting resumed Webber informed me and the rest of the board that Björn was receptive to the DBL proposal. I sat there in the helpless position of a minority owner while it was decided that I should work with DBL on the financing alternative that the board had chosen.

Coming to life again, I reported on international developments. Seibu had announced that its Björn Borg sales had increased by 25 per cent in Japan and by 60 per cent in Taiwan in the first quarter of 1989 compared to the first quarter of 1988. From those results we concluded that our strategy was working. The Milan incident had not hurt sales, because the Björn Borg trademark was well established in those markets and Borg the man did not affect them. They had reached the point that we intended to achieve in all markets. Seibu had also accepted for sale in the Japanese market one of the first produced lines designed by BBDG, the tennis collection.

In Canada our negotiations for a Björn Borg Sports Club at Whistler Mountain were continuing as planned, while I had informed Saul Schoenberg that no more investments should be made in the American market in the immediate future and that we would reduce our costs unless our revenues met projections.

The other reports by each of the divisional heads confirmed that all our activities were going according to plan. The board adjourned to a warehouse outside Stockholm, where the first prototype of the special Björn Borg Shop had been built. The shops were to be manufactured in Sweden, packed in ready-to-assemble parts and sent out to various markets. We had invested several million and were ready to open shops around the world.

I think that all of us on the board felt we were on target. But one thing bothered me – and Håkan Frisinger, too, it seems. Following this board meeting, he said, with a certain emphasis, 'The most important thing for a board is that its members have only the best interests of the company in mind. There must never be any doubt about that. I am uncertain about the Englishmen on that point.' No, it didn't feel like we were all on the same team. Björn, Webber and Jakobi were playing on one side of the field,

Frisinger and I on the other. Björn Gullström occupied a middle ground. Personally, I relied a great deal on Frisinger's experience, and I couldn't understand why Björn and the Englishmen didn't do the same.

To my surprise, Björn invited me to a party at Viking's Hill the first Saturday in June. I was in Monte Carlo, where BBDG was to hold its first design conference that weekend. I had neither the time nor the desire to go to the party, but Ingmar Alverdal phoned me and urged me to come. In the end I reluctantly allowed myself to be talked into it.

As far as I knew this was the first real party Björn had had at Viking's Hill despite the fact that he had lived there since 1986. There were about twenty guests and the party began in the afternoon. The high point and real reason for the party was the Jerry race. A Jerry boat is a one-man boat with an outboard motor; it's small, fast and somewhat unstable and fun to drive. Björn and I had each bought one the summer before. He and Ingmar had rounded up a sufficient number of them to allow us to have the race.

Everyone took the race very seriously. We would start at the pier, go around a small island in the bay and return to the pier, a distance of about a mile.

'I'll bet you won't even get in the boat,' Björn grinned at me, and Rune agreed.

I would have good reason to laugh later, for I won my heat and went on to the finals, while Björn was last in his and was eliminated. And not only that. When he began to step out of his boat on to the pier, the boat tipped to the side and he fell in the water with a big splash right in front of me and the cheering party-goers.

'God punishes some people directly,' I said to Rune, who was standing next to me.

Despite these minor setbacks Björn was happier and more open than he had been for a long time. It was one of those days when he let his sun shine upon me, and it shone brightly. He seemed almost to forget the other guests. I had a feeling that he was not being very sincere.

Loredana, on the other hand, was not having one of her better days. She was surly the entire evening and stayed in the background. Some of the guests had brought their children, who, of course, made a lot of noise, running all over the garden and the big house. Loredana became even more sullen when a couple of the children explored the room that had been furnished for Robin, discovered the bed in the shape of a Ferrari that she had ordered for him from the car maker and began playing on it. She chased the children out of the room and was even more subdued afterwards. Björn's mother watched her with rising irritation. Later, when she passed the sofa where Björn and I were sitting, she snapped, 'Look how she's behaving! What a terrible hostess. What will the guests think?'

Björn ignored his mother's remark. He had made up his mind to have a good time and nothing was going to disturb him. I hardly reacted, either, for Margaretha had always been critical of her son's choice of women.

The next board meeting was to be held in London on 26–27 June. Before that time we were to provide DBL with all the information it needed to make an exact appraisal of the company in its efforts to secure financing for us. This appraisal would differ from Price Waterhouse's six months earlier in three ways: it would take Johan Denekamp's worst-case figures into consideration, it came after the Milan incident and we now had sales figures.

Orders for 404,000 items of clothing had been placed in the spring for delivery in the autumn. The comparable figure the year before had been 127,000 items under the old Björn Borg Menswear label. Our most important market, Scandinavia, was right on budget, with sales totalling $6.8 million. This meant that Björn Borg clothes were achieving a profit in Sweden for the first time since Eiser started producing them in 1983. The preliminary budget for 1990 showed sales of $9.8 million and a profit for BBDG Scandinavia of $1 million.

Björn and I frequently discussed the situation. He seemed entirely convinced that DBL would have no problem finding the financing.

'You can relax,' he said. 'Things are fine now. It's going to work out.'

John Webber confirmed this. To my great surprise, he had taken matters entirely into his own hands and met DBL representatives in London without informing me or the other members of the board. That was difficult to understand, for I was the one who had been instructed by the board to conduct our dealings with DBL. However, I was pleased that DBL was going to support us. That's what Webber's friends at DBL had said. Sometimes it really is nice to have IMG despite everything, I thought to myself.

On the basis of the sales figures and careful analysis of the company, DBL valued BBDG at $26.4 million in May 1989, which represented the lowest price an investor would be prepared to pay for the company.

Fifth Avenue is one of the best addresses in Manhattan, and Saul Schoenberg, president of BBDG-USA, opened the company's office there with some fanfare on 21 June. As chairman of the board of our American subsidiary, I naturally joined Björn and Loredana for the occasion. Hundreds of people – buyers from the great department store chains Saks, Bloomingdales, Nordstrom and Sears, financiers and analysts from IMG and DBL, fashion makers and commentators, press and television journalists and photographers – crowded the office, showrooms and storage area. The correspondent for a Swedish newspaper described the scene:

> The waitresses were blonde and had flowers in their hair. Along with the champagne, they served herring and potato on pieces of bread no larger than one krona coins. Björn Borg was inviting the New York fashion world to a Swedish midsummer eve this Wednesday evening.
>
> Whether this Swedish version of exotic Swedish rites or the chance to be photographed with the still remembered tennis star Björn Borg was the big attraction, Björn Borg Design Group succeeded in getting a spoiled New York to flock to the company's new showrooms and offices, which have just opened in a prestigious location across the street from the Plaza Hotel on Fifth Avenue.

Earlier in the week Björn had been a guest on the popular American morning television programme *Good Morning, America*, where, in an interview worth millions in advertising, he talked about his life as a businessman and gave a fashion commentary as models paraded BBDG collections. Now he went round with a smile on his face. Wearing a light suit, a white shirt and a tie, with his hair cut rather short, Björn looked like a healthy fashion king.

'What great vibrations!' he exclaimed several times, letting himself be interviewed right and left by various people from the media.

Björn didn't like journalists, but he still loved being the centre of attention. That was fine with me, for it was good for business, at least in situations like this. Sometimes I wondered whether he would be satisfied with being 'that green rectangle', the Björn Borg image, or whether he would want to have a more prominent role. I laughed to myself a little when I saw him smiling into the cameras at the behest of the photographers.

BBDG-USA was a wholly-owned subsidiary of Björn Borg Enterprises Ltd, but it was Saul Schoenberg who bore all the responsibility. He ran the company and reported regularly to the leadership in Europe. Saul had been conscientious and very careful in building up the company; now he had to show us that he could also *sell* BBDG products. Judging on the opening, it seemed that he would make a go of it.

CHAPTER TWENTY ONE

'I'm going to bomb Stavsborg'

Julian Jakobi hosted a barbecue in his garden on the evening before the board of directors was to meet in the city at the law firm of Nabarro Nathanson, which often acted for IMG London. In addition to Julian's family, those attending included his assistant at IMG, Tim Sice, Björn and Loredana, Håkan Frisinger, Stig and me.

'Isn't Keith Harris here? He should be here, shouldn't he?' Björn asked when we arrived. He had been at Julian's for a number of hours, going over some papers.

The rest of us Swedes also wondered where the head of DBL's London office was. The most important point on the board's agenda was the issue of financing, and Keith was to make the presentation. Of course he should have been at the party.

'Oh dear,' exclaimed Julian in embarrassment. 'I thought Keith knew we were meeting here. I'll go phone him straight away.'

He reached Harris, who showed up half an hour later, as smiling and pleasant as always.

The meal was prepared and served on the terrace. Björn complimented Jakobi on the attractive garden furniture and asked him where he had bought it. Julian blushed and mumbled something. The fact was that Björn had given him the furniture as a wedding present. Oh, well. The mood was generally relaxed, although most of us were thinking about the meeting the next day, a meeting that we hoped would solve our liquidity problems once and for all.

Later that evening Julian came over to me with a document in one hand. It was Björn's and my partnership agreement. I realised that this was what Björn and Julian had been working on that afternoon.

'We'll go in and look at it, and then you'll sign it,' Julian said.

I was completely taken aback. Why was there such a hurry all of a sudden? Stig and I followed Björn and Julian into the house.

'But I can't sign this now,' I said. 'Good lord, it's an important document.'

'You must sign this evening,' Björn insisted. 'Otherwise there won't be any deal with DBL tomorrow.'

'What are you doing, Björn?' I asked. 'Do you mean I'm not to have the chance to go over the final version with my lawyer?'

He shrugged his shoulders. 'I just want to test you – do you understand?'

It was a typical Björn Borg reply. I wasn't entirely sure how he wanted to test me, but I began to understand what he was after. I knew, and so did Björn, that DBL thought BBDG's leadership was very competent, a prerequisite if the company were to succeed. The fact that I was highly respected by DBL made Björn insecure. Was I going to try to get the upper hand over him via DBL? He obviously considered such a bizarre development fully possible. If I signed the partnership contract, which regulated his and my rights and duties, before DBL came into the picture, however, the balance would be 'restored'. That would guarantee that Björn would continue to be in full control.

Julian asked Stig to help me go through the agreement, and I decided, not for the first time, to acquiesce. For the sake of the enterprise'. . .

I read through the document, which outlined our mutual rights and obligations. There were only two points that required any discussion. Our contract with Whistler Mountain contained provisions for a luxury sports cabin, and Björn wanted to add a clause to our agreement stating that the cabin was to be his private property and not the company's. Since he would be the one to use it most, I agreed. For my part, I demanded that it should be expressly stated that Björn was giving exclusive use of his name to Björn Borg Enterprises Ltd. This, of course, was the foundation upon which our company rested. At first Björn objected, but he thought it over and agreed; of course, Björn Borg Enterprises Ltd had the sovereign rights to his name. After that, Björn and I signed our partnership contract.

The board meeting started at 10.45 the next morning in Nabarro Nathanson's conference room. The first item concerned financing. I reviewed the information that had been presented to DBL and we agreed that it was complete. In addition, we agreed that $4 million was a sufficient amount of bridge financing to open letters of credit that would allow the manufacturers to begin production of the autumn fashions we had sold. We wanted to have that line of credit as insurance in the event that DBL had not yet found optimal, long-term financing. We decided to delay a vote on the question until Keith Harris had presented DBL's proposal that afternoon.

Keith did not arrive as expected. When we could wait

no longer, we phoned his office. He sounded very confused.

'I don't know what has happened,' he said. 'There's some problem in the US. I think it's best for you to come over here, because it might take some time.'

This news did not in and of itself need to alarm us, but we adjourned the meeting until seven o'clock the next morning so that Gullis, Stig and I could go to DBL's offices to find out what had happened and await further news.

There was a lot going on in DBL's office. About ten people were working on the question of BBDG's financing, and they were running all over the place, making phone calls, sending faxes and talking all at once. The atmosphere was terribly tense, almost hysterical. We asked Keith what really had happened, but he just shook his head.

'I don't know. The US hasn't approved our proposal yet.'

'But you had been given the go-ahead to arrange for BBDG's financing!'

'Yes, I know, but something must have happened. It's still morning in New York – we'll just have to wait.'

Harris hadn't said a word about any problems the night before, but had seemed as relaxed and positive as ever. Now he was very upset and nervous. The situation was really confusing. What could have happened? Everything had been as good as done! We decided to stay until there was some news.

The word came at two in the morning. DBL's head office in the United States had said no; Harris was to break off negotiations with BBDG. Harris was as dumbfounded as we were. He couldn't give us any satisfactory explanation, but eventually we would learn that because of Michael Milken's questionable dealings, DBL was a giant with feet of clay and its leadership had put an end to all major engagements. DBL would declare bankruptcy just six months later in what amounted to Wall Street's greatest crash in modern times.

We returned to the hotel tired, in despair and so disappointed we could have cried. As we sat down in my room and tried to figure out what we would tell the board the next morning, the phone rang. It was Björn, who had just returned from dinner with Loredana. He wanted to know how things had gone.

'You won't believe it, but DBL said no,' I said in a low voice.

He came to my room a minute or two later.

'Who said no? Was it the Americans, the US office?'

'It seems that way,' I said.

Björn looked like the sky had fallen in. For once he had a hard time maintaining his composure. It had been his confidants who had suggested that we turn to DBL in direct contradiction of my advice that we rely on a more conservative and solid English financial institution.

Björn stood there silent for a moment. He just didn't know what to do. How was he to repair his Englishmen's failure?

'OK,' he said after a minute or so. 'How much do we need altogether to avoid finding ourselves in this situation again? Give me a figure and don't underestimate it.'

'A maximum of $10 million,' said Stig.

'Good, then I know,' said Björn. 'Go to bed and sleep now. We'll take care of this one way or another.'

At seven o'clock the next morning I informed the other members of the board that the deal with DBL had fallen apart. Björn announced that he did not want to put any more of his own money into the company, but that he was assuming responsibility for finding alternative sources of financing.

At the office in Stockholm the phone rang constantly. Subsidiaries around the world, suppliers, colleagues, creditors – everyone wanted to know what the future looked like. I maintained close contact with Björn, Frisinger, Webber and Jakobi. Following the DBL fiasco, Webber and Jakobi reverted to their tired old roles of trying to find fault. They sent IMG's Tom Sice to the United States to go over BBDG-USA's books. Sice found that Saul Schoenberg thought the prospects so promising that he wanted to buy BBDG-USA. He made a serious offer, which Björn rejected on the advice of Webber and Jakobi. Accepting the offer, it seemed to me, would have been a good way to raise money to put back into the company. Once again, the trio on the other half of the playing field was acting oddly: one moment our US subsidiary was a burden, but the next moment an excellent opportunity to sell it was rejected.

Björn had promised to try to arrange for the financing we needed, but I guarded against his possible failure by making a number of calls of my own from Stavsborg. Through a firm in Monte Carlo, I found out that a Canadian company called Midanco was interested in investing in BBDG. I contacted Midanco immediately, and it sent two of its analysts to Stockholm to examine our books. Although Björn came to Stavsborg to meet the analysts, he seemed to be surprisingly uninterested in what they had to say.

Midanco made an offer of $10 million for 25 per cent of the shares, which was in line with the Price Waterhouse appraisal. All of us thought it was a very advantageous offer. All of us except Björn. He rejected the offer and the Canadians had to return home empty-handed.

When I asked Björn what he was doing, he said that he had a better offer from his financiers. Just who they were or what their offer was he could not tell me yet. He promised to get back to me. Once again I foolishly relied on him.

Immediately after the London meeting Björn had asked to have Price Waterhouse's written appraisal sent to Viking's Hill. In early July he had flown to Italy to meet the financiers he had in mind. When he returned I went to Viking's Hill. Everything was coming to a head and I wanted to have it out with him about Jakobi and Webber's find-a-fault tactics; about the strange relationship between the two of us; about the events in Milan, without which we would have had access to all the credit in the world; about his endless suspicions, which meant we could never predict what he would do from one moment to the next; about his parents' continued influence over him; and about rumours that led me to suspect he was continuing his drug habits.

Everything was at risk. I was thinking about the company and my colleagues and myself. I would personally lose my entire fortune if the company were forced to close because we were unable to find financiers. And who *were* his financiers, anyway? Björn had remained very quiet on that point.

I found Björn sitting in a lounge chair on the terrace.

'Björn, I want you to clear things up for me. This simply can't go on any longer. Everyone is waiting for the news. You have to tell me what's happening! If I'm the problem and you don't have confidence in me any more, then I'll resign. You can continue without me. Appoint another managing director, if you wish. All you have to do in that case is to buy me out. I'll sell my shares on the spot.'

He looked at me and smiled his normal self-confident smile. 'No, no, it's nothing like that. We're going to fight. We can't give up now.'

'But how are things going with the financing? When are you going to know?'

'I haven't got anything definite yet,' he said. 'But I can tell you that it's 99 per cent done. It's going to work out.'

'Can't you tell me who's involved?'

'No, not yet. They are Italian investors, but they want to remain anonymous for the time being. In any case, they're interested in investing $10 million, and for that they want 30 per cent of the shares. I'm to have 55 per cent and you 15.'

There he went again. He had power and he flaunted it. He was playing with me like a cat with a mouse.

'No, wait a minute – I'll have 57 per cent and you, 13 . . . Yes, that's exactly how we'll do it.'

'Do I have any choice?' I asked.

'No,' he grinned.

As I drove back to Stavsborg I was at my wits' end. I had been bombarded by questions from people nervous about the company's future for weeks and I hadn't known what to answer. And now I'd had this humiliating meeting with Björn, who wouldn't tell either me or the board anything about his plans for financing the company! His plan to reduce my share of the company to a mere 13 per cent was something I didn't have the energy to worry about for the moment. The most important issue was whether he was telling the truth about having financiers who were ready to invest in BBDG. I had an uncomfortable feeling about that, but there was nothing I could do except wait until the next board meeting, scheduled for Thursday, 13 July.

On Wednesday evening Håkan Frisinger, John Webber and Julian Jakobi arrived to spend the night at Stavsborg, where the meeting was to be held the next day. Stig had come out earlier in the week, and he and I had worked with our colleagues in the firm on a revised liquidity budget for the coming year. Late that evening the two Englishmen and I sat in my library discussing the future. Eventually we got around to talking about the new monies. I had spent a lot of time wondering who the new investors were and now I had a chance to find out.

'Where is the money coming from, anyhow?' I asked.

'We don't really know,' John said.

'You must be kidding. Of course you know!'

'No, and that's the truth. He hasn't told us.' He squirmed in his chair. 'Just as long as it isn't Mafia money, for if it is, I don't want to be involved in this any more.'

'Why would you think it's Mafia money? I thought the three of you had worked this out together.'

It came as a total surprise to me that John and Julian weren't privy to Björn's plans. I later found out that it was true. Stig told me he had bumped into Julian at an airport in Paris and he was boiling with rage. Julian had been on his way to Milan to meet the new financiers when Björn had got word to him by phone that he needn't come. But Mafia money? That must have been very unlikely. I was more and more confused.

The next morning the two Björns, Gullström and Borg, had each driven out and joined us for breakfast. Afterwards Håkan opened the meeting and immediately gave Björn the floor.

Looking happy, Björn told us, 'I have decided to invest another $10 million in share capital in Björn Borg Enterprises via a company that I own and control completely. Of that, $2 million has already been sent from a Swiss bank to my account in Liechtenstein.'

He said that the money would be in his account no later than 17 July for further transfer to Björn Borg Enterprises Ltd. The remaining $8 million was to arrive between 18 and 21 July. The company was Italian, and he once again assured us that he controlled it completely.

As chairman of the board, Håkan repeated what Björn had said and asked him to confirm that his summary was correct.

'Yes,' Björn said without a moment's hesitation.

Sighs of relief were heard around the table – BBDG had been saved!

There was one person who remained unconvinced. During a break in the meeting Björn Gullström took Håkan aside and suggested that Björn's information should be checked. Gullström himself offered to call the Swiss bank to check whether the transfer had been ordered. Frisinger immediately said no.

'When the majority shareholder tells us something, we have to believe it. If someone doesn't rely on him, then that person should question his continued membership on the board.'

Following Björn's positive news, Stig presented the

revised liquidity budget that we had put together during the week, giving an account of the expenditures and revenues for the coming year. Everyone was satisfied. The new monies would suffice. The meeting ended with a feeling that everything was under control. I looked at Björn, who appeared a bit pensive.

When he noticed my gaze, he smiled. 'Trust papa, everything will be fine.'

Anna and Cissi were also at Stavsborg at the time. I thought it was good for my daughters to be around to see with their own eyes what was happening, even if they did so from some distance. They, too, had been worried, of course, but now they could ask Håkan Frisinger, for example, anything they wanted to know about the company, and he would take time to explain. Now that the crisis was over we planned to take a holiday together. I had been working nearly two years with just a few days off now and then, and it was high time for me to slow down. But first I had the pleasant task of spreading the good news. I called the office in Monte Carlo first, then the one in New York, then Singapore and then some of our creditors. There were sighs of relief and words of satisfaction all around.

Two days later I was sitting in my library and watching television with Eva, Anna, Cissi and a couple of friends when the phone rang.

'It's for me,' I said immediately and went out in the hall to answer it. Somehow I knew who it would be. In my bones I had known the call would come and what it would be about.

341

'Hi,' said Björn. 'I'm awfully sorry, but the Italians have backed out.'

He was lying, I was sure of it.

'Lasse, we have to issue a press communiqué immediately to announce that we've failed to secure our long-term financing.'

He had never used such terms before. It sounded as if someone had told him what to say. I immediately protested.

'Never! We can't do that. The first thing we have to do is to call an extraordinary meeting of the board. I'm going to call Håkan and tell him that the money isn't coming. I'll call you later!'

I hung up without another word. He's lying, I thought. He must be crazy! And the first thing he wants to do is to go to the press? Are the employees to learn from the newspapers that we haven't any financing?

I went back to my family and friends, and told them that it was Björn who had called and what he had said. They were as upset as I was.

I reached Frisinger at his summer cottage outside of Gothenburg. I told him the news.

'This doesn't make any sense. The money had already been sent!'

Of course, I thought, it had been sent to Björn's account in Liechtenstein.

'What do you intend to do?' Håkan asked.

'Fight to the last. Try to find a new investor.'

'Do that, but you have only a week. If you haven't found the money by then, we will have to stop paying our bills. There's no more time left. Otherwise the members of the board can be held personally responsible.'

I phoned Björn.

'I've spoken with Håkan and we've decided to hold an extraordinary meeting of the board on Thursday. I don't intend to give up. Now *I'm* going to look for a solution.'

He sounded flabbergasted. He muttered something and then we hung up.

Thoughts were flying around in my head. How was I going to find someone willing to invest $10 million? I had only a week and it was the middle of the summer holidays. I paced back and forth like a lost soul. The first thing to do was to find someone who could come up with the money. And then that someone would have to take the time to go through all our books and documents and reach a decision. All that in just less than a week . . .

I began phoning every possible contact I could think of, and I asked Håkan if he would do the same. When the situation seemed entirely hopeless the phone rang. It was Peter Gyllenhammar, one of the most successful Swedish financiers of the 1980s. He owned the Mercurius Group, which specialised in buying up companies with problems, restructuring them and making them profitable. I had met Gyllenhammar when I decided to rent out Stavsborg. It was too expensive and impractical for me to live at Stavsborg when I had to spend so much time at our headquarters in Monte Carlo. Gyllenhammar had indicated his interest through an agent and had come out a number of times to look the place over.

'How are things going? When can I move in?' he asked.

'I'm sorry, but I guess I'm not going to be renting the place out after all,' I said, and then told him the whole story.

'Let's forget about Stavsborg,' he said at once. 'Let's

343

discuss what I can do for BBDG instead. I'll come out tomorrow.'

Thus began the most intensive work week of my life.

We were lucky to locate Gunnar Ström in Monte Carlo, where he was on holiday. He and Stig had immediately to go over all the available figures and information about BBDG that were in the main office there.

Gyllenhammar moved into Stavsborg on a temporary basis and examined the figures as they arrived by fax from Monte Carlo. When it came to discerning the reality behind the numbers and interpreting annual reports he was one of the cleverest people I have ever met. Gyllenhammar literally swallowed the information. He asked precise questions, analysed the answers and went on to the next task. After two days Peter was ready to discuss with the leadership of Mercurius whether they should make an offer for part of BBDG.

I tried to contact Björn several times, but without any success. He was usually out in the archipelago. Eventually, however, I reached him.

'It might work out in the end after all,' I told him. 'Peter Gyllenhammar and Mercurius are interested.'

Björn was silent.

'Gyllenhammar wants to meet with you. He is here at Stavsborg. Can you come over?' I continued.

'What's the point?' He sounded totally indifferent.

'What the hell do you mean? We can save the company, damn it!'

'Yeah, yeah . . . we'll see whether they make an offer.'

That was a very strange reaction to what was obviously our last chance. The alternative was to close down the company. At least he promised to come to the extra-ordinary board meeting that was to be held on Thursday.

I phoned Håkan on Tuesday.

'It sounds entirely unbelievable,' I said, 'but it looks as if we might save the company.'

I told him that Mercurius were considering making an offer for a share of the stock in BBDG.

'Now we need your help, Håkan,' I said.

He immediately jumped into his car and drove the 300 miles from Gothenburg to Stavsborg. While Frisinger was still in his car, Björn phoned me in a rage, for reasons I could not even guess.

'What the hell are you doing?' he screamed.

He went absolutely wild. 'Well, quit it, damn it! I forbid you to do any more! I'll come out and bomb Stavsborg if you don't stop!'

For the first time during this period I was really frightened. This was madness. A normal majority share-holder would have cheered if it suddenly seemed that his company could be rescued from a threatened bankruptcy. I wondered what Gyllenhammar would have thought had he been listening to the conversation. It was clear that Björn had already decided to close down the company at any price, but *why*?

Håkan arrived in the afternoon and immediately began to negotiate with Gyllenhammar, who had got the approval of his group to continue discussions. Tim Sice, Jakobi's assistant, was there too. He was in constant contact with his principals, Björn, John and Julian, negotiating and reporting to them on how things were developing.

Frisinger said that it was important that the offer be in

writing and that it be confirmed by Mercurius's board. For his part, Gyllenhammar insisted that Gotabanken continue to be BBDG's main bank. Frisinger immediately called Ulf Holmström at Gota International in Gothenburg, who promised to present the question of the bank's leadership as soon as possible. A few hours later Holmström called to say that the bank had decided to back us up.

On Wednesday Peter Gyllenhammar got written confirmation of the final offer from the members of his board. Mercurius would purchase 32 per cent of the shares for $9.4 million. Björn would own 51 per cent, thereby remaining the majority shareholder and retaining control of the company, while I would have 17 per cent. Björn was also given an option to buy back Mercurius's shares for the same price plus reasonable interest on the money. The contract would secure the survival of the company, the employees' jobs and payments to the suppliers and other creditors.

On Wednesday evening we once again sat in the library at Stavsborg and thought about the next day's board meeting.

'Well done,' said Håkan. 'I am very impressed by the fact that you have been able to find new investors so rapidly. Let us now hope for the best.'

'Thank you,' I said. 'Without you we couldn't have done it.'

There was a nervous and cautious mood in the kitchen the next morning. No one had much of an appetite; everyone simply nursed their coffee instead. Björn was the only one we were waiting for. Neither John Webber nor Julian Jakobi was on hand, which was very strange. Björn

Gullström had come out the day before, and I could see how tense and pale he was. Was this the day that he and Björn would part company after so very many years? If this was the end, then I certainly felt Gullis deserved a better one. He had been a steady rock for Björn for nearly two decades.

Björn came in and said hello, whereupon Frisinger immediately took him aside. As chairman of the board, he had asked to meet privately with the majority shareholder before the board meeting began. They went upstairs for a few minutes.

When they came down, Frisinger shook his head in resignation and said, 'It's just as well we get this over with as soon as possible.'

We sat down at the kitchen table. Håkan phoned Webber and Jakobi in London so that they would be able to participate by phone.

'The only thing to do is to go directly to the heart of the matter,' said Frisinger, taking up a document and opening the meeting. 'We have received an offer from the Mercurius Group, which I have in my hand.' He briefly presented the contents of the offer.

Björn immediately asked, 'Is it signed?'

'Yes, and it has been confirmed by Mercurius's board of directors,' said Frisinger.

Björn asked to see the document to confirm with his own eyes that it had been signed. He looked at the papers for a few seconds and then returned them.

'The only thing remaining to do is to vote,' Frisinger continued. 'Personally I think it's a good offer and I vote in favour of accepting it.'

I voted in favour, as did Björn Gullström. Björn voted against. Frisinger picked up the phone and asked Webber and Jakobi for their votes. Both voted against acceptance. Jakobi added that he did not have sufficient faith in the ability of the company's leadership to run the business with sufficient competence when it came to expenditures. I immediately thought to myself: then why doesn't he accept the offer and propose that I and the other officers be relieved of our duties? Webber explained his vote by saying that he thought the offer of $9.4 million was not large enough to finance our activities. The truth is that it would have been more than enough. Frisinger didn't reveal what he was thinking, but simply continued according to the rules of procedure.

'I find that the votes are three against three. I therefore refer the question to the shareholders. Do you wish to discuss the matter privately between yourselves?'

'No,' said Björn. 'There's nothing to discuss. We're closing down.'

Håkan then declared, 'As I no longer enjoy the confidence of the majority shareholder, I request permission to resign.'

Gullis announced that he was resigning for the same reason. Frisinger picked up the phone once more and the unimaginable happened. Webber and Jakobi, who had both voted with Björn, also resigned! Remaining on the board were Björn Borg and Lars Skarke, who had completely different and incompatible interests.

'There's not much to add. The only thing that remains is to dismantle the company and face bankruptcy,' said Frisinger.

348

'Exactly,' said Björn, getting up.

I looked over at Gullis, who was standing and leaning over a bench. His face was ashen, and I could see his anger. Later he would tell me that Björn had called him the day before on his mobile telephone, and that when he had found out that Gullström was on his way to Stavsborg he had screamed, 'You have one second to tell me where you place your complete loyalty – one second!'

Gullström had replied as calmly as he could, 'I don't have any such loyalty, Björn. I do what I think is right.'

Björn had immediately hung up.

I patted Gullis on the back and went to my library. Sitting there all by myself, the tension left me and my tears began to flow. I felt beaten, destroyed. I had lost everything I had fought for and believed in. And some seventy people would lose their jobs, people who had believed in me and Björn. What we had lived and worked for was dead and about to be buried. Björn had let us all down. Why hadn't he simply got rid of me and let the others continue? Lost in my own thoughts, it was a minute before I felt the presence of someone else in the room. It was Björn. He came up to me and said in a completely unemotional voice, 'If anything important comes up you can phone me. I'll be at home.'

I sat there, unable to answer. A few minutes later, I heard his Ferrari start up and kick up gravel as it left the yard.

Everyone went around without saying a thing, deep in his own sorrow and disappointment. The silence was broken when Anna, Cissi and Eva came home. I had sent them off for a while; they knew it was an important day.

'How did it go?' they asked.

'Björn said no.'

'He's crazy. Why did he do that?' asked Anna.

'I don't know. Ask Håkan,' I said tiredly.

A while later I phoned Peter Gyllenhammar.

'Björn rejected your offer.'

'OK, those things happen,' he said. 'Whose offer did he accept, then?'

'No one's. Björn is closing down.'

'What?' After a long silence a shocked Gyllenhammar said, 'That can't be true. This is the worst destruction of capital I've ever heard of!'

When I followed Håkan out to his car later and we said our farewells, he looked at me for a long while. Then he told me what had happened upstairs before the meeting. Without looking him in the eye, Björn had immediately rejected the Mercurius offer. He hadn't even shown any interest in hearing what Frisinger had to say to him. Björn had simply uttered seven words without any further explanation: 'I have decided. I am closing down.'

'It was the damned Englishmen,' said Håkan, shaking his head in frustration. 'They succeeded in filling the poor boy's head with fantasies.'

No, Håkan, I thought as I waved goodbye. They were simply minor characters in a play that was driven by other, much darker and more powerful forces. The emptiness and helplessness overwhelmed me. I couldn't hold back my tears.

I believe that Björn Borg could have continued with his career to become the greatest tennis player the world has ever known. But he'd had enough of being on the road, and he'd discovered something he liked even more than tennis. Drugs.

Cocaine is a more evil drug than you can imagine. It robbed Björn of his career, and he didn't even realise it until it had all but gone.

The Björn on the tennis courts was a million light years away from the Björn that I knew. Living in the public eye, he had been forced to keep so much of himself a secret. The fact that this super-fit tennis ace smoked around 60 cigarettes a day would certainly have been frowned upon, as would his constant use of prostitutes and, later on in his career, his blatant abuse of cocaine. Yet these are the sad truths about Björn Borg, five-times Wimbledon champion.

Today he half-heartedly continues to go about his business as the tennis world's elder statesman, while in his private life he is reclaiming those years of childhood which were stolen away by the game. Although no longer an official resident of Sweden, he resides mainly with his parents at Alstaholm on Sweden's Varmdo Island or their villa at Cap Ferrat.

A paranoid man and an only child, he hides away from adult responsibilities within the bosom of his family.

Our friend Christer Gustafsson sums it up: 'Björn Borg is a grown man, 37 years of age, and yet he still has to cut the umbilical cord. It's a sick end to what could have been a magical fairy story.'

With clever investments, he will never want for money, although his view of the world is warped and tarnished by experience. Like a little boy, it is once more his mother's love which shields him from pain.

Epilogue

Björn Borg left my house and my life without a word of explanation. I didn't understand why then, but I have thought about it a great deal and I think I know now. I think it began on that flight from Nice to Stockholm, when I told Björn I no longer wanted to be friends with him, but simply his business partner. Björn had not had very many real friends, and I had been someone not only to share the good times, but to turn to when he was having troubles. I wasn't the first person to learn that no one can distance himself from Björn Borg without retribution. Following that incident Björn wanted to take revenge on me, and he wanted to do it in a very thorough way. I was to lose my honour and my money.

Björn's public explanation for what he did was that he risked losing control of BBDG if new investors such as the Mercurius Group had come into the picture. But that's exactly what he did do, he lost control. With Italian financiers Björn started a new company, to which he transferred the trademark and the contracts that our company had developed in the name of BBDG. Then he sold 50 per cent of the shares in the new company Björnlex, thus losing control of it. The Italian businessmen who Björn told us had backed out had done exactly the opposite, they had stepped in.

Whatever they paid him, money was certainly not Björn's problem. When he moved back to Sweden, he had about $50 million in his trust fund abroad. When he left the country a few years later the trust fund had grown to about $56 million. Björn still has his fortune, whereas I and others have been ruined.

Aside from the economic loss, Björn's actions amounted to a great personal disappointment for me and for all of us who believed in him and put our energies into BBDG. The person who perhaps took it hardest of all was Björn Gullström, Björn's loyal adviser and constant support for sixteen years.

Björn Borg became an international sports celebrity when he was just a teenager. There was too much money and too much attention. He came to take everything for granted and to put himself on a pedestal. Unlike the Roman field commander, Björn had no slave to whisper in his ear that he was mortal.

But I have no such illusions, about Björn or myself. I had to try to understand what had happened. And I knew that I also had to let others know. The truth had to be told.